BANKING REGULATION OF UK AND US FINANCIAL MARKETS

Banking Regulation of UK and US Financial Markets

DALVINDER SINGH
Oxford Brookes University, UK

Routledge
Taylor & Francis Group
LONDON AND NEW YORK

First published 2007 by Ashgate Publishing

Published 2016 by Routledge
2 Park Square, Milton Park, Abingdon, Oxon OX14 4RN
711 Third Avenue, New York, NY 10017, USA

Routledge is an imprint of the Taylor & Francis Group, an informa business

British Library Cataloguing in Publication Data
Singh, Dalvinder
Banking regulation of UK and US financial markets
1. Banking law - Great Britain 2. Financial services
industry - Law and legislation - Great Britain 3. Banking
law - United States 4. Financial services industry - Law
and legislation - United States
I. Title
346.4'1082

Library of Congress Cataloging-in-Publication Data
Singh, Dalvinder, 1970-
Banking regulation of UK and US financial markets / by Dalvinder Singh.
p. cm.
Includes index.
ISBN 978-0-7546-3971-8 (alk. paper)
1. Banking law--Great Britain. 2. Financial institutions--Law and legislation--
Great Britain. 3. Financial Services Authority (Great Britain) I. Title.

KD1715.S57 2007
346.41'082--dc22

2007003824

ISBN 13: 978-0-7546-3971-8 (hbk)

Contents

Preface		*vii*
Acknowledgements		*ix*
List of Abbreviations		*xi*
1	**Modernisation of Financial Regulation**	**1**
	Introduction	1
	Financial Stability	2
	The Formal Regulation of Banks	8
	A New Era for Financial Regulation	14
	The Scope of the FSA's Responsibilities	17
	Reflections on the UK's Adoption of a Single Regulator	25
	The US Approach to Bank Supervision	31
	Conclusion	42
2	**Legal Aspects of Prudential Supervision**	**45**
	Introduction	45
	The Function of Regulation and Supervision	46
	The FSA Risk-based Approach	49
	Deposit-taking Business	54
	The US Regulation of the Business of Banks and Safe and Sound Requirements	69
	Conclusion	76
3	**Corporate Governance and Banking Supervision**	**79**
	Introduction	79
	Corporate Governance	80
	The Position of Depositor Creditors	82
	The Financial Services and Markets Act 2000	84
	The Principles for Businesses	86
	The Common Law Position of the Directors and the Senior Management Role	97
	The US Position on the Bank Director	105
	Conclusion	110
4	**Enforcement Powers and Banking Supervision**	**113**
	Introduction	113
	The Enforcement Strategy	114
	Deterrence and Sanctions	117

	The Historical Position: The Bank's Enforcement Strategy	121
	The Financial Services and Markets Act 2000	125
	FSA Powers of Investigation	127
	FSA Enforcement Powers	128
	The FSA and Cooperation with Overseas Authorities	135
	FSA Sanctions and the Human Rights Act 1998	137
	Reflections on the FSA Approach to Enforcement	139
	The US Experience of Enforcement	144
	Conclusion	150
5	**The Role of the External Auditor and Skilled Person**	**153**
	Introduction	153
	The Audit of Bank Accounts	154
	Professional Guidelines	157
	The Auditor's Liability to the Client	163
	The FSA's Use of External Auditors	167
	The Role of External Auditors in the USA	173
	Conclusion	178
6	**Legal Accountability of Financial Regulators**	**181**
	Introduction	181
	Public Responsibilities	182
	Liability of Financial Regulators	186
	Alternative Mechanisms of Accountability	191
	Exception to Statutory Immunity: The Tort of Misfeasance in Public Office	199
	The US Approach to Accountability of Federal Bank Regulators	210
	Conclusion	216
Index		*219*

Preface

The financial services industries across the world have undergone a considerable level of change over the last several decades as a result of the liberalisation of capital movement, advancement of information technology, dismantlement of barriers between parts of the financial services industry and the growth of more sophisticated financial instruments. And the regulatory structure that governs the financial markets has had to change as well to cope with the new developments in the marketplace. In some quarters a move towards a single regulator has taken place; other countries have attempted to re-examine their regulatory system to in the light of such changes. These changes have invariably required some adjustment of the underlying system of bank prudential regulation and supervision.

This work focuses on the system of regulation and supervision in the UK and US in its broadest sense. It concentrates on the legal and policy aspects of modernisation of financial regulation, financial stability, prudential regulation and supervision of banking, corporate governance, enforcement sanctions, the use of external auditors and legal accountability of financial regulators. It tackles these issues critically by using an interdisciplinary analysis of the subject matter; first to reflect on the approach taken by the FSA, and secondly to look at the approach to some of the matters in the USA to examine and describe the rules that govern banking business.

Acknowledgements

I would like to thank a whole host of people who have assisted me in completing this work. I would like to thank those who have commented on earlier draft chapters of the work, namely Joanna Gray, Andrew Campbell, Peter Cartwright, Steven Griffin, Geoffrey Wood, Kern Alexander and Peter Edge. I would like to thank Heidi M. Schooner in the USA who provided comments on those aspects of the work. All errors and mistakes, however, are my sole responsibility.

I would also like to thank a number of other people as well who have helped me along the way namely Andrew Haynes, Charles Chatterjee, Barry Rider and Chizu Nakajima. I would also like to thank Rosa M. Lastra and J. J. Norton for their individual advice. My thanks also go to the Department of Law, Oxford Brookes University, for the generous support they gave me. I would like to thank Pam Bertram and Margaret Younger at Ashgate who were so patient and helpful.

Finally my thanks go to close friends, relatives and my family – mother and brothers. But above all to my wife Sarbjit, my daughter Amaryn and son Arvind, to whom I would like to dedicate this work.

List of Abbreviations

BHC	Bank holding company
BCCI	Bank of Credit and Commerce International
DTI	Department of Trade and Industry
FDIC	Federal Deposit Insurance Corporation
FFIEC	Federal Financial Institutions Examination Council
FHC	Financial holding company
FRB	Federal Reserve Board
FSA	Financial Services Authority
FSA 1986	Financial Services Act 1986
FSMA 2000	Financial Services and Markets Act 2000
JMB	Johnson Matthey Bank
LOLR	Lender of Last Resort
MoU	Memorandum of Understanding
OCC	Office Comptroller of Currency
OTS	Office of Thrift Supervision

FSA related acronyms

APER	Statements of Principle and Code of Practice for Approved Persons, available at http://fsahandbook.info/FSA/html/handbook/APER
AUTH	Authorisation, available at http://fsahandbook.info/FSA/html/handbook/AUTH
COAF	Complaints Against the FSA, available at http://fsahandbook.info/FSA/html/handbook/COAF
COMP	Compensation, available at http://fsahandbook.info/FSA/html/handbook/COMP
COND	Threshold Conditions, available at http://fsahandbook.info/FSA/html/handbook/COND
DEC	Decision Making, available at http://fsahandbook.info/FSA/html/handbook/DEC
DISP	Dispute Resolution: Complaints, available at http://fsahandbook.info/FSA/html/handbook/DISP
ENF	Enforcement, available at http://fsahandbook.info/FSA/html/handbook/ENF
FIT	The Fit and Proper Test for Approved Persons, available at http://fsahandbook.info/FSA/html/handbook/FIT

IPRU	Interim Prudential Sourcebook for Banks, available at http://fsahandbook.info/FSA/html/handbook/IPRU-Bank
PRIN	Principles for Businesses, available at http://fsahandbook.info/FSA/html/handbook/PRIN
SUP	Supervision, available at http://fsahandbook.info/FSA/html/handbook/SUP
SYSC	Senior Management Arrangements, Systems and Controls, available at http://fsahandbook.info/FSA/html/handbook/SYSC

Chapter 1

Modernisation of Financial Regulation

Introduction

In the UK a consolidated system of regulation has been adopted to govern the deregulated markets that emanated from the 'big bang' in the 1980s and developed thereafter. The Financial Services Authority (FSA) acquired responsibility, as a single unified regulator, over the industries that make up the financial system for the purposes of prudential regulation and supervision and conduct of business. The move towards a single regulator has inevitably impacted on the role of the Bank of England (the Bank), with the transfer of bank regulation to the FSA. However, the responsibilities of the FSA and the Bank are interdependent with respect to maintaining financial stability and market confidence, which is a key rationale for regulation. In contrast the US position is more complex. It has a unique regulatory structure with a number of 'bank' regulators in addition to securities and insurance regulators. The USA has experienced a number of very significant spates of bank failures that have given rise to a considerable emphasis on bank safety when it comes to dismantling the barriers between banks and other financial services. As a result of this it has adopted a regulatory framework that now allows conglomeration but with the caveat of protecting the interests of banks. This caveat is in no way unique to the USA but the timing of it is something that makes it important to consider in comparison to the UK experience.

The first section of this chapter outlines the link between financial stability and the need for prudential supervision, because no examination of prudential supervision can take place without some outline of the importance of financial stability. It then introduces the role of the Bank as 'lender of last resort' (LOLR), a mechanism to maintain financial stability and market confidence in times of crisis, and highlights that bank supervision is necessary to reduce moral hazard that arises from the existence of the LOLR and other safety-net systems, namely deposit insurance. The second section simply outlines the introduction of a formal system of banking and financial services regulation up to the subsequent transfer of those responsibilities to the FSA. It is important to introduce the regulatory experience in the financial services sector because of the synergy between these areas. It highlights that the underlying policy of enhancing efficiency and competitiveness in the banking and financial services industry during the 1980s and onwards led to, for instance, the growth of bank financial conglomerates. In the third section the move towards a single regulator through the enactment of the Bank of England Act 1998 and the Financial Services and Markets Act 2000 (FSMA 2000) is examined. This section also analyses the objectives and principles that underpin the FSMA 2000 and reviews the work of the FSA so far, in particular the realigning of the interests of the industry with those of consumers. A broad look at the responsibilities of the FSA is needed, beyond bank supervision, to shed light on how it deals with regulatory and supervisory issues from the perspective of practitioners and consumers. The fourth section introduces the US experience of financial modernisation, highlighting that the barriers between banks and securities and insurance businesses have been dismantled in such a way as to ensure the safety and soundness of banks. It reviews the present multi-regulator model and the concerns that arise, such as the problems of cooperation and coordination of regulatory and supervisory efforts. Nevertheless, it highlights the fact that regardless of what regulatory structure is in place, the underlying prudential supervision system needs to be sound. Finally, the fifth section will provide some concluding points and comparative observations about the UK and US approach.

Financial Stability

Financial stability is a catch-all phrase referring to a whole host of factors, both positive and negative, that have an impact on the efficiency with which an economy or financial system performs.[1] The ambiguous nature of its scope has been the focus of considerable attention in light of the crises that have plagued financial markets around the world.[2] The factors that can give rise to financial stability or instability are associated with the macro-economic environment, such as a change in prices or interest rates or exchange rate fluctuations. In addition, stability can be affected by micro-economic factors such as the efficiency with which resources are allocated, ineffective prudential supervision and general imprudence in financial markets and banks or financial institutions.[3] These factors can cause a downturn in the economy or undermine market confidence in the eyes of depositors and investors, giving rise

1 Schinasi, G. J. (2004) 'Defining financial stability', IMF Working Paper WP/04/187, October, at p. 3.

2 For an assessment of the economic costs of banking crises see Hoggarth, G., Reis, R. and Saporta, V. (2001) 'Costs of banking instability: Some empirical evidence', Bank of England Working Paper No. 144: 'The costs of financial instability are considerable, in the region of 15%–20% of GDP in some cases', at p. 7. See also Large, A. (2003) 'Financial stability: Maintaining confidence in a complex world', *Financial Stability Review*, December, 170; White, W. R. (1998) 'Mr White discusses promoting international financial stability: The role of the BIS', *BIS Review*, vol. 62, 1; Hall, S. (2002) 'Spillovers from recent emerging market crises', *Financial Stability Review*, June, 128; Haldane, A. G. (2002) 'Fixing financial crises', *Financial Stability Review*, December, 157; Haldane, A. G. (2003) 'Moral hazard: How does IMF lending affect debtor and creditor incentives', *Financial Stability Review*, June, 122; Gai, P. and Shin, H. S. (2003) 'Transparency and financial stability', *Financial Stability Review*, December, 91.

3 See Crockett, A. (1997) 'Why is financial stability a goal of public policy?', *Federal Reserve Bank of Kansas Economic Review*, vol. 4, 5; Schinasi, n. 1 above; Large, A. (2005) 'A framework for financial stability', *Financial Stability Review*, June, 135; Crockett, A. (2001) 'Market discipline and financial stability', paper presented at Banks and Systemic Risk Conference, Bank of England, 23–25 May.

in the extreme to a risk of contagion or systemic problems in the banking or financial system.[4]

The macro-economic and micro-economic factors are not mutually exclusive, but rather interdependent in an economy. Therefore, financial stability can only be ensured through cooperation between the central bank, other safety-net players and bank and financial regulators. Andrew Crockett refers to this as the micro- and macro-prudential aspects of financial stability as it links the stability of the financial system with the importance of sound supervision of financial institutions.[5] For Crockett, the macro-prudential aspect refers to 'limiting the costs of distress to the economy at large'. The micro-prudential aspect, on the other hand, refers to 'limiting the likelihood of failure of individual institutions'.[6] The link between prudential supervision and financial stability is therefore designed to minimise the adverse impact of a bank failure, for example on the efficient running of the economy or the capital markets.

A 'precondition' to financial stability is the ability of the central bank to assess financial risks in the marketplace accurately, which requires its own unique infrastructure.[7] In addition official safety nets are needed, namely LOLR (lender of last resort) and deposit insurance systems. But to mitigate the risks associated with official safety nets, effective regulation and supervision are needed to ensure banking business is undertaken with prudence.[8]

The Bank of England and Lender of Last Resort

The Bank of England functions at the centre of the UK banking and financial systems in its role of assisting the government with implementing its monetary policy and acting as the LOLR to ensure financial stability.[9] This facility is used to

---

4 Kaufman, G. (1994) 'Bank contagion: A review of the theory and evidence', *Journal of Financial Services Research*, vol. 8, 123; Kaufman, G. (1996) 'Bank failures, systemic risk, and bank regulation', *Cato Journal*, vol. 16, 1; Goodhart, C. A. E. and Illing, G. (eds) (2002) *Financial Crises, Contagion, and the Lender of Last Resort: A Reader*, Oxford, Oxford University Press; Goodhart, C. A. E. (1995) 'Some regulatory concerns', Special Paper No. 79, Financial Markets Group, London School of Economics, December, at p. 16.

5 Crockett, A. (2000) 'Marrying the micro- and macro-prudential dimensions of financial stability', *BIS Review*, vol. 76, 1.

6 Ibid., at p. 2; see also Borio, C. (2003) 'Towards a macroprudential framework for financial supervision and regulation?', BIS Working Papers No. 128, February. This paper makes the important link between macro- and micro-prudential approaches to safeguard financial stability, and depositor and investor confidence – see p. 2.

7 See IMF/World Bank Financial Sector Assessment Programme for further information on this matter, available at www.imf.org.

8 See pp. 46–48.

9 For the history of the Bank of England see Acres, W. M. (1931) *The Bank of England From Within: 1694–1900, Vols I & II*, London, Oxford University Press; Fforde, J. (1992) *The Bank of England and Public Policy 1941 1958*, Cambridge, Cambridge University Press; Clapham, J. (1944) *The Bank of England, A History 1694–1914* (vol. 1, 1694–1797; vol. 2, 1797–1914), Cambridge, Cambridge University Press; Sayers, R.

avoid a liquidity problem turning into a panic in the banking and financial system by intervening with financial support.[10] The Bank could exercise the LOLR function either by open-market operations or by providing loans to the banking system.[11] The central bank intervenes in such circumstances to stabilise market confidence and avoid unnecessary bank failures because of temporary liquidity problems.

Francis Baring first expressed the notion of the LOLR in 1797, although Thornton and Bagehot respectively are given recognition for putting forward the rationale of a formal system of financial support.[12] Bagehot proposed a restrictive interpretation of the LOLR: according to him it should be made available provided that it is used to avoid panics when banks experience temporary liquidity problems. It is given at a rate to ensure repayment is made expeditiously once the crisis is over; and it should also only be given against good forms of collateral.[13] Another important ingredient in providing financial assistance is that the central bank must act decisively and quickly without hesitation, otherwise a panic could be prolonged and could spread into other parts of the financial system which were otherwise unaffected by the original problem.[14]

The Bank has acted to avert a financial crisis a number of times over its history, for example in 1821 and 1866 with the failures at Overend, Gurney & Co.[15] In 1890

S. (1957) *Central Banking After Bagehot*, Oxford, Clarendon Press; Whittlesley, C. R. and Wilson, J. S. G. (1983) *Essays in Money and Banking: In Honour of R S Sayers*, Oxford, Clarendon Press; Richards, R. D. (1934) *The First Fifty Years of the Bank of England (1694–1744)*, The Hague, Martinus Nijhoff.

10 Friexias, X., Giannini, C., Hoggarth, G. and Soussa, F. (1999) 'Lender of last resort: A review of the literature', *Financial Stability Review*, November, 151; Humphrey, T. and Keleher, M. (2002) 'The lender of last resort: A historical perspective', in Goodhart, C. A. E. and Illing, G. (eds) *Financial Crises, Contagion, and the Lender of Last Resort: A Reader*, Oxford, Oxford University Press, at p. 73; Wood, G. (2000) 'The lender of last resort reconsidered', *Journal of Financial Services Research*, vol. 18, 2/3, 203; Lastra, R. M. (1999) 'Lender of last resort: An international perspective', *International & Comparative Law Quarterly*, vol. 48, 340.

11 Diamond, D. and Dybig, P. (1983) 'Bank runs, deposit insurance and liquidity', *Journal of Political Economy*, vol. 19, 401, at p. 417. The point about avoiding a 'bank run' and maintaining confidence in the banking system is accepted by the courts as well; see *Re Chancery plc* [1991] BCLC 712.

12 See Thornton, H. (2002) 'An enquiry into the nature and effects of the paper credit of Great Britain' (excerpts), in Goodhart, C. A. E. and Illing, G. (eds) *Financial Crises, Contagion, and the Lender of Last Resort: A Reader*, Oxford, Oxford University Press, at p. 57; Bagehot, W. (2002) 'A general view of Lombard Street' (excerpts), in Goodhart, C. A. E. and Illing, G. (eds) *Financial Crises, Contagion, and the Lender of Last Resort: A Reader*, Oxford, Oxford University Press, at p. 67.

13 For an examination as to whether a penalty rate was proposed by Bagehot see Goodhart, C. A. E. (2002) 'Myths about the lender of last resort', in Goodhart, C. A. E. and Illing, G. (eds) *Financial Crises, Contagion, and the Lender of Last Resort: A Reader*, Oxford, Oxford University Press, at p. 228.

14 See Bagehot, n. 12 above.

15 'The Bank averted a panic by advancing £4 million to creditors and other key banking institutions. The government promised the Bank a Bill of indemnity to cover the excess

the Bank acted with a consortium of banks to rescue Baring Brothers and Company, deemed insolvent as a result of its exposure to a financial crisis in Argentina.[16] The Bank put together a rescue package for Barings to prevent a panic in London and other financial centres.

In modern times the secondary banking crisis in 1971 required the Bank to 'launch the lifeboat' to avert systemic risk in the banking industry.[17] This crisis was the result of a number of factors: a lack of formal bank regulation, mismanagement of risks by banks, contraction in lending in the property market and the expansion of inter-bank markets.[18] The rescue package involved financial support from not only the Bank but also the clearing banks. In addition to the 1970s' rescue, a 'mini-lifeboat' was launched in 1991 because of a perceived systemic risk in the potential failure of a group of small banks.[19] The slump in the property market exposed a number of these banks to the threat of collapse because of the increasing number of individuals defaulting on their mortgages. In order to avert this, the Bank provided liquidity and did not disclose publicly that it had done so until the panic was averted. Although the Banking Department's financial statements reported the support, it was not explicit who its recipients were.

In a number of incidents the Bank has refused to support failing institutions but has provided support to the wider financial market to avert an ensuing panic. In Overend, Gurney & Co, the perception was that it had pursued its business interests in a 'spirit of greed' and attempted to gain high profits by taking 'extreme risk'.[20] This was also the case in the collapse of City of Glasgow in 1878, which was the result of high levels of fraud. In the case of Bank of Credit and Commerce International (BCCI), support was refused on the grounds that its closure was due to large-scale fraud. As a result of the BCCI closure the Bank had to provide liquidity support to a group of Asian banks innocently affected.[21] These banks experienced difficulties in borrowing in the wholesale market due to having no previous track record of dealing in such markets. The collapse of Baring Brothers and Company in 1995 was the result of the activities of a rogue trader at its non-bank subsidiary in Singapore going undetected. Barings was bought by the Dutch bank ING, but it was felt it did not merit a formal rescue.

The Bank did decide to provide support to Johnson Matthey Bank (JMB), because of concern about the likely impact of its failure on confidence in the gold

---

of the statutory limit, on condition that advances and discounts should be at a rate not less than 10%. This rate eventually alleviated the panic.' See Acres, n. 9 above, at p. 531.

16 Clapham, n. 9 above, vol. II, at p. 326.

17 Bank of England (1978) 'The secondary banking crisis and the Bank of England's support operations', *Bank of England Quarterly Bulletin*, April, at pp. 230–236; Reid, M. (1982) *The Secondary Banking Crisis 1973–75*, Basingstoke, Macmillan.

18 Bank of England, ibid., at pp. 230–231.

19 Logan, A. (2000) 'The early 1990s small banks crisis: Leading indicators', *Financial Stability Review*, December, 130.

20 Acres, n. 9 above, at pp. 546–547.

21 Wood, n. 10 above, at p. 219.

bullion market.[22] The support given to Johnson Matthey Bankers (Minories Finance) was sufficient to allow it to continue in business and make sure it could repay the indemnity granted to it. The £52.2 million support package included dividends from the settlement of a case against its former auditors, Arthur Young, and the recovery of part-provisions that enabled the Bank to pay members of the London Bullion Market Association for their contribution to the support operation. The remainder of the dividends were used to reimburse the Bank for its contribution.[23]

The LOLR facility is traditionally considered the preserve of the banking system; however, it can be used to avoid liquidity problems in the wider financial system.[24] In some circumstances the central bank could view an institution as 'too-big-to-fail', so intervention with some kind of financial assistance is considered necessary in light of the serious impact the failure could have on the financial stability of an economy or marketplace.[25] Furthermore, the systemic risk associated with securities business led the Bank of Japan to act as LOLR to Yamaichi Securities firm because it potentially gave rise to very serious systemic concerns.[26] The fact that it was part of a financial conglomerate with entities undertaking banking business was a key reason to curb worries that a securities house was being supported in this way by the Bank of Japan.

Moral Hazard and Constructive Ambiguity

The LOLR facility is necessary to reduce the possible adverse risks associated with temporary liquidity problems affecting the stability of the financial system. However,

22 Bank of England (1985) *Report and Accounts*, at pp. 34–35; Hall, M. (1987) *Financial Deregulation, A Comparative Study of Australia & the United Kingdom*, Basingstoke, Macmillan, at p. 114; Fay, S. (1987) *Portrait of an Old Lady: Turmoil at the Bank of England*, Middlesex, Viking, at p. 141–155.

23 Bank of England (1990) *Report and Accounts*, at p. 11.

24 See Corder, M. (2004) 'Assessing risks from UK non-bank financial sectors', *Financial Stability Review*, December, 119; Scott, H. S. and Iwahara, S. (1994) 'In search for a level playing field: The implementation of the Basel Capital Accord in Japan and United States', Occasional Paper 46, Group of Thirty, Washington, DC, at p. 1. This paper makes the point that a liberal safety net in a jurisdiction can place banks from other jurisdictions with stricter safety nets at a competitive disadvantage.

25 Soussa, F. (2000) 'Too-big-to-fail: Moral hazard and unfair competition?', in Halme, L., Hawkesby, C., Healey, J., Saapar, I. and Soussa, F. (eds) *Financial Stability and Central Banks: Selected Issues for Financial Safety Nets and Market Discipline*, London, Centre for Central Banking Studies, Bank of England, at p. 5; Roth, M. (1995) '"Too-big-to-fail" and the stability of the banking system: Some insights from foreign countries', *Business Economics*, October, 43. This also leads to the concern of concentration of financial power – see Goodhart, C. A. E. (1988) 'Bank insolvency and deposit insurance: A proposal', in Arestis, P. (ed.) *Contemporary Issues in Money and Banking*, Basingstoke, Macmillan, at p. 50.

26 For an excellent analysis of this issue and the broader points about managing financial crisis see Nakaso, H. (2001) 'The financial crisis in Japan during the 1990s: How the Bank of Japan responded and the lessons learnt', BIS Papers No. 6, October, at pp. 9–11.

the existence of the LOLR does give rise to a number of concerns that require central banks and prudential regulators to gauge carefully when support is given, namely moral hazard and 'too-big-to-fail' connotations. The risk of moral hazard emanates when a banking institution takes on an unmanageable level of risk in light of the fact that the central bank, 'ready' with a support facility such as the LOLR, may intervene to bail it out of trouble if it is thought that the institution's failure could adversely affect the stability of other institutions or confidence in financial markets as a whole. The issue of moral hazard is exacerbated by the policy of intervening with financial support if the institution is considered 'too-big-to-fail'.[27]

However, the risk of moral hazard is reduced by the ambiguity surrounding the use of the LOLR, which is void of codification in any significant way. This indicates two things: first, formal rules are not always necessary to determine regulatory action; and secondly, the central bank can operate on the basis of an informal obligation to maintain confidence.[28] This is to ensure that the LOLR facility is only sought and given in the most exceptional of circumstances at the discretion of the central bank. The lack of transparency in the provision of the LOLR, called 'constructive ambiguity', ensures that banks do not become complacent but act in a prudent manner.[29] In addition to the lack of formalisation of the LOLR, the 'too-big-to-fail' principle is similarly void of rules to prevent undermining market discipline. The formalisation of these two principles to ensure more consistency in their application could increase the likelihood of moral hazard as a whole, as it would provide market participants with the opportunity to manoeuvre in such a way as to ensure support is given. Constructive ambiguity places the risk of bad decisions squarely on the shoulders of the senior management of a bank. The mechanisms to ensure financial stability and the risks associated with orchestrating a financial rescue provide just some of the reasons why some form of bank supervision is necessary.

The Rationale of Bank Regulation and Financial Supervision

Bank regulation refers to the rules banks are required to comply with, and supervision refers to the monitoring process undertaken by a regulator. The concept of prudence is integral to bank regulation and supervision: it connotes the idea that regulation requires bank activities to be undertaken with reasonable care. Indeed, bank regulation and supervision can be referred to as prudential regulation and supervision. Bank supervisors use a number of tools to regulate banks, namely capital adequacy,

27 FDIC (1997) *History of the Eighties – Lessons for the Future*, Chapter 7, 'Continential Illinois and "too-big-to-fail"', at p. 236, available at www.fdic.gov/bank/historical/history/235_258.pdf; Roth, n. 25 above.

28 The exception to this general policy is the position in the USA, where it is explicitly articulated in 12 CFR, § 201; for an examination of the use of LOLR in the USA see Schwartz, A. J. (1992) 'The misuse of the Fed's discount window', *Federal Reserve Bank of St Louis*, September/October, 58.

29 Corrigan, E. G. (1990) *Statement Before US Senate Committee on Banking, Housing and Urban Affairs*, Washington, DC; Goodhart, C. A. E. and Huang, H. (1999) 'A model of last resort', Discussion Paper 313, Financial Markets Group, London School of Economics, January, at p. 33.

consolidated supervision, large exposure rules and deposit insurance.[30] These forms of control are necessary because banks function on a small asset reserve and hold a large proportion of illiquid assets, which makes them susceptible to failure. This fragility is heightened by the fact the inter-bank market is made up of a network of large, unsecured creditor and debtor relationships, thus the failure of one bank could lead to the collapse of others.[31] In addition to these factors highlighting the need for bank supervision, the legal obligation a bank has to its customer depositors is also limited. The bank-customer relationship of debtor and creditor provides that a bank does not have a continuous obligation to account for its decisions as to how it uses depositors' money: the bank can place deposits at any risk provided it can pay the deposited money on demand.[32] This exposes a troubled bank to what is known as a 'bank run', a situation where bank customers seek 'their money' from the bank because they think it will collapse.

The Formal Regulation of Banks

A separate formalised system of regulation and supervision was first introduced with the passing of the Banking Act 1979 as a result of the secondary banking crisis.[33] However, shortcomings in the 1979 Act were exposed with the JMB collapse, which led to its repeal and the enactment of the Banking Act 1987.[34] The 1987 Act abolished the two-tier system of authorisation, considered to be at the heart of the problem. It put in its place a single system of authorisation, which was applied to all institutions

30 See pp.56 66 and pp. 191–193.

31 Freixas, X., Curzio, G., Hoggarth, G. and Soussa, F. 'Lender of last resort: A review of the literature', in Goodhart, C. A. E. and Illing, G. (eds) (2002) *Financial Crises, Contagion, and the Lender of Last Resort: A Reader*, Oxford, Oxford University Press, at p. 33.

32 See pp.82–84.

33 For a very interesting examination of whether legislation was necessary see Landhman, R. H. (1976) 'A need for new legislation?', *Credit: Quarterly Review of the Finance House Association*, vol. 17, 78, at p. 80; HMSO (1976) *The Licensing and Supervision of Deposit-Taking Institutions*, London, HMSO, Cmnd 6584, p. 3; Ryder, F. R. (1980) 'The Banking Act 1979', *Journal of Business Law*, vol. 92, 93; Bank of England (1980) 'Banking supervision and the Banking Act', *Bank of England Quarterly Bulletin*, June, 205; Bank of England (1975) 'Banking supervision: Statutory control or self-regulation', *Bank of England Quarterly Bulletin*, December, 367. The enactment of the Banking Act 1979 also ensured compliance with First Council Directive 77/780/EEC on the coordination of laws, regulations and administrative provisions relating to the taking up and pursuit of the business of credit institutions.

34 *The Committee to Consider the System of Banking Supervision*, Cmnd 9550, London, HMSO, June 1985; *White Paper on Banking Supervision*, Cmnd 9695, London, HMSO, December 1985. Many were sceptical about the flexibility the 1987 Act provided, in particular the large measure of discretion it allowed the Bank to carry out its responsibilities – see Parliamentary Debates, House of Commons, Standing Committee E, Banking Bill, Third Sitting, 18 December 1986, Mr Nelson MP, col. 79 and Ian Stewart MP, cols 80–81.

accepting deposits in the course of their business. Notwithstanding the formalisation of prudential supervision, the discretion-based style of supervision continued to be encouraged, even after the failures of BCCI and Barings.

The closure of BCCI is considered to be one of the major banking frauds of the twentieth century, and called into question the Bank's methods of prudential supervision.[35] The cause of BCCI's closure in the UK was the discovery that widespread fraud and mismanagement had rendered it insolvent. The closure exposed a catalogue of failures and irregularities that were found to have existed before revocation took place. The evidence called into question whether the Bank acted early enough to reduce the damage caused by the closure. The Bank contended that implementing restrictions on an authorised institution could result in a collapse in confidence, causing a run on a bank's assets. The decision to implement restrictions thus needed to be balanced against the interests of BCCI's depositors, and the closure therefore only came when the Bank was given overwhelming evidence of fraud and misconduct. The Bank's view was that there had been insufficient evidence to justify BCCI's closure until it received the report pursuant to s. 41 of the 1987 Act.[36] Bingham LJ in his report did not undermine the existing regime of banking supervision, but he did make recommendations to change the way the Bank utilised its resources; encourage a higher degree of alertness and inquisitiveness in its supervisory staff; and improve internal communication.[37]

The collapse of Barings brought to the fore the concern surrounding bank securities trading. Nick Leeson's activities resulted in massive losses totalling £827 million at Barings Futures Singapore, causing its parent company Barings Bros & Co. to be placed in the hands of the administrators.[38] The Dutch bank ING bought Barings for a nominal sum of £1. The collapse was a surprise because Barings was one of the most established merchant banks in the City of London with a history spanning

---

35 *Inquiry into the Supervision of the Bank of Credit and Commerce International* (1992) The Right Honourable Lord Justice Bingham (Bingham Report), London, HMSO. 'The inquiry required five points to be considered:

1. What did the United Kingdom authorities know about BCCI at all relevant times?
2. Should they know more?
3. What action did the United Kingdom authorities take in relation to BCCI at all relevant times?
4. Should they have acted differently?
5. What should be done to prevent, or minimise the risk of, such an event recurring in the future?', at p. iii. This is analysed on pp.199–210.

36 *Fourth Report from the Treasury and Civil Services Committee, Banking Supervision and BCCI: International and National Regulation*, Session (1991–92), at p. xiv.

37 Bingham Report, n. 35 above, at p. 182, para. 3.9.

38 *Report of the Board of Banking Supervision Inquiry into the Circumstances of the Collapse of Barings*, 18 July 1995 (Barings Report), London, HMSO, at para. 1.2; Barings Futures (Singapore) Pte Ltd investigation pursuant to section 231 of the Companies Act (Chapter 50) *The Report of the Inspectors appointed by the Minister for Finance*, M L C San and N T N Kuang Partners of Price Waterhouse, 6 September (1995); Norton, J. J. and Olive, C. D. (1996) 'Globalization of financial risks and international supervision of banks and securities firms: Lessons from the Baring debacle', *International Lawyer*, vol. 30, 301.

200 years. While its collapse did not bring about legislative changes, it did produce an extensive reassessment of banking supervision, including a review by Arthur Andersen of the Bank's supervision and surveillance.[39] One focus of the review was the 'appropriateness and effectiveness' of supervision and surveillance. It advised that the existing style of supervision should be retained, but clearer standards and objectives were considered necessary to clarify the Bank's approach to supervising deposit-taking institutions. These were to include, *inter alia*, a more systematic approach to supervising institutions by introducing a risk-based approach.[40]

These bank failures were not entirely attributable to a systemic defect in the supervisory process. Nevertheless the failures did highlight the importance of regulators maintaining their vigilance and arraigning non-compliance with stricter adherence to prudential controls.[41]

The Bank of England and Regulation of Financial Services

The role of the Bank is traditionally analysed in terms of banking regulation and supervision, but it also exercises a significant amount of influence over the financial system as a whole[42] through its surveillance responsibility over many parts of the UK's capital markets for the purpose of monitoring economic stability and performance. It also ensures the orderly conduct of the financial markets. Thus it became the 'voice' of the City of London, ensuring that the *status quo* in terms of regulation was maintained[43] and managing the culture of regulation over the financial markets through its influence with the government. It was also a key architect of the dismantlement of the restrictive practices surrounding the London Stock Exchange in the 1980s.[44] In addition to this change, the Financial Services Act 1986 (FSA 1986)

---

39 Arthur Andersen & Co SC (1996) *Findings and Recommendations of the Review of Supervision and Surveillance* (Arthur Andersen Report), London, Arthur Andersen Consulting.

40 Ibid., at para. 44.

41 For an examination of these issues see pp. 45–68.

42 For background to the pre-Financial Services Act 1986 position see Rider, B. (1978) 'The British Council for the securities industry', *Revue De La Banque*, vol. 17, 303; Rider, B. and Hew, E. (1977) 'The regulation of corporation and securities laws in Britain – The beginning of the real debate', *Malaya Law Review*, vol. 19, 144, at p. 155; Rider, B. (1979) 'Self regulation: The British approach to policing conduct in the securities business, with particular reference to the role of the City Panel on Take-Overs and Mergers in the regulation of insider trading', *Journal of Comparative Corporate Law and Securities Regulation*, vol. 1, 319.

43 Seventh Report from the Select Committee on Nationalised Industries, Session (1975–76) The Bank of England, London, HMSO, at pp. xliv–xlv, paras 94–98.

44 For background see Ayling, D. E. (1986) *The Internationalisation of Stockmarkets: The Trend towards Greater Foreign Borrowing and Investment*, London, Gower; Hall, J. B. M. (1986) 'Reform of the London Stock Exchange: The prudential issues', *Banca Nazionale del Lavoro*, vol. 13, 167; Plender, J. (1987) 'London's big bang in international context', *International Affairs*, vol. 4, 39; Gilligan, G. P. (1997) 'The origins of UK financial services regulation', *Company Lawyer*, vol. 18, 167; Bank of England (1983) 'Regulation in financial markets', *Bank of England Quarterly Bulletin*, December, 499,

introduced a structure of self-regulation within a statutory framework to oversee investment business.[45] The enactment of the FSA 1986 was essentially designed to restore investor confidence after a number of financial failures and weaknesses in the previous self-regulatory structures.

The body given overall control of the regime, under the FSA 1986, was the Securities and Investments Board (SIB).[46] The responsibility for appointing and removing the chairman and other members of the SIB lay with the Treasury and the Governor of the Bank of England.[47] This power vested in the Governor of the Bank highlighted the importance of ensuring that the people appointed to run the SIB understood the culture of regulation and supervision required by the City of London. The parties on the board of the SIB were thus not only politically acceptable but also acceptable to the industry. Concern for the overall cohesion of the regulator and industry could be seen with the appointment in June 1988 of Sir David Walker (a non-executive director of the Bank of England) to replace Sir Kenneth Berrill; a lawyer by profession replaced by an economist. The new appointment recommended by the Bank ensured that the regulatory regime of the SIB would complement the approach considered acceptable to the City of London.[48]

The SIB ensured that the designated 'self-regulatory organisations' (SROs), 'recognised professional bodies' (RPBs) and 'recognised investment exchanges' (RIEs) performed their delegated powers over their respective forms of investment business in accordance with the principles it laid down. The initial five SROs were whittled down to three during the 1990s: the Personal Investment Authority (PIA), the Investment Management Regulatory Organisation (IMRO) and the Securities Futures Authority (SFA). These SROs provided prudential and conduct-of-business rules relative to the investment business under their responsibility. This reduction in the number of SROs was the result of concerns raised, in the wake of several SRO

---

at p. 500; Gower, L. C. B. (1984) *Review of Investor Protection*, Cmnd 9125, London, HMSO; Department of Trade and Industry (1985) *Financial Services in the United Kingdom: A New Framework for Investor Protection*, Cmnd 9432, London, HMSO; Gower, L. C. B. (1988) '"Big bang" and City regulation', *Modern Law Review*, vol. 51, 1, at p. 10.

45 Hudson, R., Keasey, K. and Littler, K. (1997) 'Retail financial services regulation since the Financial Services Act 1986', *Review of Policy Issues*, vol. 3, 23. Cf. Hinchcliffe, J. M. (1997) 'The manifest failure of the Financial Services Act: A comment on Hudson, Keasey and Littler', *Review of Policy Issues*, vol. 3, 37; Hudson, R., Keasey, K. and Littler, K. (1997) 'The manifest failure of the Financial Services Act: A reply to Hinchcliffe', *Review of Policy Issues*, vol. 3, 49. For a focus on consumer protection see generally Llewellyn, D. T. (1993) 'Reflections on recent UK experience of financial regulation', *Butterworths Journal of International Banking and Financial Law*, September, 375.

46 Department of Trade and Industry (1989) *Possible Changes to the Financial Services Act 1986*, 1 March, London, DTI; Financial Services Act 1986 (Delegation) Order 1987 (SI 1987/942), which transferred powers under s. 114(1) of the Financial Services Act 1986 to the SIB set out in Sch. 7 of the FSA 1986.

47 Ibid., Sch., 7, para. 1(2).

48 See Rider, B. and Abrams, C. (1997) *Guide to the Financial Services Act 1986*, Bicester, CCH Editions, at p. 60.

failures, about their effectiveness. The latter period of the SROs' existence witnessed the Maxwell affair and the pensions mis-selling scandal that exposed limitations at IMRO. After the former débâcle Andrew Large conducted a review of financial services regulation.[49] A number of concerns were raised, in particular the lack of clear objectives for the financial services industry and a suspicion of regulatory capture.[50]

The PIA had responsibility for prudence and conduct of business in the insurance industry. In light of the fact that insurance products came within the definition of investment business for the purposes of the FSA 1986, the PIA was the body responsible for conduct-of-business rules. In addition, the Department of Trade and Industry (DTI) was responsible for prudential regulation during the early days of the PIA, but this responsibility was passed on to the Treasury in 1998. The powers conferred on the PIA could only be exercised if they did not conflict with the responsibilities of the prudential regulator under the Insurance Companies Act 1982 (ICA 1982). The separation of the prudential and conduct-of-business regulatory functions gave rise to a number of problems, such as a clear approach to dealing with the collapse of Equitable Life as a result of its annuity policy.[51] The PIA's jurisdiction did not involve prudential matters, as it was prohibited under the ICA 1982 from dealing with these. Indeed, it was required to liaise with the DTI and subsequently the Treasury on such issues as enforcement decisions. The approach the PIA generally adopted came under particular criticism in a review of retail financial services during the mid-1990s, calling into question the way in which it failed to regulate effectively individuals who sold such services.[52] In addition, a call was made in some quarters to revamp retail financial services regulation by consolidating the various regulators.[53]

The growing recognition of the SROs and their regulatory responsibilities led to abandonment of the notion of 'membership', as this was more of a hindrance than a positive attribute. The three remaining SROs introduced an authorisation process for institutions and individuals. In many respects this emanated from a desire by the SROs to move away from the traditional idea of 'self-regulation', which had spawned negative connotations of regulatory capture instead of producing an efficient way of allowing practitioners to ensure that regulation worked effectively. According to a 1995 Treasury and Civil Service Committee report, the SROs attempted to project themselves as effective regulators rather than self-regulatory bodies serving members' interests. The report deemed the notion of self-regulation a 'misnomer'.[54] Nevertheless, the pensions mis-selling scandal tarnished the reputation of the

49 Large, A. (1993) *Financial Services Regulation: Making a Two Tier System Work*, London, Securities Investment Board.

50 Ibid., at p. 8.

51 See a review of the Equitable Life episode on pp. 29–31.

52 Treasury and Civil Service Committee (1995) *The Regulation of Financial Services in the UK*, Sixth Report from the Treasury and Civil Service Committee, London, HMSO, 13 July, at paras 69–71.

53 Ibid., at p. 24; FSA *Annual Report 1998–1999*, at pp. 34–35, compares the number of visits undertaken by the previous regulatory bodies. It clearly highlights that the PIA undertook significantly fewer visits than other regulators.

54 Treasury and Civil Service Committee, ibid.

existing regime to the extent that a re-examination of the financial services industry was warranted, particularly in view of the excessive time taken to settle the claims of victims. Moreover, the regulatory system was not the appropriate method to regulate complex financial institutions.

The regulatory approach adopted by the FSA 1986 and the Banking Act 1987 promoted competition and innovation by enabling cross-authorisation in other financial services.[55] Whilst both focused on safeguarding specific public interests, the key objective of the Acts and the way they were implemented was to promote the pursuit of efficiency in the financial markets.[56]

The blurring of demarcation lines between traditional forms of business required coordination of supervision across the regulatory jurisdictions of the SIB, the SROs and the Bank. The Bank needed to understand how the latter institutions worked prudentially and how, with the growing involvement of banks in securities business, they could affect banking institutions.[57]

The financial institutions in the UK expanded significantly into other businesses in light of this regulatory approach as a result of the initial dismantlement of barriers to entry that distinguished the various markets and their participants.[58] Consequently, deregulation blurred the distinction between previously discrete business activities and forged their synergy.[59] The outcome of deregulation was the growth of financial conglomerates – groups that undertake more than one type of financial activity.[60] The benefits of such conglomerates are said to be for consumers, in terms of a wide variety of financial products and competitive prices, rather than enhancing the efficiency of the marketplace through economies of scale.[61]

---

55 Bank of England (1986) 'UK approach to financial regulation', *Bank of England Quarterly Bulletin*, March, 48; Bank of England (1984) 'The business of financial supervision', *Bank of England Quarterly Bulletin*, March, 46; Bank of England (1987) 'Change in the Stock Exchange and regulation of the City', *Bank of England Quarterly Bulletin*, February, 54, at p. 58.

56 Bank of England (1986) 'Supervision and competitive conditions', *Bank of England Quarterly Bulletin*, June, 242.

57 This is notwithstanding the fact that prudential supervision did evolve to cope with new forms of risk. See Bank of England (1985) 'Banking risks in an evolving market', *Bank of England Quarterly Bulletin*, June, 217; Bank of England (1990) 'Some current concerns of a banking supervisor', *Bank of England Quarterly Bulletin*, June, 219; Bank of England (1988) 'The co-ordination of regulation', *Bank of England Quarterly Bulletin*, August, 364, at p. 365.

58 See generally Maycock, J. (1986) *Financial Conglomerates: The New Phenomenon*, London, Gower; Mullineux, A. W. (1986) *UK Banking After Deregulation*, London, Croom Helm, at p. 30.

59 OECD (1992) *Banks Under Stress*, Paris, OECD, at p. 15; OECD (1989) *Competition in Banking*, Paris, OECD, at p. 9.

60 OECD (1995) *Financial Conglomerates*, Paris, OECD, at p. 35.

61 Ibid., at p. 70; see also Llewellyn, D. T. (1992) 'Banking in the 1990s: Challenges and responses. Part 1', *Butterworths Journal of International Banking and Financial Law*, November, 528, at p. 529: 'The most efficient firms would become yet more efficient and the average efficiency of the industry would rise', suggesting that efficiency does not increase across the board and leads to a monopoly position. For an examination

The twenty-first century is no exception to this continued change in the financial system. However, it has experienced a period of great consolidation in the respective markets rather than an expansion into other financial sectors, as was the case in the 1980s and 1990s.[62] This is clearly evident with the various mergers and acquisitions that have taken place in the banking industry – to enhance market share of the retail financial services sector, for instance.[63] Consequently the trend towards financial conglomeration in the 1980s and 1990s is being cautiously reassessed, with a move to enhancing the core business with an appropriate mix of other complementary financial services rather than creating a financial supermarket in the traditional sense.[64]

A New Era for Financial Regulation

The Labour Party's manifesto, up to the election in 1997, had declared its intention to overhaul the financial services industry but did not indicate the extent of this overhaul, nor that it would include banking supervision.[65] This only manifested itself when Labour succeeded the Conservative Party in the 1997 general election. The Chancellor of the Exchequer emphasised that reforms were necessary to ensure investor confidence and the overall well-being of the economy and those employed in it.[66] He pointed out the importance of the reforms, which would include the transfer of banking supervision. The Bank was meant to be somewhat appeased by the fact that the Chancellor wanted it to be fully involved in the new proposals. The Governor's public opposition was cautious; the unique position of banks in the economy rendered them open to certain risks.[67] This vulnerability obliged the

---

of the misconceptions about the efficiency advantages of financial conglomerates in the USA see Wilmarth, A. E. (2002) 'The transformation of the US financial services industry, 1975–2000: Competition, consolidation, and increased risks', *University of Illinois Law Review*, vol. 2, 215.

62 OECD, n. 59 above, at pp. 9–14; OECD, n. 60 above, at pp. 10–12; Group of Ten (2001) 'Consolidation in the financial sector', Summary Report, January; Ruding, H. O. (2002) 'The transformation of the financial services industry', Occasional Paper No. 2, Financial Stability Institute, March. For analysis of the US position see Berger, A. N., Demsetz, R. S. and Strahan, P. E. (1999) 'The consolidation of the financial industry: Causes, consequences, and implications for the future', *Journal of Banking and Finance*, vol. 23, 135.

63 Datamonitor (2004) *Banks in the United Kingdom: Industry Profile*, at p. 7.

64 Ruding, n. 62 above, at pp. 6–9.

65 Labour Party (1997) *Business Manifesto: Equipping Britain for the Future*, April, at p. 4.

66 House of Commons Debates, 20 May 1997, col. 510.

67 Bank of England (1997) 'Transfer of banking supervision', press release, 20 May. Prior to this policy initiative, the separation of monetary and banking regulation was considered in Treasury and Civil Service Committee (1993) *The Role of the Bank of England*, First Report, vol. 1, 8 December; and the separation of it was strongly challenged – see memorandum submitted by Sir Nicholas Goodison, Minutes of Evidence taken before the Treasury and Civil Service Committee, Wednesday 3 November 1993, 116–118.

central bank to monitor banks more closely than other financial institutions, thus the new system of regulation could never be void of the Bank's involvement. Indeed, appointment by the government of Howard Davies, deputy Governor of the Bank of England, as chairman of the FSA seemed natural given the formal links between the various heads of financial regulation and the Bank. The Chancellor declared that in this appointment he was drawing upon the 'resident expertise' of the Bank.[68]

The Bank of England Act 1998 and the Memorandum of Understanding

The Bank of England Act 1998 set out the initial steps towards a single, unified regulatory body with the transfer of banking supervision to the FSA and, amongst others, the personnel of the Supervision and Surveillance Division.[69] This ensured that the specialist skills required to supervise banks were securely placed under the wing of the FSA.[70] But the main thread of the 1998 Act was that it bestowed upon the Bank the right of independent action in matters of interest rate policy.

The Bank's relationship with the Treasury and the FSA is outlined in a memorandum of understanding (MoU).[71] This stipulates how the three organisations are expected to work together.[72] Central to the role and function of the Bank is the monitoring of stability in the financial system. The idea of the financial system incorporates not only the banking sector but also those institutions in the wider financial marketplace that are able to affect stability. In accordance with the MoU the Bank is required to monitor the infrastructure of the payments system, both domestically and abroad. In this respect the Bank is required to monitor systemic risk in general. The FSA is required to monitor the financial institutions it regulates. The Bank is responsible for warning the FSA of possible problems in the domestic and international payment systems that could affect the UK financial markets.

The MoU does not define the role of the LOLR function.[73] According to the MoU, the Bank, with its LOLR role, has the facility to ensure stability to avert systemic damage to financial markets. The power to exercise the LOLR function is not prescribed in formal rules, but is a discretionary power to be exercised in order to 'avoid a serious disturbance in the UK economy'.[74] The MoU does not define 'systemic damage', which means that assessment of when instability has systemic

---

68 House of Commons Debates, 20 May 1997, col. 511.

69 Bank of England (1998) *Report and Accounts*, at p. 15; ss. 21 and 22 of the 1998 Act respectively; Blair, M., Cranston, R., Ryan, C. and Taylor, M. (1998) *Blackstone's Guide to the Bank of England Act 1998*, Oxford, Oxford University Press.

70 1998 Act, s. 17; see specifically Goodhart, C. A. E. (2000) 'The organisational structure of banking supervision', Special Paper No. 127, Financial Markets Group, London School of Economics, October, at p. 41; Lastra, R. (1999) 'Banking regulation in the 1990s', *Journal of International Banking Law*, vol. 13, 45, at p. 45.

71 Bank of England (1997/98) *Memorandum of Understanding between HM Treasury, The Bank of England and the FSA* (MoU), Banking Act Report, at pp. 37–39.

72 See 1998 Act, Part III: 'Transfer of Supervisory Functions of the Bank to the Financial Services Authority'.

73 Bank of England, n. 69 above, Core Purpose No. 2, at p. 8.

74 MoU, n. 71 above, at p. 39, para. 11.

implications is left to the concerted judgement of the three bodies. The MoU has in effect reverted to Bagehot's original suggestion that the Bank should be the LOLR to the whole financial system and not simply the banking system.[75]

The MoU sheds little light on when the LOLR should come into play, leaving its operation in an ambiguous state to prevent complacency in the market, as discussed before. In many respects it preserves the opacity of this role by avoiding a statutory codification of its functions. The Bank is required to cooperate closely with domestic and international financial supervisors to avoid systemic damage. The LOLR, as its name makes clear, is utilised only in the most exceptional circumstances, after consultation with the Treasury and the FSA. The key operational responsibilities of the Bank and the FSA are split in terms of 'lead operator'. In cases where the problem originates in the payment and settlement system, the Bank will be 'lead operator'; in the event of problems originating in the FSA's domain, it will be 'lead operator'. The Bank will be the ultimate source of liquidity.[76] It is unfortunate to say, but it will take a financial crisis to assess whether the arrangements under the MoU are the most efficient way of dealing with such incidents.

The Financial Services Authority

The unique way the FSA is incorporated as a private company limited by guarantee[77] implies that regulation is endogenous: it is rooted within the market and detached from government intervention in terms of its day-to-day responsibilities. However, the fact remains that, like any other body exercising public functions, the FSA is accountable to Parliament and the judiciary.[78] It functions at arm's length from the Treasury, but the Treasury retains overall responsibility for the activities of the FSA and the financial markets. The Treasury has a number of 'holds' on the FSA: the FSA submits its annual report (including a report by the non-executive directors) to the Treasury for examination, and it is then the responsibility of the Treasury to submit that report to Parliament;[79] the Treasury also has responsibility for appointing and removing the chair and executive members of the FSA's governing board.[80] It also commissions reports relating to the efficiency and effectiveness of the way the FSA utilises its resources,[81] and conducts inquiries into regulatory failures that raise

75 Ibid.

76 Ibid., at p. 39, para. 12.

77 FSMA 2000, s. 1.

78 FSA (1998) *The Open Approach to Regulation*, July; for an analysis of the background to the status of the FSA see Law Society Policy Directorate (1998) *Memorandum of the Law Society 'Financial Services and Market Bill'*, Memorandum by the Company Law Committee No. 367, November, para. 2.1. See also Lomnicka, E. (2000) 'Making the Financial Services Authority accountable', *Journal of Business Law*, January, 65; Davies, H. (1999) 'Financial regulation and the law', *Company Financial and Insolvency Law Review*, vol. 3, 1.

79 FSMA 2000, Sch. 1, para. 10.

80 FSMA 2000, Sch. 1, paras 2 3.

81 FSMA 2000, s. 12.

concerns about financial stability or undermine consumer interests.[82] The power to commission inquiries is formal and not *ad hoc*, as in the previous system of regulation.[83]

Independent regulatory bodies such as the FSA have grown in importance for a variety of reasons, the most significant being that the complexity of society requires specialised bodies to take responsibility for politically sensitive areas.[84] For example, the increasing complexity of the financial services industry is one important factor that led to the consolidation of regulators into a single regulatory body. Secondly, the independent regulator is said to have the expertise to undertake such responsibilities[85] – the complexity of the risks and the convergence of the risk profiles of financial institutions are another reason for placing the various regulatory specialisations under one roof to monitor them more efficiently.

It is also important to ensure the independence of the regulator. This requires reassurance that day-to-day responsibilities are carried out apolitically and that the general public interest is being taken into account as a whole.[86] This means there are not only political but also bureaucratic, industrial and consumer interests that the regulator is required to take on board, and is indeed held accountable to.[87]

The Scope of the FSA's Responsibilities

The FSA has the overall regulatory responsibility for deposit-taking businesses, investment businesses (encompassing regulation of recognised investment exchanges) and insurance businesses. The FSMA 2000 amalgamates the central components of previous regulatory regimes, designating one authority to make rules governing regulated and prohibited activities, authorisation and exemption, continuous supervision, enforcement powers and the establishment of an appeal process. The introduction of the FSMA 2000 transferred to the FSA the 'regulation of financial services and markets; to provide for the transfer of certain statutory functions relating to building societies, friendly societies, industrial and provident societies and certain other mutual societies; and connected persons'.[88]

The FSA is required to undertake these responsibilities in accordance with the objectives and principles set out in the FSMA 2000, which provides a foundation for the decisions the FSA takes to fulfil its responsibilities.[89] These objectives and

82 FSMA 2000, s. 14.

83 FSMA 2000, s. 17.

84 Day, P. and Klein, R. (1987) *Accountabilities: Five Public Services*, London, Tavistock; Baldwin, R. and Hawkins, K. (1984) 'Discretionary justice: Davis reconsidered', *Public Law*, Summer, 570.

85 Baldwin and Hawkins, ibid., at p. 579.

86 Froud, J. and Ogus, A. (1996) '"Rational" social regulation and compliance cost assessment', *Public Administration*, vol. 24, 221.

87 FSA, n. 78 above, at pp. 4–5.

88 Preamble to FSMA 2000.

89 FSA (1997) *Financial Services Authority: An Outline*, October; FSA (1999) *The Financial Services Authority*, August; FSA (1998) *Financial Services Authority: Meeting*

principles provide the context for more precise rules and guidance to assist the FSA to undertake its activities with some assurance that it is compliant with them. In many respects the formalisation of regulation governing the financial system by the FSA ensures the degree of discretion in regulation is 'confined', 'structured' and 'checked' to avoid an abuse of power.[90] Collin Diver contends that the success of an administrative body depends on the precision of its rules and on gauging whether the following three tests are satisfied. First, a rule needs to be 'well-defined', 'universally acceptable' and appropriate to the activities of regulated parties. Secondly, the rule needs to be 'accessible': it needs to applicable without being burdensome. Third, rules need to be 'congruent' to the intended objectives.[91] Diver's tests of the effectiveness of regulation provide a useful approach to assess the work of the FSA so far. Moreover, the structuring of regulation sheds a significant amount of light on the way the interests of the various parties are dealt with in the financial services industry. The FSA has attempted to construct a regulatory structure that engages a suitable mix of past and present techniques for the purpose of consolidating its role in pursuit of the new, formally stated objectives.[92]

The objectives place a duty of conduct upon the FSA, and this makes it accountable for its decisions in terms of those objectives. Being declared objectives, they are the yardstick measures to determine whether it is fulfilling its responsibilities. This level of accountability is a positive development from that of the previous regime, whose objectives had never received formal statement and could therefore not be the arbiters of its performance quite so easily. In view of the FSA's position in law in this matter, its objectives do not elaborate a list of formal duties it is obliged to fulfil; rather, those objectives are simply expressions of intent. The political process and the formal Practitioner and Consumer Panels play a significant part in the accountability process.[93]

The FSA's Objectives

In exercising its responsibilities the FSA focuses on the objectives of market confidence, public awareness, protection of consumers and reduction of financial crime.[94] While the FSA has not purported to place these objectives in order of importance, it is fitting that market confidence is first as it captures a broad range of factors connected with depositor and investor confidence that directly or indirectly include reference to the other objectives. The first two objectives introduce the idea of the financial system, which suggests that they are rather more nebulous, whilst the latter two require regulated firms and persons to take direct responsibility for

---

Our Responsibilities, August; FSA (2000) *A New Regulator for the New Millennium*, January.

90 Davis, K. C. (1980, c. 1969) *Discretionary Justice: A Preliminary Enquiry*, Westport, CN, Greenwood Press, at p. 4.

91 Diver, C. (1983) 'Optimal precision of administrative rules', *Yale Law Journal*, vol. 93, 65, at p. 67.

92 FSA (1998), n. 89 above, at p. 14.

93 Ibid., at p. 9.

94 FSMA 2000, s. 2(2); see also FSA (1998), n. 89 above, at pp. 16–18.

implementing measures to protect consumers and reduce the incidence of financial crime. These two objectives focus on the integrity of the UK financial system, and their reach extends territorially in light of the fact that financial markets are globally integrated. For example, an incident overseas involving a regulated firm could have a negative impact on the reputation of the UK financial system if that firm is permitted to undertake regulated business in the UK.

The First Objective: Market Confidence The first objective requires the FSA to focus its attention on the importance of maintaining confidence in the financial system, which includes reference to financial markets, exchanges and regulated activities.[95] This objective is in many respects the mainstay of well-functioning markets in ensuring that depositors and investors have confidence in the financial markets in which they hold their deposits and make their investments. The objective of market confidence provides a broad rationale for possible intervention, whether it is do with, *inter alia*, an individual firm, a sector of the industry or consumer interests. The wide ambit of responsibility with which the FSA is conferred means that it needs to have a strong understanding of what is happening in the domestic and international financial markets so it can monitor the risks emanating from them and assess how they can impact on market confidence. The FSA has put in place its own systems to report on matters which may affect it achieving its objectives, with its annual domestic and international regulatory outlooks. For example, during the slowdown in the economy and equity markets in 2002 the FSA focused on the effectiveness of risk management systems in firms to assess how robust they were in such conditions, and called in some cases for improvements.[96] In its *Financial Risks Outlook 2004* the pressure on firms to comply with a myriad of international and EU measures was something the financial services industry needed to take seriously given the enforcement implications that arise once these are implemented into domestic law,[97] which seem unabated in 2005.[98] The pressures of the 'geopolitical environment' in 2006 with the threat of terrorist activities, for instance, are said to require regulated firms to reassess their risk management systems and contingency plans on a day-to-day basis to deal with the disruption that could arise from such events.[99] However, maintaining market confidence paradoxically does mean that certain firms will be allowed to fail, and depositors and investors need to be aware of that risk.[100] The FSA has highlighted that its approach is not to put in place a 'zero-failure regime', which would lead to a high level of moral hazard.[101] This normally accrues when formal mechanisms of support such as LOLR and deposit protection schemes exist within a system of regulation and are initiated to support those experiencing problems.

95 FSMA 2000, s. 3(1).

96 FSA (2002/03) *Annual Report*, at p. 103.

97 FSA (2004) *Financial Risks Outlook*, at p. 89.

98 FSA (2005) *International Regulatory Outlook*.

99 FSA (2006) *Financial Risks Outlook*.

100 See above, Financial Stability and the Bank of England and Lender of Last Resort, on pp. 2–7.

101 FSA (2003) *Reasonable Expectations: Regulation in a Non-zero Failure World*, September. See pp. 49–53.

The complexity of achieving market confidence also requires cooperation between the FSA, the Bank and the Treasury, as manifested in the MoU, due to the interdependence of financial stability, monetary stability and the regulation of financial institutions. For instance, the Bank would conduct its own surveillance of the financial markets for the purposes of stability to form its own understanding of market trends both domestically and internationally.[102]

The Second Objective: Consumer Awareness The second objective of cultivating public awareness is about enhancing the public's understanding of the financial system.[103] The innovative importance attached to this is elevated by its necessity, due to the systemic failure in the pensions and mortgage industries to sell their financial products with the appropriate level of care so that consumers are aware of the risks associated with the products. Therefore it comes as no surprise that the highest proportion of enquires to the FSA are regarding pensions and endowment mortgages.[104] The objective is premised on the idea that a consumer who is aware of the risks in various financial products is one who can make good investment decisions. The FSA has placed a considerable amount of regulatory resources into enhancing the level of financial literacy among the general public.[105] Its 2005 consumer awareness report addressed the degree of awareness of what the FSA does and the level of confidence the public had in its work, highlighting for instance the degree of uncertainty among the public surrounding the possibility of a financial firm collapsing.[106]

The obligations individuals enter into when buying financial services are not normally short term, but rather long-term commitments exposed to changing market conditions which can negatively impact on the value of financial products. Consumers need to be aware of that fact so they can challenge some of the assertions in promotional literature produced by regulated firms, but this is ultimately dependent on their level of financial literacy, which is affected by their socio-economic background.[107]

However, this is not to say that individual consumers have the right simply to challenge financial services companies on the basis that the returns on an investment were not what they expected when markets did not perform as previously anticipated. The FSA places the responsibility for informing consumers about financial products and the risks associated with them squarely on the shoulders of the regulated firms

102 See above, Financial Stability and the Bank of England and Lender of Last Resort, on pp. 2–7.

103 FSMA 2000, s. 4(1).

104 FSA, n. 96 above, at p. 15; for an analysis of consumers and financial services see Cartwright, P. (2005) *Banks, Consumers and Regulation*, Oxford, Hart.

105 For example, FSA (2005) *Consumer Awareness of the FSA and Financial Regulation*, July.

106 Ibid., at p. 17.

107 FSA (2000) *Better Informed Consumers. Assessing the Implications for Consumer Education of Research by BMRB*, April.

and approved persons.[108] It emphasises the importance of treating consumers fairly as part of its governance strategy.[109] In the light of the issues highlighted, specific emphasis has been placed on internal processes to handle complaints at firms. Moreover, enforcement actions have been taken by the FSA against firms when it has serious misgivings about the robustness of their procedures.[110] This involves, for instance, the sale of endowment mortgages. For example, Abbey Life and Scottish Amicable were fined £1 million and £750,000 respectively for, *inter alia*, mis-selling endowment mortgages, and required to pay compensation in the region of £120–160 million and £11 million respectively to those customers.[111] While the fines indicate a strong stance against individual failures, they need to be considered in the light of the overall gap in endowment mortgages, which will be in the region of £30–50 billion over the next couple of decades.[112]

The Third Objective: Consumer Protection The third objective is consumer protection, a key rationale for financial regulation.[113] The FSA has put a significant amount of emphasis on consumer protection rather than purely the efficiency of the financial markets, which distinguishes it from the previous regulatory systems.[114] The FSA has indicated that it does not advocate excessive regulation for the protection of consumer interests, although it has increased the scope of its work to cover financial products that were outside its purview to realign the interests of consumers and financial providers, so that the former's interests are dealt with more fairly. But an overemphasis on consumer-related regulations is not appropriate: firstly, because no amount of regulation is capable of protecting consumers from all risk; and secondly, a regulatory order should not attempt to attain an objective of absolute protection. Nevertheless, the FSA has certainly attempted to realign the interests of the industry and consumers to deal with the expectations gap that exists between them.[115] This has resulted in the FSA putting in place measures to ensure customers are treated fairly, such as publishing its *Treating Customers Fairly – Building on Progress* in 2005 to deal systematically with customers who are treated unfairly as a result of bad advice and inappropriately designed products which do not make their inherent risks as clear as possible.[116] Enforcement action has also been taken against firms that have either produced misleading financial literature, failed to deal with customer complaints efficiently or mis-sold financial products. For instance, in the latter case

108 For example, Principle 6, Customers' Interests, Principles for Businesses, places a responsibility on the firm to 'pay due regard to the interests of its customers and treat them fairly'. This is further explored on pp. 86–88.

109 FSA (2003/04) *Annual Report*, at p. 26.

110 For an analysis of enforcement issues see pp. 125–144.

111 FSA, n. 96 above, at p. 21.

112 FSA, n. 109 above, at p. 8.

113 FSMA 2000, s. 5(1).

114 FSA (1997), n. 89 above, at p. 30.

115 This is analysed in more detail on pp. 27–31.

116 FSA (2005/06) *Annual Report*, at p. 27.

Royal Liver Assurance in 2006 was fined £550,000 for mis-selling with-profits savings policies.[117]

The FSA is required to assess the appropriate level of consumer protection. To do that it needs to be mindful of the risks associated with individual financial products and the degree of experience and understanding consumers may have of them. This must be measured against the general principle of *caveat emptor*, which is interpreted to place little more than a broad onus of duty on consumers to take responsibility for their investment decisions.[118] In order to mitigate the risk to consumers, the FSA has devised principles to govern the way regulated firms undertake their business so that they do not undermine consumer interests by treating them unfairly. It places that obligation on both the regulated firm and individual senior management. Furthermore, it has required that regulated firms incorporate consumer interests into strategic plans to achieve compliance.[119] Ultimately, the interests of consumers are formally protected, to a limited extent, with a compensation scheme for losses that may accrue from the failure or closure of a regulated firm. But consumers still bear a significant degree of risk from the loss, as such schemes only provide 100 per cent compensation up to a certain level.[120] The proportion not recoverable could be claimed through the liquidation process.[121] This form of co-insurance can be called into question on the grounds that the small depositor would find it impossible to assess the extent to which a regulated firm is risk-averse.[122]

The Fourth Objective: Reducing Financial Crime The fourth objective introduces a responsibility to reduce financial crime.[123] Financial markets need to maintain a significant degree of integrity, avoid being associated with the proceeds of crime and seek to prevent a climate where fraud is prevalent. This objective does not require the FSA to devote resources to eliminate financial crime. It takes a rather more pragmatic approach by requiring the markets to reduce the likelihood of financial crime occurring. In many respects the former approach would require a disproportionate amount of resources because it is impossible to measure accurately the size of the problem and eliminate it. It is important to emphasise that this objective transcends the whole financial system, so it is vital that no one sector is more susceptible than another either to receiving the proceeds of crime or in its propensity for other forms of criminal activities. It is reasonable to suggest that the FSA as a single regulator is

117 Ibid., at p. 28.

118 Davies, H. (1999) 'Building the Financial Services Authority: What's new?', 1999 Travers Lecture, London Guildhall University Business School, March, available at www.fsa.gov.uk/speeches/1999/march/11031999.htm, p. 4; HM Treasury Response to the Joint Committee's First Report, available at www.fsa.gov.uk/development/legal/f...t_committee/first_report/hmt_response.htm, para. B.

119 FSA, n. 96 above, at p. 104.

120 See pp. 181–218.

121 Campbell, A. and Cartwright, P. (2001) *Banks in Crisis: A Legal Response*, Aldershot, Ashgate, in particular p. 151.

122 See pp. 191–193.

123 FSMA 2000, s. 6(1).

best placed to ensure this is the case, so that a level playing field exists in relation to the compliance costs associated with reducing financial crime across the industry.

The responsibility of achieving this objective is placed on regulated persons, who need to be aware of how their business can be a channel for the proceeds of crime.[124] In addition, they need to devote adequate resources to reducing the likelihood of abuse by insiders, i.e. employees involved in fraud or dishonesty. The concerted move towards reducing financial crime has placed considerable emphasis on, for instance, regulated persons to know their customers. This has been an important mantra not only domestically but also internationally, in line with best practice in this area.[125] Various events in the international community have also placed more emphasis on 'knowing your customer' for the purpose of combating terrorist financing. These political concerns have required regulated firms to devote a considerable amount of resources to reducing the likelihood of them being used for these kinds of purposes. For instance, designated money-laundering officers are assigned the responsibility of putting in place measures suitable for arraigning financial crime. Firms are required to have in place appropriate systems to deal with record keeping, customer identification and internal reporting procedures to prevent, *inter alia*, money laundering. The FSA has, where it has considered it necessary, taken enforcement action against firms that have not put in place appropriate anti-money-laundering compliance functions. For instance, Royal Bank of Scotland was fined £750,000 for a breach of money-laundering rules applying to customer identification.[126] In the case of Northern Ireland Insurance Brokers, permission to carry on regulated activities was revoked after suspicions that senior management had assisted clients in providing false information about their addresses.[127] Indeed, such requirements are not just the responsibility of firms but also individuals who fail to comply with anti-money-laundering procedures.[128]

The FSA Principles

The FSMA 2000 sets out a number of regulatory principles intended to underpin the new regulatory objectives, namely efficiency and economy, role of management, proportionality, innovation, the competitiveness of the UK and competition.[129] In the discharge of its functions, the FSA must take into account whether a new measure is an efficient use of regulatory resources. Whether regulatory actions have a sufficiently high level of certainty to be measurable is debatable.[130]

---

124 FSA Handbook, *Money Laundering* (ML).

125 Ibid., (ML3); see also FSA (2003) 'Identification of existing customers by regulated firms', briefing note, July; FSA (2003) *Reducing Money Laundering Risk: Know Your Customer and Anti-Money Laundering Monitoring*, August. For international standards see information published by the FATF, available at www.fatf.org.

126 FSA, n. 96 above, at p. 57.

127 Ibid.

128 FSA, n. 116 above, at p. 20.

129 FSA Principles, available at www.fsa.gov.uk/objectives/1_principles.html.

130 Ferran, E. and Goodhart, C. A. E. (2001) *Regulating Financial Services and Markets in the 21st Century*, Oxford, Hart, at p. 157.

The FSA has a formal obligation to have a regard for the ability of financial markets to compete with their international counterparts. The increasing internationalisation of markets and the interaction of various participants in those markets have made the capital markets much more interdependent. This interdependency is also a feature of specific product markets, such as those for derivatives and core equities (the source of the derivatives), where price movements are closely correlated.[131] This principle formalises to some extent the traditional *de facto* measures of the previous regulatory and supervisory authorities. For example, the Bank had maintained that its style of supervision ensured the competitiveness of UK financial markets by maintaining a level playing field across financial sectors and jurisdictions. However, there was a perception that the Bank's style of supervision was one that encouraged a 'lax regulatory environment' to promote the City of London.

Competition policy is an integral part of structuring regulation and supervision. This obligation requires the FSA to dismantle obstacles that might impede or distort that ability to compete because of the structure it has put in place. In short, the FSA is required to maintain a level playing field between the various sectors of the financial industry.[132] Recent policy guidance obliges the FSA to carry out an analysis of competition and, on the basis of its findings, determine whether a policy decision it is contemplating will facilitate competition and innovation in the market.[133] It also needs to estimate the impact of a policy initiative on London (the financial centre), and to assess the costs and benefits of the burdens and restrictions which may arise if that policy were implemented. The guidance elaborates on 'effective competition' by highlighting the importance of achieving the best possible level of 'social welfare', whether for the consumer or the firm. In general terms, it maintains that efficiency and costs are improved through competition, hence the importance of not stifling competition.[134]

The FSA Consumer and Practitioner Panels

The FSA has established two formal panels, the Practitioner and Consumer Panels.[135] The formal panel of practitioners has a general duty to consult about FSA policy and market developments.[136] In many ways what the new regime provides is the best of 'self-regulation' practice: close links with the industry and a competent adviser base for policy formulation, without ceding the power of authorisation, supervision and enforcement to that base. The Practitioner Panel has attempted to place distance between itself and the FSA in terms of any suggestion that it is simply an FSA forum

131 See SEC Staff Report (1987) *The October 1987 Market Break*, US SEC Division of Market Regulation, at pp. 3–6.

132 FSMA 2000, s. 3(e) (g). It is not surprising that the Association of British Bankers advocated competition to be an objective of regulation within the new regime – see Joint Committee on Financial Services and Markets (1999) *First Report*, Appendix 13, para. 4.

133 FSA (2000) *Making Policy in the FSA: How to Take Account of Competition. A Guide to Competition Analysis in Financial Services* (Guide to Competition), July.

134 Ibid., at p. 7.

135 FSA (1998) n. 89 above.

136 FSMA 2000, ss. 9 and 10 respectively.

for practitioners.[137] The establishment of the Consumer Panel provides balance in the policy formation process and places the interests of consumers on the regulatory agenda. This move reduces the perception of regulatory capture by the providers of financial services.[138] The introduction of the Consumer Panel on an equal footing to the Practitioner Panel has brought with it a considerable degree of tension between their respective interests. The assessment below indicates some of the general concerns, rather than detailed issues of the FSA's approach to prudential regulation, about moving towards a single regulator and its objectives and principles.

Reflections on the UK's Adoption of a Single Regulator

The move away from multiple regulators to a single-regulator approach with the establishment of the FSA was a bold step in the light of the sheer size of the UK financial services industry and the importance attached to it in terms of its overall contribution to the economy. The move to a single regulator inevitably avoids a firm having to deal with different regulatory bodies overseeing similar areas of its business.[139] Indeed, the 1999 Practitioner Panel report indicated the dissatisfaction of financial institutions with the previous regulatory bodies,[140] with the exception of banks and building societies, which regarded their respective regulators quite highly.[141] The 2004 report confirms the reluctance about any possible return to the old systems of regulation,[142] and indeed the adoption of the single regulator was 'positively supported'.[143] But the move to a single regulator was never going to mean that the problems of the past would effectively be eliminated: as the FSA is an amalgamation of the past regulatory bodies it has had to deal with failures that have continued on after it took over the regulatory helm of the financial markets, such

137 FSA (1997) 'Practitioner involvement', consultation paper, October. This was more forcefully iterated in a speech by chairman Donald Brydon at the FSA Annual Open Meeting, 18 July 2002, at p. 1.

138 Financial Services Consumer Panel (1999) 'Financial Services Consumer Panel calls for changes to the Financial Services Bill to safeguard consumers', press release, 13 April.

139 For a UK perspective see Briault, C. (1999) 'The rationale for a single national financial services regulator', FSA Occasional Paper, May; Davies, H. (1999) n. 78 above. Ferran, E. (2003) 'Examining the United Kingdom's experience in adopting the single financial regulator model', *Brooklyn Journal of International Law*, vol. 28, 257. For a broader international perspective see Abrams, R. K. and Taylor, M. (2000) 'Issues in the unification of financial sector supervision', IMF Working Paper WP/00/213, December; Schooner, H. M. and Taylor, M. (2003) 'United Kingdom and United States responses to the regulatory challenges of modern financial markets', *Texas International Law Journal*, vol. 38, 317; Mwenda, K. K. and Fleming, A. (2001) 'International developments in the organisational structure of financial services supervision', paper presented at seminar hosted by the World Bank Financial Sector, 20 September.

140 Financial Services Practitioner Panel (1999) *Report*, at p. 28.

141 Ibid., at p. 15.

142 Financial Services Practitioner Panel (2004) *Report*, at p. 21.

143 Ibid., at p. 12.

as the pension and endowment mortgage mis-selling scandal.[144] This has required a realignment of the objectives of efficiency and investor protection and awareness much more than was the case in the past. Nevertheless, a clear distinction between the FSA and the past system does exist, in that it has attempted to modernise and put in place a risk-based approach founded on a consolidated prudential system of regulation and supervision to control the financial services industry.[145]

The move to a single regulator and the enactment of the FSMA 2000 does mean that a single approach to regulation and supervision is more likely than with a plurality of regulators attempting to provide a level playing field. According to the 2002 report practitioners thought that a single regulator would have more of an understanding of the business as a whole and 'simplify compliance process'.[146] This to some extent removes the inconsistencies between the various parts of the industry. For example, the limited regulation and supervision of the insurance industry needed to be brought into line with its banking and securities counterparts to ensure more regulatory consistency across the financial services industry.[147] However, the amalgamation of a whole host of regulators under a single body will take time to bring about a 'single regulatory culture'. Indeed, the bringing together of the different cultures of regulation and experience is itself no easy task. The plurality of regulatory cultures cannot be eradicated by simply subsuming them into a single framework of regulation and supervision, even if it is risk based. For example, with the single regulator made up of a whole host of regulators it could mean that banks are no longer considered unique, as they were viewed by bank regulators, but just another financial institution.[148] A single regulator may be able to see group activities better from a group compliance point of view, but the specialisation and knowledge an individual regulator may have of a single group entity is something that cannot simply be ignored. Indeed, while certain aspects of business are centralised for specific efficiency purposes, a considerable number of issues give rise to specialised compliance matters on a day-to-day basis that warrant specialist regulators at hand for guidance. This is not to suggest that regulators are in some respect quasi-managers of risks in a financial institution, but a degree of assistance is necessary to build dialogue between the FSA and the regulated to avoid issues escalating into material non-compliance.[149] In order to deal with this issue the FSA has put into place a new organisational structure to reflect the financial services industry better, building on the integration of prudential regulation and conduct-of-business divisions.

---

144 Financial Services Consumer Panel (2000) 'Consumer Panel calls for tougher action on mis-sold endowments', press release, 3 October.

145 See pp. 48–53.

146 Financial Services Practitioner Panel (2002) *Report*, at p. 107.

147 Financial Services Consumer Panel (2001) 'Consumer Panel welcomes extension of FSA regulation to mortgage advice and insurance brokers', press release, 12 December; Financial Services Consumer Panel (2001) 'FSA must protect all consumers under new general insurance regulation', press release, 14 December.

148 See Corrigan, G. E. (1982) 'Are banks special?', in *Annual Report Federal Reserve Bank of Minneapolis*, available at www.minneapolisfed.org/pubs/ar/ar1982a.cfm.

149 This is a criticism highlighted by the Practitioner Panel. See pp. 139–140.

The Practitioner Perspective The Practitioner Panel is at the forefront of examining and commenting on the work of the FSA as it affects the providers of financial services, whether they are firms or individual advisers. The expectations of the financial industry of the FSA were at the outset high, in particular in terms of providing a better regulatory environment on the premise of 'strong regulation as a whole'.[150] However, whether or not strong regulation is needed across the board has been at the forefront of concerns in an industry which consists of a complex mix of individual, small and large, retail and wholesale providers of financial services. Indeed, of particular concern is the lack of a clear demarcation line between the retail and wholesale sectors.[151] The existing distinction between provider and consumer used by the FSA is considered too simplistic. According to the Practitioner Panel the lack of a clear demarcation line undermines the UK's competitiveness internationally.[152]

The move towards stronger regulation has brought with it a sense of 'overkill' in the eyes of the industry in terms of the burden of regulation.[153] This is particularly the case with compliance costs, which they say have not been apportioned appropriately between retail and wholesale sectors. The view of the wholesale sector is a concern in light of the fact that it is generally perceived to require less regulation than its retail counterpart. The 2004 report indicated that at least 80 per cent of large firms thought the current regulatory regime was 'too great a burden' on the industry.[154] The weight of regulation is suggested to have undermined rather than benefited the interests of consumers; and these interests were considered to have been given greater weighting than the FSA's other objectives.[155] While the FSA is set up as a separate legal entity distinct from government, practitioners were of the opinion in the 2002 report that this was a formal separation rather than of any substance, in that the FSA was following the government's concern to protect consumers.[156] In many respects the growing responsibility of firms and individuals providing financial services emanates from the enhanced position of consumers in financial regulation, in particular the principle of 'treating customers fairly'.[157] One must also highlight the fact that the industry considers the approach taken by the FSA to have hindered the development of new products and services, and undermined its general obligation to ensure the competitiveness of UK financial markets.[158] The Practitioner Panel has called for a review of the way the retail and wholesale sectors are dealt with, so that the burden of regulation is less with respect to the wholesale end of the industry where investors are more sophisticated. In addition to the costs of regulation, another significant hindrance has been the costs of compliance incurred

150 Practitioner Panel, n. 142 above, at p. 22.

151 HM Treasury N2 Plus 2 Review: The practitioners thoughts on what should be included, available at www.fs-pp.org.uk/inquiry_responses.html.

152 Ibid., at p. 1.

153 Practitioner Panel, n. 142 above, at p. 26.

154 Ibid., at p. 31.

155 Ibid., at p. 28.

156 Practitioner Panel, n. 146 above, at p. 109.

157 See Principle 6, Principles for Businesses.

158 Practitioner Panel, n. 142 above, at p. 5.

by the industry. The 2004 report indicated that most practitioners from both retail and wholesale sectors thought compliance costs were unreasonably high, and were likely to continue to increase.[159] These issues have also led to concerns about the overall competitiveness of the UK financial services industry being undermined. Finally, another criticism of the FSA in the 2004 report is the lack of assistance in providing guidance to regulated firms.[160] This reduces the positive dialogue between the regulated and regulator to discuss how effectively rules can be applied, and is heightened when there is a perception that the regulator is prone to use enforcement sanctions rather than dialogue.[161]

The Consumer Perspective The events of the 1980s and 1990s are inextricably linked to the interests of lay consumers who have been mis-sold financial products.[162] This required a realignment of the various interests that make up the financial services industry at the provider and consumer ends. This issue can be illustrated by the financial costs of the pension mis-selling scandal, which will result in a compensation bill of approximately £11.5 billion and cost the industry £2 billion for the review it had to conduct to deal with the cases.[163] Indeed, the move towards financial conglomeration and more competition has tended to affect the volume of providers and prices in the marketplace rather than working to create more informed customers. The Consumer Panel, like its practitioner counterpart, has tried to gauge the needs of those it represents to see how effective the FSA has been in addressing consumer concerns.[164]

The two objectives of financial regulation – consumer awareness and protection – provide the basis for assessing the effectiveness of the FSA and the financial services industry. The traditional idea of consumer protection has tended to be concerned with, *inter alia*, protection against fraud, mis-selling of financial products and compensation when consumers lose money through these or by the failure of financial institutions. Indeed, the way the regulator acts in such cases through enforcement actions and compensation is a means of assessing the FSA's approach to protecting consumer interests.[165] In addition to the importance attached to consumer protection, the level of consumer awareness of financial products has been brought to the fore by the FSA, in light of the fact that the more consumers are aware of

159 Ibid., at p. 34.

160 Ibid., at p. 66.

161 Ibid., at p. 68.

162 Financial Services Consumer Panel (1999) *Annual Report*, at p. 15; Financial Services Consumer Panel, n. 144 above.

163 Financial Services and Markets Tribunal, *Rayner, E. T. & Townsend, J. R. v. The Financial Services Authority*, July 2004, at p. 3.

164 Financial Services Consumer Panel (2000) *Consumers in the financial market: Financial Services Consumer Panel annual survey of consumers 2000*.

165 Financial Services Consumer Panel (2004) 'Submission to the Treasury Committee's inquiry into "Restoring confidence in long-term savings"', January, at p. 7; HM Treasury (2003) *Review of the Financial Services & Markets Act 2000 (FSMA) – The Financial Services Consumer Panel's Priorities*, at p. 2; see also Financial Services Consumer Panel (2003) *Research Report: Consumer Concerns in Great Britain*, Spring.

the different financial services and providers, the more likely they are to be able to avoid the problems indicated above. Indeed, the issues of consumer awareness and protection are now seen as inextricably linked to one another.

The failure of the financial services industry to deal adequately with consumers has been a major issue for the FSA. For example, Equitable Life was just one of the major débâcles it had to contend with at the commencement of its responsibilities, as this put a number of existing and new pension policyholders in the position of losing considerable amounts of money on their policies. The difficulties at Equitable Life occurred because of the gross failures of management to mitigate the problems arising from their approach to calculating annuity rates.[166] The company's guaranteed annuity rate exceeded market rates and gave rise to excessive liability in the region of £1.5 billion. This was exacerbated by a House of Lords judgment that the Equitable Life board's decision to change its annuity rate to secure some kind of future for the business was detrimental to existing policyholders as it was a breach of its contract.[167] This ultimately led to the decision by Equitable Life to put its business up for sale in an attempt to secure a future for its new customers; this was unsuccessful, as a buyer failed to materialise.

The Equitable Life débâcle gave rise to considerable criticism of the regulatory regime overlooking the insurance sector, resulting in misgivings about the previous regulators. This led to a number of public investigations into the whole affair, the Baird Report,[168] the Penrose Report[169] and the Parliamentary Ombudsman's Report.[170] A significant proportion of the problems occurred before the FSA came into existence, when the DTI and the Treasury were responsible for regulating the insurance industry – the FSA took responsibility as prudential regulator from 1 January 1999. It was criticised for, *inter alia*, not notifying consumers fully about the problems associated with Equitable Life so they could avoid buying policies that were relatively unmarketable by other providers without some sort of financial penalty.[171]

The Baird Report investigating the FSA's role in the Equitable Life scandal highlighted a number of weaknesses in the FSA's approach to managing the problems in the interests of policyholders, even though it noted that the 'die was cast' by the time the FSA took over.[172] A number of recommendations were specific to the

166 Consumer Panel (2004) ibid., at pp. 37–48.

167 *Equitable Life Assurance Society v. Alan David Hyman* [2000] 1 All ER 961.

168 *Report of the Financial Services Authority on the Review of the Regulation of the Equitable Life Assurance Society from 1 January 1999 to 8 December 2000, which Her Majesty's Government is submitting as Evidence to the Inquiry Conducted by Lord Penrose* (Baird Report), 16 October 2001, at p. 186.

169 *Return to an Order of the Honourable House of Commons Dated 8 March 2004 for the Report of the Equitable Life Inquiry. The Right Honourable Lord Penrose*, HC290 (Penrose Report).

170 Parliamentary Ombudsman (2002/03) *The Prudential Regulation of Equitable Life. Part 1: Overview and Summary of Findings*, HC 809-1 (Parliamentary Ombudsman Report).

171 Baird Report, n. 168 above, at p. 181.

172 Ibid., at p. 187.

prudential regulation of insurance, or lack thereof.[173] The FSA was said to be not 'proactive' enough to seek out the problems, and failed to coordinate adequately the prudential and conduct-of-business issues, which were separate in the old regime and brought together in rudimentary form under the auspices of the FSA at the time. The Baird Report suggested better coordination and exchange of information between the two divisions to avoid some of the problems associated with Equitable Life, which were interdependent and so required a more integrated approach to addressing the situation regarding annuity rates.[174] This was echoed by the Parliamentary Ombudsman's Report, which stated that with hindsight the prudential regulator could have emphasised the concerns about annuity rates to its conduct-of-business counterpart.[175] The Baird Report recommended a more 'intrusive and involved' form of prudential regulation, similar to that experienced in the banking sector.[176] This is also indicated in the Penrose Report, in which the level of scepticism in dealing with regulated firms was considered wanting.[177] The Penrose Report criticised the FSA for not keeping abreast of the issues surrounding the sale of Equitable Life, thereby placing new policyholders at risk.[178] However, the Parliamentary Ombudsman found no evidence that the FSA failed to envisage a sale not going ahead in light of the early interest by prospective buyers. Indeed, the report highlighted the sensitive issue of balancing allowing the company to continue to do business with the interests of existing and new policyholders as the major reason for not intervening to stop it pursuing new business during the period when it was looking for a buyer.

The criticism levelled at the FSA needs to be put into some form of context. The FSA had not, at the time, put into place its single regulatory regime, which may have led to a more efficient way of dealing with the problems associated with Equitable Life. Indeed, the Parliamentary Ombudsman concluded that the FSA's acts or omissions did not amount to maladministration in its investigation into the matters arising from the débâcle. According to Callum McCarthy, the modernisation of the regulatory regime that oversees the insurance industry needs to ensure that the industry meets the needs of consumers by making sure it has the 'hard financial resources necessary to back the promises they make to their policyholders'.[179] This will help to ensure that the expectations gap between the returns consumers can anticipate and the promises made by insurance providers about potential returns is better aligned to reduce the likelihood of another débâcle such as this. The events at Equitable Life highlight the gaps in prudential regulation between the sectors of the financial services industry, and the need to ensure better consistency so that consumers are not adversely affected.

173 Ibid., at pp. 188–189.

174 Ibid., at pp. 201–202.

175 Parliamentary Ombudsman Report, n. 170 above, at p. 7.

176 Baird Report, n. 168 above, at p. 206.

177 Penrose Report, n. 169 above, at p. 709.

178 Ibid., at p. 725.

179 Financial Services Authority (2004) 'FSA statement on the Equitable Life inquiry FSA/PN/022/2004', press release, 8 March.

The expectations gap between regulated firms as providers and consumers of financial services has been widened by the fact that consumers lack the appropriate level of understanding to be able to judge between 'good' and 'bad' financial products.[180] Indeed, the sheer number of participants and their competition for business results in more confusion rather than assisting consumers with making better choices between financial products. This was the opinion of the Consumer Panel in its response to the Treasury regarding long-term savings.[181] It places heavy criticism on the shoulders of firms, which it considers have generally failed to reduce the informational asymmetry between consumers and providers in marketing their products, and highlights the reluctance of firms to rectify problems when mis-selling is evident and provide compensation in a timely manner. In the light of this the Consumer Panel is supportive of the enforcement approach taken by the FSA and the high-profile fines it has exacted. In its 2003 annual report the panel contends that it is these kinds of actions of which firms take note.[182] However, the panel also recommended a move towards forming a league table of offending firms to force them to deal with customers more fairly, in addition to the FSA's current approach of publicising individual enforcement decisions. While the FSA enforcement actions have mainly been supported by the Consumer Panel, it is critical of the FSA's general approach to ensuring that firms comply with its policy initiatives and contends that the FSA does not intervene enough in this regard.[183] It criticises the FSA's approach of simply accepting the industry's views, giving rise to, for example, consumers buying inappropriate financial products.[184]

The US Approach to Bank Supervision

The US system of prudential regulation and supervision of banking is without doubt a complex structure, in that it is not centralised in a single regulator but is the responsibility of a number of separate and independent regulators. Kushmeider contends explicitly that it is a system 'no one building a [financial regulatory] system anew would want to duplicate'.[185] This is exacerbated by the fact that bank regulation and supervision are separate from other functions to ensure financial stability, namely LOLR and deposit insurance, giving rise to competing responsibilities and claims. In addition, the adoption of a dual system of chartering banks to undertake banking business adds to the complexity.

180 Financial Services Consumer Panel submission to the Treasury Committee's inquiry into 'Restoring confidence in long-term savings', January 2004.

181 Ibid., at p. 4.

182 Financial Services Consumer Panel (2004) *Annual Report Highlights 2003/04*, at p. 2.

183 Financial Services Consumer Panel (2004) *Annual Report*, at p. 7.

184 See Chapter 4 in this volume.

185 Kushmeider, R. M. (2005) 'The US federal financial regulatory system: Restructuring Federal Bank regulation', *FDIC Banking Review*, vol. 17, 1.

The Dual Banking System

The dual banking system consists of two formal methods of chartering commercial banks (authorising them to undertake the business of banking): at the state level and at the federal level.[186] This is a consequence in many respects of the constitutional make-up of the USA, based on both a state and a federal system of governance.[187] Historically, state-regulated banks issued their own notes. This was before the federal government intervened to introduce, at a federal level, a national currency to support its war efforts at the time.[188] The Office Comptroller of Currency (OCC) was placed at the helm of the national currency to manage it.[189] The dual banking system was a by-product of the legislation to introduce the national currency, and put an end to states issuing their own banknotes. Indeed, the expectation was that state-chartered banks would abandon their state charter for a federal charter. But the introduction of the new federal charter did not result in a mass exodus from the state system, even when a subsequent punitive tax was imposed on state banknotes to force them to change.[190] The result was two formal systems of chartering: the bank regulator in the individual state charters the state banks, and the OCC charters national banks pursuant to the National Bank Act 1864.[191] But the dual banking system is not rigidly divided into two parts – a state bank could convert its charter to a national charter and vice versa.[192] According to Kenneth Scott, 'the core of the dual banking system is the simultaneous existence of different regulatory options that are not alike in terms of statutory provisions, regulatory implementation and administrative policy'.[193] Nevertheless the complexity of the dual system gives rise to a common conclusion that the present arrangements would not in hindsight be the system of regulation

186 For an examination of the dual banking system see OCC (2003) *National Banks and the Dual Banking System*, September, in particular the limited powers of the state to intervene in the supervision of national banks, at p. 16; Schooner, H. M. (1996) 'Recent challenges to the persistent dual banking system', *St Louis University Law Journal*, vol. 41, 263, at p. 267; Butler, H. N. and Macey, J. R. (1988) 'The myth of competition in the dual banking system', *Cornell Law Review*, vol. 73, 677. For a critique of some of the limits of the dual banking system, in particular the utility of state involvement in banking regulation and supervision, see Wilmarth, A. E. (1990) 'The expansion of state bank powers, the Federal response, and the case for preserving the dual banking system', *Fordham Law Review*, vol. 58, 1113, at pp. 1239–1255.

187 Redford, E. S. (1966) 'Dual banking: A case study in federalism', *Law and Contemporary Problems*, vol. 31, 749; Butler and Macey, ibid., at pp. 682–683.

188 The National Currency Act 1863 and subsequently modernised with the enactment of the National Bank Act 1864.

189 12 USC, § 1.

190 Schooner, H. M. and Taylor, M. (1999) 'Convergence and competition: The case of bank regulation in Britain and the United States', *Michigan Journal of International Law*, vol. 20, 595, at p. 610.

191 12 USC, § 1; see Comptroller of the Currency, n. 186 above.

192 For conversion from national banks to state banks see 12 USC, Chapter 2, § 214(a).

193 Scott, K. E. (1994) 'The dual banking system: A model of competition in regulation', *Stanford Law Review*, vol. 30, 1, at p. 41, cited in OCC, n. 186 above, at p. 3; Schooner, n. 186 above, highlights the costs of converting from one charter to another, at p. 272.

and supervision that would be put in place to oversee US banking.[194] Their separate charters and membership ultimately increase the complexity of the whole structure.

In addition to these two chartering systems, membership of the Federal Reserve and the Federal Deposit Insurance Corporation (FDIC) also plays a significant role.[195] The FDIC and the FRB have prudential responsibilities to oversee the activities of their members in addition to the primary regulators.[196] National banks are required to be members of the Federal Reserve and the FDIC.[197] Membership of the FDIC is automatic once a national bank becomes a member of the Federal Reserve, giving it access to the public deposit insurance fund.[198] State member banks have the option to choose to come under the jurisdiction of the Federal Reserve[199] and thus the FDIC. Membership means the banks are under the umbrella of their chartering authority, as well as the Federal Reserve and the FDIC, for the purposes of supervision and enforcement to a lesser or greater extent to fulfil their individual responsibilities.[200] For example, a national bank will be chartered by the OCC, which will have responsibility for its prudential supervision; the FDIC will have supervisory and enforcement responsibility to fulfil its obligations to the deposit insurance fund; and the Federal Reserve will have responsibility over its access to the discount window and reserve requirements.

The Individual Regulators

The primary regulators have the main responsibility for prudential regulation. The primary regulatory bodies are the Federal Reserve,[201] the OCC,[202] the FDIC[203] and the Office of Thrift Supervision (OTS),[204] which are the primary federal supervisors of approximately 5,321, 2,031, 949 and 936 institutions respectively. These statistics highlight both the size of the banking system and the responsibility each regulatory authority has. At a domestic level the OCC and the FDIC are ultimately the main authorities responsible for bank regulation, supervision and examination.

The regulation and supervision of the business of banking has evolved over a considerable period of time, most notably through legislative means codified in

---

194 Kushmeider, n. 185 above, at p. 1.

195 12 USC, § 1813 (d)–(e).

196 'Banking institutions and their regulators', available at www.ny.frb.org/banking/regrept/BIATR.pdf. This matrix provides a 'simple' outline of the primary regulators and membership system in the US system of regulation and supervision, deposit insurance and emergency liquidity support provided therein.

197 12 USC, § 282; Board of Governors of the Federal Reserve System (1994) *The Federal Reserve System: Purposes and Functions*, Washington, DC, available at www.federalreserve.gov/pf/pf.htm, at p. 13.

198 12 USC, § 1814 (b).

199 12 USC, § 321 and § 282 respectively.

200 See for instance 12 USC, § 325 326.

201 See www.federalreverse.gov/.

202 See www.occ.treas.gov/.

203 See www.fdic.gov/.

204 See www.ots.treas.gov/.

various places in Title 12 Banks and Banking of the United States Code (USC); this is divided into 49 chapters, giving rise to a considerable level of complexity.[205] The responsibilities of the FDIC,[206] the OCC,[207] the FRB[208] and the OTS[209] are broadly speaking set out in separate chapters; these make up the 'Appropriate Federal Banking Agency'.[210] In addition, a significant proportion of responsibility is conferred on the individual federal regulators as administrative bodies separately within the Code of Federal Regulations (CFR) designating administrative powers.[211] The primary regulators have also devised their own styles of regulation, supervision and enforcement which are set out separately in their individual manuals.

The OCC is responsible for chartering and supervision of national banks. Pursuant to s. 27(a)–(b) of 12 USC,[212] it is authorised to grant national bank charters and is responsible on an administrative level, as provided in CFR s. 4.2, for overseeing national banks, with powers to regulate, supervise and exercise enforcement actions in accordance with federal laws. The OCC can appoint examiners to national banks 'as often as the [OCC] shall deem necessary',[213] and these banks are required to make reports about their 'condition', regarding their financial health in terms of assets and liabilities for instance, to the OCC.[214] The OCC is also responsible for ensuring that national banks operate in a safe and sound manner.[215] But it must be mindful that it achieves its other regulatory goals, which are to 'promote competitiveness for national banks' and 'improve efficiency of examinations and supervision, including reducing supervisory burden'.[216]

The Federal Reserve is at the 'helm' of the banking system in its capacity as central bank to manage monetary stability.[217] It acts as a central source of liquidity and a single-note issuer.[218] The Federal Reserve puts emphasis on combining its responsibilities for monetary policy and bank supervision to gauge the prudential stability of the banking system.[219] It has specific responsibility for supervising

205 For a historical account of the evolution of bank regulation at both state and federal levels see Davis, A. K. (1966) 'Banking regulation today: A banker's view', *Law and Contemporary Problems*, vol. 31, 639.

206 Title 12 USC, Chapter 16.

207 12 USC, Chapter 1.

208 12 USC, Chapter 3.

209 12 USC, Chapter 12.

210 12 USC, § 1813 (q) (1)–(4).

211 12 CFR.

212 12 USC, § 21–27.

213 12 USC, § 481.

214 12 USC, § 161.

215 See generally pp. 69–72.

216 OCC (1996) *Bank Supervision Process*, at p. 1; OCC, Comptroller of the Currency Administrator of National Banks (2005) *A Guide to the National Banking System*, Washington DC, April, at p. 3.

217 Federal Reserve Act 1913; Board of Governors of the Federal Reserve System, n. 197 above.

218 Board of Governors of the Federal Reserve System, ibid.

219 Ibid., at p. 72; for some observations about the dual responsibility see Kushmeider, n. 185 above, at p. 12.

financial holding companies, bank holding companies, state charter banks and foreign bank operations.[220] The oversight the Federal Reserve exercises over the respective holding companies is deemed necessary for the purposes of gauging the groups' safety and soundness. This gives rise to a necessity to cooperate and seek relevant information from the other primary regulators rather than making duplicate examinations of a bank and its subsidiaries.[221]

The FDIC was established in 1933 after the huge spate of bank failures in the 1920s and 1930s.[222] It was set up to insure 'the deposits of all banks and savings associations'.[223] FDIC membership gives rise to a further layer of prudential supervision for the purpose of safeguarding the deposit insurance fund.[224] The FDIC is the primary regulator and supervisor of state-chartered banks that have decided not to become members of the Federal Reserve system, which are categorised as non-member banks.[225] Its most important function is the administration of the deposit insurance fund, which provides protection of up to $100,000 to an individual depositor.

The Federal Financial Institutions Examination Council (FFIEC) was set up in 1979 to assist the federal bank regulators to enhance the level of uniformity and consistency in their supervisory, examination and enforcement practices.[226] The move towards creating a single body to coordinate and enhance consistency between the regulators should not come as a surprise: it is designed to reduce the potential inconsistency that might arise from the fact that a number of regulators have overlapping responsibilities to oversee the activities of federally regulated banks. In addition to enhancing the level of consistency, another concern is to reduce unnecessary regulatory burdens that might arise as a result of federal regulators' actions. The FFIEC periodically publishes interagency notices on, for example, the importance of notifying and coordinating information about possible enforcement decisions taken by a federal regulator with other regulators.[227]

A number of problems could arise with a multi-regulatory system of prudential regulation, as it requires a significant amount of cooperation and communication for it to operate efficiently to reduce the likelihood of bank non-compliance – failures have resulted from a lack of coordinated work. It will be shown that the

220 Board of Governors of the Federal Reserve System, n. 197 above, Chapter 5, Supervision and Regulation. For bank holding companies see Bank Holding Company Act 1956 as amended 12 USC, § 1841; foreign banks, International Banking Act 1978 as amended 12 USC, § 3101.

221 For example, FRB (2000) 'Framework for financial holding company supervision', Supervisory Letter SR 00-13, 15 August.

222 Banking Act 1933, Public Law 73-66.

223 12 USC, § 1811(a).

224 12 USC, § 1811 1832.

225 12 USC, § 1815.

226 12 USC, § 3301 3308, in particular 3305; for information about the Federal Financial Institutions Examination Council see www.ffiec.gov/default.htm.

227 FFIEC (1997) 'Interagency coordination of formal corrective action by the Federal Bank regulatory agencies', revised policy statement, February, available at www.fdic.gov/regulations/laws/federal/rpsi.pdf.

complexity of the system means issues are not always communicated efficiently between the regulators across the financial services industry, let alone the banking industry. Nevertheless, the US system of regulation is considered 'appropriate' to undertake the task of overseeing the finance industry, but the emphasis is on better coordination between the respective regulators so that the activities of bank-financial conglomerates can be better monitored.

The USA Moves Towards Regulatory Consolidation

The move towards regulatory consolidation in the banking system dates back to the 1930s and continued intermittently into the 1990s.[228] However, this has been unsuccessful due to the underlying confidence in the regulatory system that prevails, despite a number of misgivings. This issue is obviously heightened with the move in some quarters now towards a single-regulator model governing the financial system, or even a single bank regulator.

The multi-agency approach has advocated that competition between the regulators results in a diminution of unnecessary regulation and supervision. Alan Gart illustrates the idea of 'competing in laxity' by pointing out that some regulators lured new members with the incentive of reducing the burden of regulation.[229] Moreover, Gart highlights that competition existed between the regulators regarding, for instance, the permissible business activities they allowed their members to pursue, and gave rise to pressure to ensure the multi-regulator model is retained.[230] The most significant concern was the large number of bank failures, which undermined confidence in having such a multitude of bank regulators. This led to criticism of the rigour with which these institutions were examined. The findings of a General Accounting Office (GAO) review highlighted a number of misgivings across the board in all the regulatory bodies; for instance, the Federal Reserve Board failed to supervise the activities of financial holding companies sufficiently, in particular intra-group transactions.[231] Moreover, the GAO report highlighted the lack of coordination between regulators with supervisory responsibilities. It pointed to the failure of the Bank of New England as an example where the OCC as the examiner of the lead bank and the Federal Reserve responsible for examining the holding company did not discover the fact that it was about to collapse.[232] The report proposed the establishment of a Federal Banking Commission and the dismantlement of the OCC and the FDIC. However, the rationale for change at the time could not provide a conclusive solution as to the future role of the Federal Reserve, given the importance attached to combining bank regulation and management of monetary policy.[233]

228 GAO (1996) 'Bank oversight: Fundamental principles for modernizing the US structure', GAO/T-GGD-96-117.

229 Gart, A. (1993) *Regulation, Deregulation, Reregulation*, New York, John Wiley & Sons, at p. 140.

230 Ibid., at p. 143.

231 GAO (1994) 'Bank regulation: Consolidation of the regulatory agencies', GAO/T-GGD-94-106.

232 Ibid., at p. 2.

233 Ibid., at p. 6.

Notwithstanding the various proposals for reform, the move towards a single bank regulator has not to date borne fruit.

The wholehearted move towards universal banking was reined in by the overarching concern about the fragility of the banking system.[234] The vulnerability of the official safety net for insured institutions has been a major consideration.[235] The position pre-1930s was a different picture, with an active policy of allowing commercial banks to pursue securities activities.[236] The fragility of the banking system was heightened during the 1930s when thousands of banks failed and the Great Depression ensued. The policy-makers at the time thought that the fragility of the banking system was exacerbated by its involvement in securities business. Consequently, the separation of commercial bank and securities businesses, in the form of deposit-taking and lending and underwriting securities respectively, was enacted with the passage of the Banking Act 1933, colloquially referred to as the Glass-Steagall Act. This Act also attempted to avoid concentration within the financial system by dismantling the universal banking model.[237] Subsequent research into the failures during the Great Depression called into question the premise on which the Glass-Steagall Act was passed, suggesting that depression ensued from the economic circumstances at the time rather than systemic failures in the conduct of bank securities business.[238] Benston contends the abuses and conflicts of interest associated with banks involved in securities business at the time were exaggerated.[239] The Glass-Steagall Act was considered, therefore, to be a political reaction to mete out appropriate measures to curb the excesses of those deemed to be the culprits for the Great Depression.

---

234 GAO (1987) 'Bank powers: Insulating banks from the potential risks of expanded activities', GAO/GGD-87-35, April; GAO (1988) 'Bank powers: Issues related to the repeal of the Glass-Steagall Act', GAO/GGD-88-37, January; GAO (1988) 'Testimony, using "firewalls" in a post-Glass-Steagall banking environment', GAO/T-GGD-88-25, April; GAO (1995) 'Testimony, financial regulation: Modernization of the financial services regulatory system', GAO/T-GGD-95-121. For examination of the regulatory structures that oversee the securities markets see GAO (1995) 'Testimony, financial regulation: Benefits and risks of merging SEC and CFTC', GAO/T-GGD-95-153, May.

235 GAO, GAO/GGD-88-37, ibid., at p. 16; GAO, GAO/T/-GGD-95-121, ibid., at p. 6.

236 See Edwards, F. R. (1979) 'Banks and securities activities: Legal and economic perspectives on the Glass-Steagall Act', in Goldberg, L. G. and White, L. J. (eds) *The Deregulation of the Banking and Securities Industries*, Lexington, MA, Lexington Books, pp. 273–291, at p. 275.

237 Shull, B. (2000) 'Financial modernization legislation in the United States: Background and implications', UNCTAD Discussion Paper No. 151, UNCTAD/OSG/DP/151.

238 Benston, G. (1990) *Separation of Commercial and Investment Banking: The Glass-Steagall Act Revisited and Reconsidered*, Oxford, Oxford University Press; White, E. (1986) 'Before the Glass-Steagall Act: An analysis of the investment banking activities of national banks', *Explorations in Economic History*, vol. 23, 33; Calomiris, C. W. (2000) *US Bank Deregulation in Historical Perspective*, Cambridge, Cambridge University Press.

239 Benston, ibid.; Senator Carter Glass contended that the abuse of the banks' powers to undertake securities business at that time undermined the safety and soundness of the banking system.

The key features of the prohibition on bank securities business were articulated in ss. 16 and 21 of the Glass-Steagall Act.[240] These provisions prohibited member banks and securities firms respectively from entering into each other's business. Sections 20 and 32 of the Act prevented the use of affiliations and intra-group directorships and employees to circumvent the general prohibition. However, the broad prohibition indicated in these sections includes exceptions to the general rule. First, the restrictions did not apply to state-chartered banks or non-member banks. Secondly, banks could still underwrite government securities. Thirdly, the general prohibition did not apply to banks' overseas operations, where they could undertake a variety of securities activities. In addition to these direct exceptions, the attitude towards a bank's equity holding of non-bank entities was relaxed by the Federal Reserve.[241] The Federal Reserve required the implementation of firewalls to ensure the risks associated with these securities subsidiaries did not adversely affect the safety and soundness of the banking system. The OCC also permitted national banks to undertake other business activities through a separate subsidiary. The regulators have thus played an active role in enhancing the efficiency of the financial system, albeit separately by allowing the growth of bank-financial conglomerates.[242]

The Gramm-Leach-Bliley Act 1999

The move towards the dismantlement of barriers between banks, securities firms and insurance businesses formally came about with the enactment of the Gramm-Leach-Bliley Act 1999 (GLB).[243] The Act's remit is not to provide for a wholesale change to the regulatory structure for the dismantled financial services industry, but to take away the barriers that had prevented financial conglomeration between banks, securities and insurance firms.[244] The objective of the 1999 Act is to encourage the growth of financial conglomeration to enhance the efficiency of the financial system in the USA. However, it does not allow the co-mingling of investment and commercial banking under the same roof, as seen in a 'universal bank' model. The legislation in that respect is not a complete overhaul of the previous system, but only provides incremental change. It retains in part a functional system of regulation where financial businesses are overseen by their respective bodies: the Securities Exchange Commission, the State Insurance Commissioner and the state or federal regulators will respectively regulate the securities, insurance and bank businesses.[245] But at the helm of this system is the Federal Reserve, with the responsibility of being

240 Namely ss. 16, 20–21 and 32 of the Banking Act 1933. Equally important, the Act established the Federal Deposit Insurance Corporation.

241 Shull, n. 237 above, at p. 6.

242 See pp. 69 70.

243 Public Law 106-102, Gramm-Leach-Bliley Act 1999: 'To enhance competition in the financial services industry by providing a prudential framework for the affiliation of banks, securities firms, insurance companies and other financial service providers, and for other purposes.'

244 Ibid., § 101, 103 and 104 respectively.

245 See Titles II and III. For a critical analysis of functional regulation of a financial services industry where barriers are eroding away, giving rise to financial conglomeration, see

'lead regulator' to the financial system as a whole by acting as the consolidated supervisor of financial holding companies (FHCs). In particular the Federal Reserve is to act as the 'umbrella supervisor for financial holding companies, and State insurance regulators' for the purposes of coordinating supervision of FHCs with a bank and an insurance firm.[246]

The 1999 Act extends a bank holding company's scope by giving it the right to form an FHC[247] which can engage in activities of a financial nature or 'incidental to such activities' or 'complementary to a financial activity'[248] provided 'it does not pose a substantial risk to the safety and soundness of depository institutions'. The FRB in consultation with the US Treasury is empowered to decide what activities are 'financial in nature' or may be 'complementary' to financial activities.[249] The provision and the long list of activities included indicate that the idea of 'financial in nature' is interpreted broadly.[250] The restrictions on banks' affiliation with commercial businesses have been relaxed somewhat: FHCs can in certain circumstances hold shares in commercial companies for a limited period, after which they need to be divested.[251] The significant premise for the decision to extend the scope of activities in which an FHC can engage is the safety and soundness of the deposit-taking institution.[252]

The Federal Reserve is conferred formal oversight of both bank holding companies (BHCs) and FHCs for the purposes of consolidated supervision. The respective functional regulators are required to provide examination reports to the Federal Reserve.[253] It can, on the findings of these reports or its own examination of the holding companies and their subsidiaries, take the necessary action to deal with their activities if they pose, *inter alia*, an adverse risk to the deposit-taking institution or the deposit insurance fund.

Schooner, H. M. (1998) 'Regulating risk not function', *University of Cincinnati Law Review*, vol. 66, 441.

246 Public Law 106-102, n. 243 above, § 307.

247 It amends the Bank Holding Company Act 1956, § 4; Public Law 106-102, n. 243 above, § 102.

248 Public Law 106-102, n. 243 above, § 103 (s. 4 (k) (1) (A) and (B)).

249 Ibid., § 103 (s. 4 (k) (3)).

250 Ibid., § 103 (s. 4 (k) (4) (A)–(I)).

251 Ibid., § 103 (s. 4 (n)).

252 In some instances a firewall is also allowed to be put in place; see Public Law 106-102, n. 243 above, s. 46, 'Safety and Soundness Firewalls Applicable to Financial Subsidiaries of Banks' for insured state banks. In addition, to curb the risks associated with the title of 'too-big-to-fail', for some financial holding companies the Federal Reserve is required to look into the 'feasibility' of financial holding companies holding 'a portion of their capital in the form of subordinated debt to enhance the discipline within such groups by such creditors': Public Law 106-102, n. 243 above, § 108 (a) (1).

253 Public Law 106-102, n. 243 above, § 111, 112 and 115.

Reflections on US Financial Modernisation

The move towards formal dismantlement of barriers between the various sectors of the financial system has led to a review of how best to regulate prudentially the financial conglomerates and the risks that emanate from their activities. Consequently, the US method of regulating the financial system has come under pressure to handle complex institutions and conglomerates better.[254] The US regulators have made incremental changes to oversee better the domestic and international services its financial intermediaries undertake. US bank regulators have for a considerable length of time had in place a risk-focused approach to regulating complex banking operations.[255] In light of international measures, the USA has put in place, for instance, consolidated supervision of some securities and insurance firms that operate in the EU so that US firms comply with the Financial Conglomerates Directive.[256] While the prudential regulation of financial services is sound within the respective sectors, the lack of coordination and cooperation between the regulators in dealing with cross-sectoral issues does cause concern and warrants a review of the current regulatory structure.[257] According to Wilmarth, the type of business organisation encouraged post-GLB will potentially place unreasonable demands on the federal safety net to extend its coverage to non-bank activities in the light of the potential systemic risk that could result from part of a large financial conglomerate getting in trouble, whether it is the banking or non-banking part.[258]

The key problem associated with the multi-agency approach governing banking, securities and insurance businesses is the level of communication and cooperation, and indeed competitiveness, between the regulators. This is especially the case when issues to do with one part of a financial conglomerate transcend into other regulatory domains.[259] The issue of regulatory confidentiality means that information about firms cannot be readily passed on to other interested regulatory bodies.[260] To mitigate this problem, in the banking system the FFIEC was established at the federal level.[261] The FFIEC is said to have been successful in setting common principles and standards, but has been reluctant to widen its scope to incorporate securities and insurance businesses to reflect the nature of the industry post-GLB.[262] While the FFIEC is a

254 GAO (2004) 'Financial regulation: Industry changes prompt need to reconsider US regulatory structure', GAO-0561. This section relies on this report to provide the remit for the analysis; Wilmarth, n. 61 above, pp. 454–456.

255 See Lichtenstein, C. C. (2005) 'The Fed's new model of supervision for "large complex banking organisations": Coordinated risk-based supervision of financial multinationals for international financial stability', *Transnational Lawyer*, vol. 18, 283. See pp. 72–76.

256 See GAO, n. 254 above, at p. 30.

257 See generally GAO, n. 254 above, at pp. 8 10.

258 Wilmarth, n. 61 above, at pp. 303–304.

259 A gateway for example does exist in 'significant financial or operational risks that may be evident'; see 12 USC, § 1831l, Coordination of risk analysis between SEC and Federal banking agencies.

260 GAO, n. 254 above, at p. 97.

261 See n. 226 above for information about the FFIEC.

262 GAO, n. 254 above, at p. 98.

formal mechanism to coordinate efforts better between the federal regulators, other informal methods of communication also exist to alleviate day-to-day problems.[263] However, the level of competitiveness between the regulators has led, for instance, to failures at banks being exacerbated by a lack of coordination between regulators in resolving the problems that have arisen.[264]

The issue of FHCs requires the FRB to seek the cooperation of securities and insurance regulators to assist it to supervise their activities, which can be elevated to presidential level if a crisis is serious enough. However, coordination between the regulators on a day-to-day level to supervise FHCs does pose problems, with issues such as fraud not being detected when it transcends into other financial sectors.[265] For example, a 2001 GAO report recommended better information-sharing between bank, securities and insurance regulators to eliminate the possibility of individuals working in one part of the financial services industry when they have been banned in another sector.[266] The issue of monitoring risks that emanate from other sectors has also been heightened in the securities industry. The pressure for better coordination between regulators has been emphasised at a political level post-1987 with the stock market crash and after the attacks of 11 September 2001. But according to the GAO report, while *ad hoc* coordination systems are in place there is no 'systematic sharing of information', and this undermines the assessment of risks that can adversely affect other areas of the industry.[267] For example, the rescue of Long-Term Capital Management (LTCM) showed how regulators were only interested in protecting the interests of their own firms' link to the hedge fund rather than dealing with issues that crossed over into other regulatory jurisdictions.[268] The GAO report highlights that 'functional specialization has drawbacks as well, including the inability to take advantage of the economies of scale and scope'.[269] This regulatory structure overseeing financial conglomerates does not mirror the way they manage their activities across the companies they have formed under holding structures. Wilmarth explains how FHCs manage their affairs, and indeed protect their reputation, in a more centralised rather than decentralised manner which does not reflect the fragmented regulatory structure, even though consolidated supervision is exercised.[270] The incremental changes adopted in GLB, such as firewalls between banks and non-banks, are not robustly supervised, calling into question their actual utility to prevent transactions between the companies in a holding structure.[271]

The strengths of the current system lie with its sheer size, specialism and flexibility in the way regulation is implemented.[272] The GAO report notes the ability

263 Ibid., at p. 99.
264 Ibid., at p. 100.
265 Ibid., at p. 105.
266 GAO (2001) 'Financial services regulators: Better information sharing could reduce fraud', GAO-01-478T.
267 GAO, n. 254 above, at p. 109.
268 Ibid., at p. 110.
269 Ibid., at p. 113.
270 Wilmarth, n. 61 above, at p. 456.
271 Ibid., at pp. 456–457.
272 GAO, n. 254 above, at p. 114.

of regulators to be more sophisticated and innovative, rather than adopting a single approach across the system.[273] Whether it is principles- or rules-based depends on the regulators' choice of how best to oversee the activities for which they are responsible. Notwithstanding the strengths of the current regulatory system, the GAO puts forward a number of 'options' for change; these vary from adopting a single-regulator model to setting up a single body to oversee large, complex financial groups.[274] However, the introduction of GLB warrants further examination of how FHCs are regulated, possibly with the adoption of a lead regulator to coordinate the examination processes of the entities associated with the holding company. The lead regulator could act in cases when a problem arises in one particular entity to help coordinate the dissemination of information between the respective regulators.

Conclusion

This chapter has attempted to place the regulation and supervision of banking in the context of financial stability. The separation of bank supervision and central banking has required the FSA to adopt mechanisms to ensure it can identify matters that may affect such stability with its responsibility to achieve market confidence, one of the key factors associated with maintaining financial stability. For instance, through its domestic and international outlook reports it assists intermediaries in the financial system to monitor forthcoming risks which could threaten their compliance with the regulatory regime. This makes the FSA responsive to changes in the market-place on both a macro and a micro level. So while central banks have the traditional function of ensuring financial stability in its widest sense, a separate regulator also needs to be mindful of associated issues and have monitoring systems in place to help it make better-informed decisions when exercising its responsibilities. These other issues – consumer awareness, consumer protection and reducing financial crime – have been formally expressed separately as objectives of regulation which could undermine market confidence, and have spawned individual policy agendas under separate initiatives.

The unique risks associated with banks did not prevent the UK moving towards deregulation in the mid-1980s so that banks could participate in a broad range of financial services. In this period, as in earlier times, the Bank of England was a major influence on the culture and shape of regulation and supervision. However, despite this the financial services industry in the early 1980s and 1990s exposed considerable gaps in the style of regulation, with a whole host of scandals such as endowment mortgage and pension mis-selling. This in many respects undermined the moves to improve the prudential regulation and supervision of banks, with for instance the introduction of lead regulation to enhance the ability of banks to undertake other types of financial services. The trend towards conglomeration brought with it certain efficiencies relating to the costs associated with financial products, and indeed new products, but it failed to consider the interests and needs of consumers, such as their

273 Ibid.

274 Ibid., at pp. 129–132.

ability to understand the risks associated with the various types of financial products on offer. The past few years of FSA work have therefore seen efforts put into changing the culture of regulation so that consumer interests are just as prominent, if not more so, as issues such as industry competitiveness. This has resulted in a move by the FSA to realign the interests of consumers and financial intermediaries so that consumers are better aware of the risks associated with the financial products they are offered. In spite of this the industry has considered the move to a single regulator beneficial, in that large, complex financial services firms are now dealing with one body rather than a large number of regulators with overlapping responsibilities, as was the case in the past. A single culture of regulation and the adoption of a single risk-based approach to regulation have also brought changes to the approach to enforcement, clearer articulation of stakeholder interests in firms and alternative mechanisms of regulatory accountability.

The US experience is distinctive, with several regulators overseeing the banking system based on its federal and state forms of governance. This system of regulation, and its principle of 'safety and soundness', were heavily influenced by large-scale bank failures, leading to emphasis on protecting the public deposit insurance fund to stave off bank runs ensuing from mass withdrawals by depositors rather than the broader concern of maintaining financial stability which should be the central plank of banking regulation. While the Federal Reserve has the overarching responsibility for financial holding companies and powers of intervention of its own, it is still reliant to a considerable extent on the work of the primary regulators. The traditional emphasis on regulatory competition and rivalry, while arguably reducing the regulatory burden, has resulted in a number of cases where it has simply not worked due to a lack of cooperation and communication between the various regulators – which is similar to having discrete regulators with differing objectives examining the same issues but reaching different conclusions and indeed expectations of the regulated. The move towards deregulation in the USA, in some respects similar to that in the UK, has been designed with the safety and soundness of banks as one of its major premises, as a result of which a complete move to financial-commercial conglomeration has not been allowed as it has in the UK. Moreover, the US support for its complex system of bank regulation, even in recent times, demonstrates that provided its system of prudential supervision is considered sound then a single bank regulator is not deemed necessary. However, competing pressures for change could tip the balance in the long run, such as financial conglomeration, where a single overarching body coordinates the dissemination of information from its various parts – the inability of the current system to deal with such issues may be enough to effect change.

Chapter 2

Legal Aspects of Prudential Supervision

Introduction

The FSA is responsible for the prudential regulation and supervision of banks to provide the basis to undertake banking business. The importance of robust oversight of bank activities is evident in light of their vulnerability to failure. Prudential regulation and supervision not only cover the activities of a bank in the jurisdiction in which it is incorporated, but also extend transnationally: the regulator will require information from the bank about its activities or associated activities overseas to assess the likelihood of these adversely impacting on the interests of depositors and the stability of the banking and financial system in which the bank is incorporated. Indeed, the risks for depositors and the stability of the banking system are the main rationale for robust prudential regulation and supervision, regardless of how regulation is structured. The process of deregulation in the 1980s–1990s required a rather more sophisticated approach to regulation and supervision to capture a whole host of risks not traditionally under the purview of bank regulators. A central part of the system has therefore been capital adequacy rules to capture and cushion against the risks associated with banks undertaking securities and insurance business. These rules have attempted to create a level competitive playing field for banks and protect them from the risks inherent in their activities.

In this chapter the first section defines both regulation and supervision. The second section analyses the move towards the adoption of a risk-based approach by the FSA, and the link between the objectives of regulation and the procedures the FSA has put in place to determine the level of resources it will devote to any one regulatory area. The move towards a risk-based approach mirrors the move by the industry to a risk-based management system. This gives rise to a top-down approach to the application of regulation and supervision rather than a bottom-up approach where the focus of attention is on how the firm manages its business and risks and whether it is acting in a prudential manner. The third section introduces a definition of banking business and how firms are authorised by the FSA to undertake it. This will provide the basis to analyse the supervision of banks by the FSA, focusing on the consolidated supervision, capital adequacy and large exposure regimes that oversee a bank's activities. The rationale behind the various aspects of prudential supervision will be discussed, with a description of the main features. The importance of international cooperation through both formal and informal means will be considered, namely the statutory provisions and memoranda of understanding (MoUs) regulators enter into with one another. The fourth section introduces some aspects of US banking business. It will focus on the term 'safety and soundness', which is equivalent to exercising banking business prudentially. Finally, the adoption of a risk-based approach to the supervision of large, complex banks will be considered. While both the UK and the USA have adopted a risk-based approach, the focus does differ in light of the fact the former system applies to the whole financial services industry and the latter simply to large, complex banks rather than the whole banking system. The UK approach does not simply separate institutions in terms of size, but through a risk assessment separates institutions out into various categories of risk. These comparative observations are highlighted in the conclusion.

The Function of Regulation and Supervision

The mechanisms to protect the banking system consist of a number of discrete but interdependent functions that may not be housed in one public body.[1] Responsibility for LOLR, deposit insurance and regulation and supervision of banks could be vested as a whole or in part in a government department, the central bank or a separately constituted public body to oversee the banking system.

The main responsibility of the regulator is regulation and supervision for the purposes of ensuring the business of banking is undertaken prudentially or in a safe and sound manner. But the terms regulation and supervision house differing responsibilities, even though many use them together, interchangeably or separately, to focus on the type of authority exercised.[2]

The literal definition of regulation in the *Oxford English Dictionary* is 'a rule prescribed for the management of some matter, or for the regulating of conduct; a government precept or direction'.[3] The function of supervision in the *Oxford English Dictionary* refers to 'general management, direction, or control; oversight, superintendence'.[4] Therefore regulation refers to the process of devising rules, whereas supervision focuses on 'advising' on how to comply with such rules, possibly through formal guidance.

The bank regulator is, depending on the mandate it has been given by the state, responsible for devising day-to-day 'secondary sources' of law such as rules, standards and guidelines that emanate from 'primary sources' such as statutes, hence the label of *de facto* law-maker.[5] In this respect regulation fulfils the regulator's statutory obligation for, for instance, prescribing rules to regulate authorisation, supervision, enforcement and the right of appeal. The supervision process refers to the regulator's responsibility to ensure that those prescribed rules are continuously obeyed. For example, the UK system centres on protecting the 'perimeter' by criminalising unauthorised activities: efforts by the UK regulator to protect the remit

1 See p. 3.

2 Federal Reserve System (1994) *Purposes and Functions*, available at www.federalreserve.gov/pf/pf.htm, at pp. 59–60. For a wider examination of regulation and supervision see Lastra, R. M. (1996) *Central Banking and Banking Regulation*, London, Financial Markets Group, London School of Economics, at p. 108.

3 *Oxford English Dictionary*, available at www.http://dictionary.eod.com.

4 Ibid.

5 Shapiro, M. (1983) 'Administrative discretion: The next stage', *Yale Law Journal*, vol. 92, 1487, at p. 1510.

of the marketplace by putting in place specific fit and proper requirements on firms and persons before they can embark on entering the market show the importance attached to the risks associated with unauthorised activities.[6] The regulator can, once a bank is authorised, undertake the responsibility of monitoring its activities through either on-site or off-site supervision,[7] and can exercise its enforcement powers to deal with incidents of non-compliance.[8] In addition to regulation and supervision, another important function bank regulators and central banks can undertake is surveillance. This function complements regulation and supervision because it contains an element of vigilance as well, thus highlighting the importance of observing those under the regulator's authority, as a whole, with a degree of scepticism.[9] Through surveillance a regulator can adjust the intensity of both regulation and supervision at a sector level or individual firm level to ensure overall financial stability.[10]

The general debate about the distinction between regulation and supervision has also focused on whether a regulator has adopted a rules- or discretion-based approach to fulfil its statutory responsibilities.[11] While regulation is suggested to prescribe how management should reach decisions, supervision allows a significant degree of judgement to be exercised in decision-making. In this respect the regulation-based approach has tended to place limits on the autonomy of management with prescriptive and restrictive rules, whereas supervision is suggested to respect the autonomy of management to comply with a broad range of standards. In terms of both regulation and supervision regulators have nevertheless the authority to intervene and deal with issues of non-compliance. Indeed, regulation- and supervision-based approaches both house elements of each other, failing which a regulation-based approach could be considered over-inclusive and a supervision-based approach under-inclusive.[12]

The traditional distinction between regulation of investment business and banking business is frequently used to give as examples of regulation and supervision

---

6 The problems of a lack of a formal system of licensing were brought to the fore during the secondary banking crisis which led in part to the introduction of the Banking Act 1979. See p. 55.

7 For example, an off-site approach is used in Switzerland where external auditors are relied upon to a considerable extent to undertake the practical aspects of supervision – see Hupkes, E. (2006) 'The external auditor and the bank supervisor: Sherlock Holmes and Doctor Watson?', *Journal of Banking Regulation*, vol. 7, 145.

8 See pp. 112 151.

9 *Oxford English Dictionary*, n. 3 above.

10 See pp. 2–3. For a historical perspective see Arthur Andersen & Co SC (1996) *Findings and Recommendations of the Review of Supervision and Surveillance* (Arthur Andersen Report), London, Arthur Andersen Consulting, July, paras 95 98; Bank of England (1996) *The Objectives, Standards and Processes of Banking Supervision*, February, at p. 7 for an examination of the importance of supervision and surveillance to avoid systemic risk.

11 Treasury and Civil Service Committee (1994/95) *The Regulation of Financial Services in the UK*, Sixth Report, p. xxxi. This is discussed further by Quinn, B. (1996) 'Rules v discretion: The case of banking supervision in the light of the debate on monetary policy', Special Paper 85, Financial Markets Group, London School of Economics, July.

12 See pp. 112–121.

respectively. The regulation of investment business has tended to protect the interests of investors with a range of conduct-of-business rules linked to the sale of financial products; these rules do not exist in commercial banking, other than the Banking Code which only provides limited forms of protection to a depositor. The separation of the two forms of business and the obligations they have to an investor and depositor are different. For example, a bank has limited or no obligation to a depositor to explain the rationale of its decisions regarding the deposit, whereas in an investment business the obligation to investors is continuous so they can judge the risks associated with the investment product bought. In light of this, the business of banking has tended to be governed with a supervision-based approach to ensure at the institutional level a bank is prudently run in terms of managing its assets and liabilities. The regulation of investment business has tended to focus on the functional aspects of the business on product lines.

Risk and Supervision

The UK financial markets, like other financial markets, experienced a considerable level of change with the advent of more sophisticated methods of dealing with assets and liabilities and better risk management techniques developed by financial intermediaries to enhance their profitability. The advancement of information technology provided a considerable level of assistance in this process of dealing with risks. The move to better risk management led to the growth of sophisticated financial products and markets for derivatives and asset-backed securitisation, to name just a few, to such an extent that they have become discrete but very large and popular financial products in their own right. The process of securitisation, for example, assists with converting a portfolio of assets into marketable securities, reducing exposure to credit risk. The combination of both deregulation and the developments in risk management techniques meant regulators could no longer focus on traditional risks associated with the business they authorised, but needed to acquire an understanding of other forms of risk. Consequently new sets of standards and regulatory techniques have been devised to deal with the activities of bank-financial conglomerates that transcend different business lines and even jurisdictions to ensure risks are managed prudentially. For example, a formal system has been adopted of supervising financial conglomerates through arrangements for lead supervision.[13]

In the UK, the Barings Bank collapse in 1995 brought to the fore questions about the methods used to decide whether banks complied with prudential standards and guidelines.[14] The approach associated with UK banking regulation was particularly targeted, as it was suggested that it lacked the context in terms of objectives and principles to gauge the degree of compliance with a whole host of prudential standards banks were required to meet on a continuous basis.[15] While the experienced judgement of regulators was necessary, it was not structured and

13 See p. 60.

14 See specifically Arthur Andersen Report, n. 10 above; Bank of England (1996) *The Bank's Review of Supervision*, 24 July.

15 Arthur Andersen Report, n. 10 above, para. 38.

checked as efficiently as possible.[16] In some respects the criticism at the time was not about whether a risk-based approach should be formally adopted but more to do with the traditional debate about whether discretion should be curtailed with the adoption of rules.[17]

This was nevertheless consumed by the focus on adopting a risk-based approach. The new approach signalled the adoption of a regulatory and supervisory system that assessed risks and regulatory resources in a more prioritised manner, giving risks the appropriate level of regulatory attention. According to the Bank a more 'systematic model of risk assessment' was needed to ensure the 'supervisory programme' was applied more efficiently across the banks it authorised.[18] This in many respects moved the Bank's decision-making authority into a more structured and ordered form so that regulatory resources and decisions could be rationally justified according to a single 'framework' of supervision rather than the 'plurality' of approaches that had previously existed.[19] The consequence of this was considerable, as it also impacted on the approach to dealing with authorised banks with a move to a more on-site method of supervision rather than an off-site system. The move was to improve the insight regulators got of a bank by being at the premises and engaging with management in the way it undertook its business. Over-relying on off-site methods of supervision did not provide the kind of insight a bank regulator required to satisfy itself of the bank's compliance. Finally, the adoption of a risk-based approach was not a replacement of the discretion-based approach with a rules-based approach; rather it was to assist the discretion-based approach. However, no sooner had the Bank and other regulators got their risk-based approach up and running than the move towards a single regulator was announced.

The FSA Risk-based Approach

The FSA adopted a risk-based approach in its regulation and supervision of regulated firms. The risk-based approach operates on two levels: at an organisation level, and at the firm level which is articulated in the 'firm risk assessment framework'.[20] The risk-

16 Ibid., para. 39.

17 *Report of the Board of Banking Supervision Inquiry into the Circumstances of the Collapse of Barings*, London, HMSO 18 July 1995. It highlights that the events culminating in the collapse of Barings did not warrant any fundamental change to the framework of regulation in the UK, at p. 251, para. 14.4. Arthur Andersen Report, n. 10 above, para. 20 pointed out the concern about the possible expectations gap which could arise if a rules- and inspection-based approach were to be implemented in the UK similar to other jurisdictions. The latter does not necessarily reduce the number of bank failures.

18 Bank of England (1997) 'The Bank's review of supervision: Major changes announced', press release, 19/11/97.

19 Arthur Andersen Report, n. 10 above, at para. 43.

20 FSA (2000) *A New Regulator for the New Millennium*, January; FSA (2000) *Building the New Regulator: Progress Report 1*, December; FSA (2002) *Building the New Regulator: Progress Report 2*, February; FSA (2003) *The Firm Risk Assessment Framework*, February.

based approach is referred to as the ARROW framework (advanced risk-responsive operating framework) by the FSA and its staff. It is not focused on compliance with the prudential requirements that exist within the Interim Prudential Source Book or the Handbook Guidelines, but encapsulates risks that exist externally and internally in the financial services industry.[21] It is specifically mindful of the interests of the wider stakeholders, such as depositors, investors and other financial intermediaries, as well as its own interests and compliance with its statutory objectives and principles.[22] The FSA highlights in its risk assessment framework that it functions to measure firm risks differently to the way firms normally manage risk.[23]

The FSA refers to the risk-based approach as a 'bridge linking the statutory objectives and our regulatory activities'.[24] It attempts to apportion resources according to the degree of risk regulated firms pose to it fulfilling its regulatory objectives.[25] The more risk a regulated firm poses to the FSA not achieving its objectives, the more resources it should put into dealing with the risk. This approach to managing regulatory resources is said to enhance the efficiency and effectiveness of supervision for both the regulated and the regulator because it allows both parties to focus attention on areas of greatest concern. It is in many respects a methodological approach to how the FSA will undertake its responsibilities of surveillance, regulation and supervision to capture the risks that may adversely impact on the UK financial services industry. The action the FSA takes to deal with a risk to its objectives is based on multiplying 'impact' by 'probability' to determine the 'priority' it needs to place on dealing with the risk.[26] In this calculation 'impact' refers to the consequence of a risk and 'probability' the likelihood of it happening. This mechanistic approach to calculating a risk does imply that all the risks are easily quantifiable and the size of the adverse risk is easily identifiable. However, while the underlying assets and liability of a regulated firm can be relatively easy to measure historically, other risks are only identifiable through judgements made during the supervision of regulated firms.[27]

The operating framework sets out the FSA's approach to its risk-based system of regulation,[28] outlining the processes it goes through to identify the risks the sector and a regulated firm pose to its regulatory objectives. The parameters of this framework are set out in a 'risk map'; the boundaries are the given objectives and principles of regulation. The FSA embarks on the process of mapping risks to its objectives and strategic aims so that it can enhance the credibility of the decisions it takes by being proactive as far as possible in its decision-making rather than reactive. The attempt to flesh out decisions and show how they are reached regarding resource allocation between the various sectors of the industry enhances the transparency of

---

21 FSA *Progress Report 1*, ibid., at p. 8.

22 Ibid.

23 FSA (2003), n. 20 above, at p. 12.

24 FSA *A New Regulator*, n. 20 above, at p. 14.

25 FSA (2003), n. 20 above, at p. 9.

26 FSA *A New Regulator*, n. 20 above, at p. 16; FSA (2003), n. 20 above, at p. 13.

27 FSA *Progress Report 1*, n. 20 above, at p. 11.

28 FSA (2002), n. 20 above, at p. 5.

this traditionally opaque area of regulation. This makes the framework unique in comparison to other risk-based systems of regulation because not only is it used to identify risks that emanate from firms but it also acts as an accountability mechanism by which government, consumers and the industry can judge how efficiently the FSA is using its resources to achieve its objectives.

The FSA embarks on the risk assessment process annually through its financial risk outlook, international risk outlook and its plan and budget for the forthcoming year. These reports provide a general idea of the 'fragility' of the external economic environment and the risks firms are exposed to, thus aiding in gauging the likelihood of risks affecting the FSA achieving its objectives. For example, in its 2005 outlook and plan the FSA highlights the large number of legislative measures that firms will be required to comply with as a considerable hurdle for them to overcome to avoid regulatory and legal risks.[29] In its first annual plan and budget the FSA was mindful of overburdening the industry with regulation.[30] The annual priorities need to be sufficiently flexible, given the nature of capital markets, to allow the FSA to deal with unforeseeable events that may unexpectedly put additional strain on regulatory resources. It is inevitable that the occurrence of a problem which is not captured by the risk-based approach will lead to a degree of criticism. However, to circumvent such criticism the FSA has set out the limits of what it can and cannot do in a publication entitled *Regulation in a Non-zero Failure World*, in which it proposes that it does not intend to achieve a position of 'zero failure' in the financial services industry.[31] This is an expectation some may have, with the presence of regulation creating an expectations gap between what the public and the regulator consider it can and cannot do to avoid institutions failing or perpetrating fraud.[32] According to the FSA, regulation does not try to 'prevent all collapses, or lapses in conduct, in the financial system'.[33] However, the FSA does undertake to educate consumers about the limits of regulation and the responsibility they have themselves to assess the risks they take when purchasing financial products, to help them mitigate the risk of loss and understand the routes to seek compensation.[34] The move towards greater consumer awareness, treating consumers fairly and mitigating the risks associated with financial products has given rise to criticism regarding the burden of regulation it has produced for the industry – challenging the industry on its commitments to consumers.

The FSA embarks upon a 'firm risk assessment' to ascertain the risk the firm poses by categorising risks into business and control types.[35] A business risk emanates from a firm's business activities;[36] a control risk is associated with the way it manages its business.[37] For example, risk to a firm's financial soundness is

29 FSA (2005) *Financial Risk Outlook*.
30 FSA (2000–2001) *Plan and Budget*, at p. 6.
31 FSA (2003) *Regulation in a Non-zero Failure World*, September.
32 FSA *A New Regulator*, n. 20 above, at p. 6.
33 Ibid.
34 See pp. 20 22.
35 FSA (2003), n. 20 above, at p. 14.
36 Ibid., at p. 91.
37 Ibid.

categorised as a business risk and the treatment of customers is a control risk. The former could impact on the FSA achieving its market confidence objective and the latter could adversely affect the consumer protection objective. The first stage of the risk assessment is to gauge the risks the firm poses by referring to the regulatory returns made in compliance with reporting requirements. This stage could simply focus on the individual regulated firm or firms as part of a group to assess the various risks they pose both individually and collectively. The FSA may consider the risks that exist overseas pose a threat to its objectives of consumer protection and reducing financial crime.[38] While the FSA indicates that regulatory resources will not be used to deal with risks that pose a threat to its market confidence and consumer awareness objectives because of the specific jurisdictional scope of those objectives, it is still vigilant of risks that could adversely affect it achieving these objectives and has used remedial tools such as enforcement sanctions to deal with risks that have crystallised overseas and affect the reputation of the UK financial markets.

The FSA ends the risk assessment by completing a risk mitigation programme to decide on the types of tools it needs to use to deal with the risks that have been identified.[39] A regulatory tools matrix sets out the possible responses the FSA can take, categorised according to whether they are monitoring (tools to monitor risks), diagnostic (tools to identify and measure risk), preventive (tools to mitigate risks) or remedial (tools to address identified risks). The FSA response rises upstream in line with the severity of the risk. The impact of the risk on the regulatory objectives determines the 'intensity' of the action it takes. Once the process is complete the regulated firm is given an individual risk assessment categorised as high, medium-high, medium-low or low impact. However, this banding of regulated firms does not necessarily mean these firms are risky institutions: a firm could be placed in the high band but pose a low risk. The FSA focuses its attention on the potential of risks crystallising to determine the category in which a regulated firm is placed. The high-impact band indicates a high probability of a risk adversely affecting the regulatory objectives should it emerge.

The response to the risk banding is set out in the FSA's regulatory tools matrix: the tools are categorised according to the risk posed by the firm. The FSA highlights that this is ultimately dependent upon the seriousness of the risk in relation to it not achieving its objectives. If the risk posed by the firm is low, no action is considered necessary. If the firm poses a medium-low risk the FSA can use a variety of tools to 'monitor', 'identify' and measure risk. Risks considered to be in the high or medium-high category would be dealt with by applying either preventive or remedial tools. If a firm poses a medium-high risk the FSA has the authority to exercise its powers to mitigate the risks. Finally, if the firm poses a high risk then the FSA can exercise its enforcement powers to deal with the problems associated with the risk.[40] The risk calculated by the FSA through its assessment is communicated to the regulated firm with the results of the risk mitigation programme, but is not publicly disclosed. The move to complete transparency of the banding process could have wider

38 Ibid., at pp. 11–12.

39 Ibid., at p. 18.

40 Ibid., at pp. 31–32.

consequences for a firm, such as a loss of business if it is considered a high risk as a result of poor internal controls although its sector counterparts are categorised as less of a risk.

The FSA risk-based approach can be described as a methodology to ensure decisions about resources are made according to the objectives and principles set out in the regulatory regime. The advantage of a single risk-based approach is that it avoids the problems associated with having to deal with the findings of different risk-based systems used under the previous regimes, as this would hinder cross-comparison of the firms. The difficulty of adopting a plurality of systems of regulation is highlighted by Michael Foot, head of financial supervision at the time: regulators would exercise their responsibilities 'at the boundaries of their industry even when they had an issue which quite clearly related to other industries'.[41] The plurality of criteria to measure the discrete risks for which the differing regulators had responsibility meant the results would be difficult to compare in light of the differing objectives. Therefore, armed with a single set of objectives and principles that transcend the processes of regulation and supervision, a single risk-based system should give rise to a more consistent approach to measuring the risk posed by a financial conglomerate.

The mechanisms described above highlight that the approach the FSA has adopted is top-down rather than bottom-up; thus it is more of an accountability tool as it enables the FSA to justify its decisions to its stakeholders. Notwithstanding this, a risk-based approach need not be so rigid and inflexible as to fail to capture the unique risks associated with the differing type of financial services firms, for example the possible impact of a bank closure on the wider economy.

The risk-based approach cannot be seen as a panacea for regulatory decisions. Like most regulatory systems it ultimately relies on past performance, which may not be an accurate indicator of future performance. It is thus crucially important to have experienced staff who are able to spot inconsistencies in the information provided. While the risk-based approach does structure regulatory decision-making in a more coherent way, it also highlights the complexity of the decisions regulators are required to make and the judgement that needs to be exercised. Regulatory discretion is thus only structured to a limited extent by adopting a risk-based approach. The categorisation of a firm as low risk is ultimately a judgement based on information provided by the firm, and there is always the possibility that the information is not entirely complete. In this respect the regulator needs to address evidence of non-compliance rigorously.[42]

In many respects the FSA approach reduces the autonomy of firms by focusing their attention on a broad range of stakeholders, as it links its responsibilities with regulatory responsibilities and outcomes. This is evident with the number of functions that are designated controlled functions, from executive to relatively junior employee level.[43]

---

41 Foot, M. (2000) 'Our new approach to regulation What will be the difference for firms', FSA, December.

42 See Chapter 4.

43 See pp. 99-101.

Deposit-taking Business

The pre-1979 Banking Act position clearly highlights that a whole host of activities were considered banking business by the Bank of England.[44] The more recent, somewhat restricted interpretation of the business of banking has generally been focused on the 'demand' side of a bank accepting deposits: the bank being a repository for money upon which an individual can draw cheques.[45] However, equally important is the 'supply' side of a bank's operations: the bank lending the money deposited in its accounts to others.[46] The regulation of bank business in the UK has focused on those institutions that are accepting deposits rather than those institutions lending money. While the business of banking comprises both accepting deposits and lending, for the purposes of bank regulation and supervision it is the 'perimeter' of the business of accepting deposits that is protected by prohibiting those who are not authorised.

The FSMA 2000 provides a general prohibition on carrying on regulated activities without authorisation,[47] with a penalty of imprisonment for up to two years. The FSA has taken a strong stance against illegal deposit-taking to protect the interests of consumers who may be caught by such activities. For example, Alan Evitts was sentenced to 18 months in jail for taking £204,000 in illegal deposits.[48] The director of enforcement, David Mayhew, provided a cautionary note to consumers indicating the risk they take of losing their money when they are lured by promises of high levels of return.[49] The court echoed similar sentiments, indicating 'its astonishment' that investors could be taken in by such absurd levels of return.[50]

The question of whether or not a person is undertaking the business of deposit-taking is not easy to determine. A 'deposit', on the face of it, is a range of possible transactions, not all of which fall within the category of banking. For example, a distinction has been drawn between deposits and payment for services in order to avoid uncertainty. Slade LJ's decision in *SCF Finance v. Masri* drew a distinction between margin payments and deposit-taking business: in the former payments were for the provision of services and were not deposit-taking business.[51] The FSA has

---

44 Morrison, I., Tillet, P. and Welch, J. (1979) *Banking Act 1979*, London, Butterworths, at pp. 2–5.

45 *United Dominions Trust Ltd v. Kirkwood* [1966] 2 QB 431, 447. For a detailed examination of the 'nature of banking' see Cranston, R. (2005) *Principles of Banking Law*, Oxford, Oxford University Press, at pp. 4 9.

46 *Comrs of the State Savings Bank of Victoria v. Permewan Wright & Co. Ltd (1915)* 19 CLR 457, 470 471.

47 FSMA 2000, s. 19.

48 FSA (2005) 'Glossop accountant jailed for illegal deposit-taking', FSA/PN/070/2005, 23 June; for a historical analysis of the way in which the 'perimeter' was regulated by the Bank of England see Singh, D. (2002) 'Enforcement methods and sanctions in banking regulation and supervision', *International and Comparative Corporate Law Journal*, vol. 4, 307, at pp. 333–335.

49 FSA, ibid., at p. 1.

50 Ibid., at pp. 1 2.

51 *SCF Finance Co. Ltd v. Masri* [1987] QB 1007, 1020–1021.

adopted the same approach to the definition of deposit-taking business by focusing on accepting of deposits as 'excluding advancements in normal commercial transactions for goods and services'.[52]

The activity of 'accepting deposits' must be undertaken 'by way of business' for it to fall within the scope of the definition.[53] The FSA has clarified the meaning of 'by way of business' by referring to the frequency with which deposits are accepted: normally on a 'day-to-day' basis rather than 'on particular occasions'. The definition centres on the frequency with which a person holds himself out to receive deposits, whether expressly or implicitly, on any normal working day.[54] This follows Slade LJ's definition of what amounts to a business activity, and also generally concurs with Hobhouse J's reasoning in *Morgan Grenfell* concerning interest rate swaps with local authorities: he refers to the 'frequency' of the party undertaking the transaction for profit for it to be by way of business. However, Hobhouse J includes even the first transaction that is executed, as it is part of 'overall business activities'.[55] This would broaden the scope of the definition of 'by way of business' if the intention was that the first transaction would be the start of such a business.

Authorisation and Permission

The first facet of regulation is authorisation to undertake a particular type of business. Authorisation serves two main purposes: it attempts to protect the marketplace from incompetent players, and encourages depositors and investors to do business confidently within a secure environment. A formal system of authorisation acts as an effective way of limiting entry to and exit from a marketplace so that it can function in an orderly manner. This ensures that deposit-taking business, for instance, is appropriately undertaken in accordance with the designated prudential standards and conduct-of-business rules with which authorised firms are required to comply. But the fact that institutions are authorised to undertake regulated activities does not preclude the risks of loss or failure arising from fraud or mismanagement. Consequently, regulation and supervision do not attempt to eliminate loss or failure in a marketplace.

The FSMA 2000 introduces the idea of permission[56] to carry on regulated activities. Application for Part IV permission requires the applicant to satisfy 'threshold conditions' on a continuing basis.[57] The FSA's powers here are broad, and include the authority to change a firm's permission status if it thinks that a regulatory objective of market confidence, consumer protection, consumer awareness or reduction of financial crime is imperilled. This allows the FSA extensive scope for exercising its decisions about authorisation. The FSMA 2000 requires the regulated

52 Auth 2.6.2G.

53 Auth 2.3.1G.

54 *SCF Finance*, n. 51 above, at pp. 1022–1023; see also *Morgan Grenfell & Co v. Welwyn Hatfield District Council (Islington LC, third party)*, 1 All ER [1995] 1, 13.

55 *Morgan Grenfell*, ibid., at pp. 13–14.

56 FSMA 2000, s. 40.

57 Ibid., s. 41.

activities to be identified so that the FSA can apply the limitations or requirements it thinks appropriate for controlling the way the activities are performed.

The FSA's Approach to Supervision

The FSA outlines its approach to supervision in its Supervision Handbook in compliance with the FSMA 2000, which places a responsibility on the FSA to put in place 'arrangements' to ascertain if a regulated firm is complying with its statutory obligations and rules and guidance.[58] The 'arrangements' the FSA puts in place need to be designed with its objectives and principles of good regulation in mind.[59] In accordance with these principles, for example, the onus is on a firm and its senior management to exercise reasonable care to undertake regulated activities in accordance with the requirements, which will ultimately need to be appropriate in terms of cost and benefit. The FSA has put in place a risk-based approach to fulfil its responsibilities of regulation and supervision so that it uses its resources efficiently to mitigate the risks that ensue from the financial services industry to it achieving its objectives.[60] In addition, the FSA has the responsibility of putting in place 'arrangements' to enforce the provisions set out in the FSMA 2000 and handbooks.[61]

The Threshold Conditions

The FSMA 2000 provides minimum criteria for granting permission to carry out regulated activities. These are referred to as 'threshold conditions'.[62] The FSA is required to ensure that those seeking authorisation can satisfy these conditions. The concept of 'threshold' indicates that these requirements need to be met at the point of entry, although the actual requirement is to comply with them continuously. The threshold conditions are broad and contain a large degree of discretion in their scope; they are complemented by a whole host of prudential rules and guides that flesh out their application[63] and are further elaborated in the Principles for Businesses,[64] Statements of Principles for Approved Persons[65] and the Interim Prudential Sourcebook for Banks.[66] These extensive rules and guidance reduce the level of uncertainty in the minds of the regulated and the regulator, thus reducing the expectation gaps that exist between the FSA and the regulated.[67]

58 Ibid., s. 6(1) of Sch. 1; SUP 1.1.2G.

59 SUP 1.1.3G. See generally pp. 23 24.

60 SUP 1.3G.

61 FSMA 2000, s. 6(3).

62 FSMA 2000, Sch. 6 includes legal status, location of offices, close links, adequate resources and suitability. See for guidance COND 1.

63 FSMA 2000, s. 138.

64 FSA, Principles for Businesses. See pp. 86–88.

65 FSA, Statements of Principles and Code of Practice for Approved Persons.

66 Interim Prudential Sourcebook for Banks (IPRU).

67 IPRU, GN: s. 2 (3)–(4).

The first threshold condition[68] is the requirement that the legal status of the entity seeking to authorise a person to accept deposits must be either a body corporate or a partnership. The second condition[69] is the requirement that the head office and registered office both be located in the UK. This enables the FSA to focus its attention on the head office, where central management and control of the day-to-day activities of the authorised person are located. The requirement is designed to avoid another BCCI scenario and complies with the Post-BCCI Directive to adopt this policy within the EU. It was found that BCCI avoided effective supervision because its centre for management was in London and its place of incorporation was Luxembourg, which prevented effective supervision of its operations.[70] The third threshold[71] incorporates another requirement of the Post-BCCI Directive: authorised persons must disclose links with other persons so that the FSA can identify the location of possible risks to the authorised person. The FSA has the right to seek information about any close link it wishes to know about, even in cases where the close link is an exempted entity. The FSA can individually discuss its requirements of notification about close links, especially in the case of non-EEA incorporated credit institutions. The close links' materiality will be assessed, as will changes in links within the banking group. The fourth threshold[72] requires that the authorised person must have adequate resources on a solo and consolidated basis to carry on regulated activities continuously. The FSA interprets 'adequate resources' to refer to the quality and quantity of financial resources as well as staff and systems of control to manage risks emanating from the business and/or its group-wide activities. The authorised person must, as part of a group, manage risks in connection with its business continuously. Extensive guidance is provided to supplement these conditions.[73] The fifth threshold condition is the suitability of the firm or the group, if it is part of a group, in terms of being fit and proper to be granted permission by the FSA to carry on regulated activities.

Reporting Requirements

The FSA relies on the cooperation of regulated firms to provide information which is 'timely', 'accurate' and 'complete' to enable it to judge how the firm is undertaking its business in compliance with requirements.[74] For example, a firm is required to notify the FSA if it is likely to fail to meet one of the threshold conditions or damage its reputation or undermine its service to customers. The FSA places considerable reliance on the firm to provide it with accurate information. Regulated firms are required to provide reports on a whole host of matters. The FSA relies on the compliance reports to fulfil a part of its supervision work. It requires financial reports on individual firm

68 COND 2.1.

69 COND 2.2.

70 Bank of England, United Kingdom Administrative Arrangements for the Implementation of the Close Links Provision of the Post-BCCI Directive, No. S&S/1996/9.

71 COND. 2.3.

72 COND. 2.4.

73 IPRU (Bank) at GN: s. 2.

74 SUP 1.5.

and group level on either an annual, half-yearly or quarterly basis. A firm is required to provide an annual report and audited accounts, and adequate information on capital adequacy and large exposures on both a solo and a consolidated basis. Only with the cooperation of regulated firms can the FSA achieve its regulatory objectives and principles. In addition, the notification and reporting obligations form the basis for the FSA completing its risk assessment to determine the impact of a firm on it achieving its statutory objectives. The obligation on the regulated firm is to provide timely and accurate reports; the FSA can exercise its authority to investigate and impose enforcement sanctions if such information is not forthcoming. It is therefore not surprising that the FSA takes a hard line on failure by firms to provide such information, highlighting how such failures seriously undermine it in achieving its regulatory objectives and indicating to CEOs the threat of enforcement sanctions in cases of failure to notify business activities and inaccurate reports.[75]

Finally, the FSA's financial reporting requirements require firms to complete returns on a whole host of prudential matters. These are explored in more detail below, in particular the historical background and their broad features.

Consolidated Supervision

In the light of the experience of the early 1970s, banking regulators recognised the effect of business operations in both home and host countries on their respective jurisdictions. This required them to focus on areas beyond their respective markets: to pay attention to the transnational operations of banks in other countries and include these operations in what is called 'consolidated supervision'. The general principle, in the Basel rules, is that 'no banking institution should be allowed to avoid supervision'. Consolidated supervision has been particularly important to reduce the likelihood of banking failures that could have systemic consequences in either host or home markets. Prominent failures such as Franklin National Bank, Banco Ambrosiano, BCCI, Barings and others have heightened the need for effective consolidated supervision and close monitoring of activities on a transnational basis.

The Basel rules have evolved through 'accords', which are broad measures of negotiated statements of intent.[76] The responsibilities of the home and host countries are derived from reciprocal rights and powers to limit the adverse effect of a bank failure in their respective jurisdictions affecting the host or home jurisdiction. The Basel Core Principles recommend that bank supervisors practise global consolidation of internationally active banks by applying 'appropriate' prudential measures to 'all aspects' of their business.[77] The Core Principles also make it mandatory that bank supervisors 'require the local operations of foreign banks to be conducted to the

75 FSA Dear CEO letter, 'Transaction Reporting', 14 December, 2005 available at www.fsa.gov.uk/pubs/ceo/transaction_reporting.pdf.

76 For an analysis of the work of the Basel Committee on Banking Supervision see Walker, G. (2001) *International Banking Regulation – Law, Policy and Practice*, The Hague, Kluwer Law.

77 Basel Committee on Banking Supervision (1997) Core Principles for Effective Bank Supervision, recommendation 23.

same high standards that are required of domestic institutions' in order to enhance the quality of regulation and supervision internationally.[78]

The EC directive on consolidated supervision places legal obligations on the home regulator to supervise bank operations effectively on a consolidated basis using the principle of 'mutual recognition', in accordance with which the host state has no power to revoke or restrict authorisation granted unless this is done in the interest of a 'general good' such as the deflection of a systemic crisis.[79] The Second Consolidated Supervision Directive (SCSD) introduced the necessity for consolidated supervision of all banking groups, in particular parent undertakings that are not credit institutions.[80] The SCSD provided consolidated supervision of credit institutions whose business includes activities listed in the Annex to the Second Banking Directive (SBD).[81]

Consolidated Supervision of UK-incorporated Banks

The FSA undertakes consolidated supervision in addition to individual 'solo' supervision of banks.[82] Consolidated supervision is not deemed a substitute for solo supervision. The FSA's consolidated supervision of UK-incorporated banks ensures that they comply with the threshold conditions of 'adequate resources' and 'suitability' for the business they undertake.[83] The main concern of the supervision regime is to evaluate on a qualitative and quantitative basis the risks that arise from the activities of the group to which the bank belongs.

Consolidated supervision is not an attempt to regulate all the activities undertaken by the group, so it is not a substitute for a single risk-based approach: it focuses on the risks that could affect the interests of the bank. These can emanate from risks to the group as a whole; over-reliance on the bank to finance other parts of the group through intra-group lending; and the risk to the bank's reputation if problems exist in other parts of the group.

Consolidated supervision is undertaken on a quantitative and qualitative basis. The qualitative approach includes the activities of industrial and insurance companies that do not form part of the consolidated returns banks are required to submit. The quantitative methods focus on those activities that form part of the consolidated returns. The adequacy of the level of capital the bank holds as part of the group's consolidated activities is referred to as the consolidated individual capital ratio. The requirements to comply with consolidated supervision include an obligation on the

78 Ibid., recommendation 25.

79 This directive and other banking directives are consolidated in a single directive: Directive 2000/12/EC of the European Parliament and Council (2000) 'Harmonisation of Prudential Bank Regulation and Supervision', 20 March, L 126/1. Opinion of the Economic and Social Committee on the 'Proposal for a European Parliament and Council Directive relating to the taking up and pursuit of the business of credit institutions', 98/C 157/03 C 157/13.

80 Ibid., Directive 2000/12/EC, Arts 53–54.

81 Ibid., Annex 1.

82 IPRU, CS: S. 4, pp. 1–4.

83 Ibid., S. 1, pp. 1–2.

bank to have in place adequate controls to ensure it can generate the information to fulfil these rules.

Lead Regulation

The concept of 'lead regulation' evolved independently of 'consolidated supervision' to manage the regulatory chain which existed to supervise multi-authorised groups of institutions across various business forms. It originated from the 1986 'big bang' and the introduction of the Financial Services Act 1986 and the Banking Act 1987 for the purposes of prudential regulation of diversified financial groups. The responsibility of the lead regulator, predominantly the Bank, when banks were part of a group was to ensure the flow of information across the various regulatory bodies and assess the compliance of the institution with the prudential regulations governing its activities.

The lead supervisor will be established on the basis of a 'predominant business test',[84] and chosen from either the Complex Groups Division or one of the divisions responsible for that particular type of business. Thus a predominantly banking group will have a lead supervisor from either the Complex Groups Division or the Banks and Building Societies Division. While the 'predominant business' might be identifiable, the FSA has not actually clarified whether it will make its decision on the basis of profit or turnover, or whether it will simply accept the traditional identification of authorisation. This will be an issue for retail banks such as Lloyds TSB, which at one point generated a large proportion of its profits from insurance business.[85] In such cases, while the financial group is always perceived to be banking-oriented, its profits resulted from insurance business. Lead supervision, however, does not replace solo supervision or consolidated supervision by the designated regulatory division, but rather is a complementary procedure for effectively supervising the diverse range of risks that emanate from a complex financial group. While lead supervision can enhance efficiency and reduce regulatory overlap in financial conglomerates through a single approach, in the UK such supervision inevitably requires cooperation with regulators in other jurisdictions.

Capital Adequacy

Capital adequacy is of crucial importance in the prudential supervision of banks' activities. In order to safeguard a bank from the risks to which it is exposed, a prescribed level of capital is required against specific risks to mitigate any chance

84 SUP 1.5; see further FSA (1998) *Supervision of Complex Groups*.

85 Lloyds' merger with TSB and earlier acquisition of Abbey Life made it the largest insurance provider amongst UK banking groups see Lloyds TSB Group plc *Annual Report and Accounts 1996*. In terms of profit from its core business area, insurance and investments made the largest contribution to the group, exceeding the contribution from retail banking and mortgages see Lloyds TSB Group, *Annual Report and Accounts 1998* at p. 16. Lloyds' interest in the insurance business was further consolidated with its acquisition of Scottish Widows Fund and Life Assurance Society for £7 billion in 1999 – see 'Wooing the widow', *The Sunday Times*, 27 June 1999, at p. 1.

of default if they were to occur. In this respect capital adequacy is said to act as a regulatory charge on the bank in its pursuit of its banking business.The more risky the business the greater the level of capital required to be held against it, and *vice versa* – if the business gives rise to a low risk less capital is required to be held against it. However, this is deemed a legitimate charge to incur in a business where the consequences of default could be catastrophic if a certain degree of capital did not exist to cushion any losses. The level of capital banks are required to hold against prescribed risks has been an issue of international importance in the light of the fact that it has consequences for the competitiveness of banks. Indeed, a catalyst for international standardisation was the move by the UK and USA to put in place their own standards in 1987. This prompted the international community, in particular the other members of the Basel Committee, to devise a minimum capital standard, agreed at 8 per cent against risk-weighted assets. The requirement to hold at least 8 per cent of capital was to prevent banks from over-committing themselves and increasing the risk of a default in their business, resulting in liquidity or insolvency problems in the extreme-case scenario. The international move towards standardisation has been to provide some consistency and a level playing field within the international community so that banks, regardless of their regulator, are required to hold the same kinds of capital and levels of capital when competing with one another. In respect to capital adequacy it is important to note that it is not a panacea to prevent bank failures: this is limited by the extent of management having the discipline to undertake business with the appropriate level of prudence.

The traditional focus of capital adequacy standards in the prudential supervision of banks has been to mitigate the loss that could occur from default in a bank's lending business, which gives rise to credit risk. However, given that banks now participate in other forms of business, in particular investment business, standards have been revised to ensure adequate kinds of capital are held to mitigate the losses that could emanate from such business, which gives rise to market risk.

The European Community also supported the move towards standardisation by introducing the Own Funds and Solvency Ratio Directives, which now form part of the Consolidated Banking Directive. The Own Funds Directive indicates what constitutes capital for the purposes of calculating the level of capital a bank holds.[86] The Solvency Ratio Directive adopts the 8 per cent ratio as the minimum requirement for the purpose of calculating the level of capital to risk-weighted assets.[87]

The picture was somewhat completed by the introduction of the Capital Adequacy Directive (CAD) as part of the international effort to bring about a coordinated approach to determining the capital adequacy requirements of investment firms and credit institutions.[88] It determines the minimum capital that banks and investment firms are required to have in order to safeguard against market and other risks associated

86 Directive 2000/12/EC, s. 1, Arts 34–39, n 79 above.

87 Directive 2000/12/EC s. 2, Arts 40 47, n 79 above.

88 Council Directive 93/6/EEC (1993) 'On the Capital Adequacy of Investment Firms and Credit Institutions', 15 March.

with their trading activities.[89] The CAD attempts to achieve equality of treatment between those in direct competition with one another based upon a common standard of assessing market risk, which includes position risk, counterparty/settlement risks and foreign exchange risks.

The CAD and the Basel Accord both introduced the concepts of 'banking book' and 'trading book' to separate the regimes for 'lending' and 'trading' business to supervise such risks separately.[90] The weightings attached to banking and trading business are rather crude, as they do not necessarily reflect the size of the risk attached to them. It therefore artificially suggests that some investments, for instance non-government securities, are more risky than others. To mitigate the inefficiencies of the standardised approach to assess market risk, banks were allowed to use their own internal management models to calculate this risk and capital requirements.

Capital Adequacy and UK-incorporated Banks

The threshold conditions require banks to have adequate resources to carry on regulated activities on a solo and consolidated basis. The Interim Prudential Sourcebook provides that the capital adequacy framework is used to determine whether a bank has a sufficient level of capital to support its activities in terms of the size of the business and the risks that emanate from it. The FSA guidelines highlight that a bank's compliance with the capital adequacy framework is not simply judged on the basis of the level of capital it holds, but also according to the kinds of risks the bank is exposed to in its business. The FSA therefore sets out some limits as to the utility of simply assessing the ratio of capital to risk. It highlights, *inter alia*, that capital is only a safety net; the quality of the assets needs to be assessed just as much as calculating the capital ratio; and not all types of risks are captured by the capital adequacy regime, such as operational and settlement risk.

The FSA regime adopts the banking and trading book division to calculate the level of capital allocated to the respective risks associated with those two broad categories of business. The banking business consists of assets that give rise to credit risk – the risk of a borrower defaulting. Notwithstanding the international adoption of the banking and trading book regime it is not always simple to categorise risks fully with the type of business, nor in some cases does the regime recognise certain risks which are associated with the business undertaken by the bank. For instance, there is no capital requirement for interest rate risk in the banking book even though it can arise from lending business. The trading book consists of assets held short term that give rise to market risks, such as movements in equities held by a bank. In addition to equities, other kinds of securities that are included are assets held for the purpose of proprietary trading (commodities) or derivatives, whether OTC or on-exchange.

89 Lavoie, C. (1992) 'Consensus on the EC Capital Adequacy Directive (CAD): What will be the future cost of securities trading?', *Butterworths Journal of International Banking and Financial Law*, August, 361; Tidball, S. (1992) 'Consensus on the EC Capital Adequacy Directive (CAD): Implications for UK institutions', *Butterworths Journal of International Banking and Financial Law*, October, 462.

90 IPRU CB: S.v1.

The trading book regime applies to those banks categorised as CAD banks that have a significant amount of trading activities as part of their business portfolio.

Capital Adequacy and Internal Models

The foregoing discussion noted that the standardised approach to capital adequacy has come under criticism because of its inflexibility on how capital-against-risk should be managed. In many respects the recognition afforded to internal models has motivated institutions to innovate in risk management strategies rather than concentrate on ensuring that they quantitatively meet the existing capital requirements and 'trigger' and 'target' ratios. Moreover, the nature of risk management, given the developments in the area, is such that many of the standardised methods for calculating capital are deemed rudimentary in comparison with the methods used by some banks and investments firms for internal purposes. These concerns required Basel and the European Commission to amend their respective capital adequacy policies to incorporate the use of internal models.[91] This resulted in a further amendment of the Basel Capital Accord and European CAD, and in the renamed CADII,[92] implemented on 30 September 1998, which allows banks to use a wider range of internal models.[93]

The models of the CADI standard approach go through a process of recognition to ensure they can be used for the purpose of capital adequacy calculation. This process includes the models themselves and the operating environment in which they function.[94] An authorised institution might have a number of models for calculating the various types of risk it is taking in its various businesses. The model review process is an integral part of the overall risk-based approach to supervision: CADI models are systematically reviewed, prior to their recognition by the FSA, during on-site visits and on the basis of pre-visit information. The review process includes a systemic assessment of the model, of the conditions to be met in using it and of the systems and controls that underpin it.

The FSA recognises the admittance by CADII of the use of internal models for measuring market risks in calculating capital requirements;[95] this was necessary because some banks had in place measuring systems that were more sophisticated than the CAD standard approach, and had to be allowed to benefit from their use. (The utilising bank is required to satisfy a number of qualitative and quantitative

---

91 Lastra, R. M. (2004) 'Risk-based capital requirements and their impact upon the banking industry: Basel II and CAD III', *Journal of Financial Regulation and Compliance*, vol. 12, 225. For a historical account see Elderfield, M. (1996) 'Basel publishes final market risk capital standards', *Butterworths Journal of International Banking and Financial Law*, March, 125; Bates, C. (1998) 'CADIII moves forward', *FT Financial Regulation Report*, January, 2; O'Neill, N. (1998) 'CADII moves forward – Proposals to amend the EU Capital Adequacy Directive', *Butterworths Journal of International Banking and Financial Law*, February, 178.

92 CADII – 98/31/EC. Lastra, ibid., at p. 236.

93 IPRU, TS: S. 1.

94 Ibid., S. 2..

95 IPRU, TV: S. 1.

standards.) Moreover, the admittance was an incentive to banks to measure market risks with more precision.

The value at risk (VaR) measure provides an estimate of the worst expected loss on a portfolio as a result of market movements over a period of time.[96] The internal models undergo a recognition process consisting of on-site visits and off-site assessment by the Traded Risk Department and external auditors. The qualitative standards[97] a model has to fulfil are extensive, and focus on internal controls, management and the resources that underpin the functioning of the model. Included in the recognition process is a programme of stress testing that can betray vulnerabilities, and a regular review by internal auditors to assess risk measurement capabilities. The 'recognition process' has quantitative standards to ensure that internal models produce a consistency of results across banks and have a 99 per cent confidence limit.[98]

There is consensus on the use of internal models.[99] However, they are not a panacea but the inevitable outcome of developments in risk measurement strategies. According to Danielsson, VaR has a number of limitations and in some respects actually increases the vulnerability of institutions because it may provide false impressions of the degree of risk to which an institution is exposed.[100] It is therefore necessary for regulators to be cautious of internal models, particularly when they are the product of the institution using them. In the USA Hendricks and Hirtle recommend regulators scrutinise information closely to ensure that an institution's true risk exposure is portrayed. Hendricks and Hirtle show a high degree of pragmatism in their attitude to regulating internal models by suggesting that their introduction does not necessitate the overhauling of regulatory expertise, but rather the maintenance of a staff with a high degree of technical skill and experience in reviewing bank trading operations.[101] This is to ensure that many of the limits of VaR models can be effectively addressed. Nuxoll provides a more cautious approach:[102] a number of assumptions exist that can call into question the reliability of the results that arise when using VaR models – for example, the assumption that the price of a portfolio of assets is reliably reflected by the price at the end of the trading day, when in practice the VaR can be calculated and indeed will change during the course of the day's trading.[103] Moreover, in a Bank of England survey one of the findings was that banks

96 Ibid., S. 2, para. 2.5.

97 Ibid., S. 4.

98 Ibid., S. 5.

99 Hendricks, D. and Hirtle, B. (1997) 'Bank capital requirements for market risks: The internal models approach', *Federal Reserve Bank of New York Economic Policy Review*, December, 1.

100 Danielsson, J. (2000) 'The emperor has no clothes: Limits to risk modelling', paper presented at conference on Rules, Incentives and Sanctions: Enforcement in Financial Regulation, Financial Markets Group, London School of Economics, May.

101 Hendricks and Hirtle, n. 99 above, at p. 9.

102 Nuxoll, D. A. (2001) 'Internal risk-management models as a basis for capital requirements', *FDIC Banking Review*, vol. 12, 18.

103 Ibid., at p. 22.

could not even agree on the simple components of a VaR calculation for a standard derivatives contract.[104]

Large Exposures

The examination of capital adequacy and consolidated supervision also requires an examination of the FSA's approach to large exposures.[105] This issue gained prominence in the UK after the collapse of Johnson Matthey Bankers. The Leigh Pemberton Report highlighted the importance of controlling large exposures with the repeal of the Banking Act 1979.[106] The EC directive on the monitoring of large exposures[107] was built on the Commission's recommendation.[108] It allows the regulator to monitor the excessive concentration of exposure to a single client, or group of connected clients, that could result in major losses or seriously affect the solvency of a credit institution.[109] The broad policy reason for the regulation of large exposures is to prevent a distortion of the competitiveness of banks by controlling the level at which they expose themselves to particular counterparties.[110] The provisions of the directive indicate the importance of laying down specific standards for exposure by a bank. The large exposure requirements operate in conjunction with solo and consolidated supervision and capital adequacy requirements for both the banking and trading sides of a business.

The Large Exposure Policy Governing UK-incorporated Banks

The FSA's approach is to monitor large exposures of banks and banking groups at a solo and consolidated level in order to gauge the extent to which the portfolio of customers is as diversified as possible to avoid excessive concentration of risks. The FSA requires a bank to set out its own policy on large exposures, including exposures to individual customers, banks, countries and economic sectors. The bank is required to have appropriate systems in place to ensure it can monitor its exposures on a daily basis. The FSA provides specific levels and requirements as to the extent a bank can commitment itself to any one kind of counterparty or group of closely related counterparties: it is required to report to the FSA if it exceeds the limit of 10–25 per cent of its capital. Only in the most exceptional circumstances is a bank allowed to exceed the 25 per cent level of capital base exposure.[111] The bank in these circumstances is required to provide notification on a quarterly basis of the

104 Ibid.

105 IPRU, LE: S.1–S. 2.

106 HMSO (1985) *Report of the Committee Set Up to Consider the System of Banking Supervision* (Leigh Pemberton Report), Cmnd 9550, London, HMSO.

107 Directive 2000/12/EC , s. 3, Arts 48–50, n 79 above.

108 European Community, 'Recommendation on common guidelines for monitoring and controlling credit institutions' large exposures', 87/62/EEC.

109 Lee, R. G. (1992) 'The monitoring and control of large exposures: A view from the United Kingdom', *Butterworths Journal of Banking and Financial Law*, vol. 4, 125.

110 Pecchoili, R. M. (1987) *Prudential Supervision in Banking*, Paris, OECD, at p. 74.

111 IPRU, LE: S. 9.

state of its exposure. The FSA would increase the level of enquiry if the level of exposure exceeds 10 per cent, but the approach relies on banks not exceeding the 10 per cent limit.

International Cooperation

The internationalisation of financial intermediaries requires effective cooperation between home and host authorities, without which regulatory oversight of their activities would be limited and could result in problems not being spotted in time to be adequately remedied.[112] This was particularly obvious in the BCCI and Barings collapses and on other occasions where cooperation was simply not forthcoming, such as in the German regulators' communications with the international creditors of Bankhaus Herstatt.[113] In the case of BCCI, the over-reliance on the Luxembourg authorities under s. 3(5) of the Banking Act 1979 contributed to continued licensing, even though the Luxembourg authorities had notified the Bank that they could not supervise BCCI and its activities effectively. International cooperation was given a statutory platform by the Banking Act 1987, which allowed the Bank the option of relying upon the judgement of the home regulator of the country in which a business is predominantly situated.[114] The continuation of BCCI's operations despite its damaged credibility was possible because it was able to retain the status of being a body under the supervision of the College of Regulators while the Bank was under some pressure in light of the problems associated with safeguarding the interests of actual and potential depositors. The BCCI closure shows that if cooperation with a regulator is not fulsome, fraud and other malpractice can flourish to the point where a financial institution becomes a liability in an economy.

The Barings collapse exposed some problems with the level of cooperation between the respective regulators, albeit the formal chain of cooperation between bank and securities regulators was not fully addressed at the time. The collapse highlighted the uncertainty with which regulators could formally cooperate with one another and a reluctance in part to cooperate in investigations. According to the Singapore Report, the initial request for interviews by the Singapore authorities was rejected by HM Treasury because it was 'of the view that there was no reciprocity in connection with the Board's work in Singapore'.[115] Requests for information had to be given adequate consideration. This decision was reversed later. Formal requests through the courts were unsuccessful because no benefit accrued to the judicial

112 Lastra, R. M. (2006) *Legal Foundations of International Monetary Stability*, Oxford, Oxford University Press.

113 Helleiner, E. (1994) *States and the Reemergence of Global Finance: From Bretton Woods to the 1990s*, New York, Cornell University Press, at pp. 171–173.

114 S. 9(3) of the Banking Act 1987.

115 Barings Futures (Singapore) Pte Ltd Investigation pursuant to section 231 of the Companies Act (chapter 50) *The Report of the Inspectors Appointed by the Minister for Finance*, M L C San and N T N Kuang Partners of Price Waterhouse, 6 September (1995).

managers in Singapore during the investigation.[116] However, in a decision relating to a request by the director of the Serious Fraud Office for documents in Singapore, the judge focused on a different point although the outcome was similar – it was decided that such matters were best dealt with by the respective regulatory authorities rather than through the courts in light of the informal cooperation the parties had already given to one another during their individual investigations.[117] According to Lai Kew Chai J, 'the decision whether to exchange any information or documents must rest with the regulators of the financial industry. They assist in formulating policies which, once decided, they also implement. They also conduct relationships with their counterparts in connection with international financial institutions. More often than not, it did not require much imagination to know that many bilateral problems could best be solved at their levels.'[118] The Board and the Singapore authorities did, however, arrange an informal exchange of notes between the investigating teams. This was deemed adequate consideration. On a wider note, the Barings débâcle called into question the role of external auditors, as the same level of cooperation between the professional bodies was not forthcoming. The extension of the investigation by the UK accountancy profession into Singapore was blocked by the refusal of the Singapore authorities to cooperate.

While countries do recognise the importance of mutual cooperation to resolve such matters, they are reluctant to undermine the trading interests of persons within their jurisdiction. This problem was highlighted by the implementation of the Hague Convention on the Taking of Evidence Abroad in Civil and Commercial Matters 1970, which resulted in many jurisdictions introducing 'blocking statutes' to prevent 'fishing expeditions' or the transfer of information that is not in the public interest to those requesting it. The UK was no exception to this move, as it introduced the Protection of Trading Interests Act 1980 in order to curb extraterritorial demands for information from another jurisdiction.

The FSA and Cooperation with Overseas Authorities

The FSA has a duty under s. 354 of the FSMA 2000 to cooperate with 'other persons', which includes similar authorities in the UK and elsewhere, by doing 'whatever it considers appropriate to co-operate'. This rather ambiguous provision, like the other duty provisions, does not impose a statutory obligation on the FSA. Instead, it has a status similar to that of the sections outlining its responsibilities under the FSMA 2000: it constitutes the platform, together with a range of formal MoUs, on which the FSA can cooperate with extra-national authorities. A memorandum of understanding is a memorandum of intent signed by the regulators rather than

116 *Re Barings Futures (Singapore) Pte Ltd; the Board of Banking Supervision v. Judicial Managers of Barings Futures (Singapore) Pte Ltd* [1996] 1 SLR 89.

117 *Re Barings Futures (Singapore) Pte Ltd; Director of the Serious Fraud Office v. Judicial Managers of Barings Futures (Singapore) Pte Ltd* [1996] 2 SLR 89.

118 Ibid., at p. 95.

an agreement between states. MoUs are essentially concerned with exchange of information or guidelines for cooperation between regulators.[119]

The MoUs the FSA has entered into with other regulators flesh out the scope of s. 354 of the FSMA 2000 on a practical level. Given that the FSA is a single regulatory authority overseeing the financial system, some of the MoUs make reference to the fact that the respective regulators could seek information and ask for assistance with enforcement matters to do with financial institutions. Indeed, in some instances the FSA has asked regulators to extend an MoU to include insurance firms rather than simply covering banks and securities firms, as is the case with the Canadian authorities.[120] However, cooperation in other jurisdictions could be problematic: for example, while a number of MoUs exist with the US bank and securities regulators, it would be difficult to include insurance as it is regulated on an individual state level rather than at a federal level.[121]

The MoU between the FSA and the China Banking Regulatory Commission is typical of most MoUs, as it puts in place reciprocal arrangements for supervising and sharing information about their respective banks.[122] The MoU refers to sharing information and notifying authorities regarding 'material supervisory concern', which refers to matters such as the 'safety and soundness' of the conduct of a bank and whether it operates according to the respective prudential standards. It also refers to 'events that would have a material adverse effect on the financial stability of banking organisations in the jurisdiction of the other authority'.[123] On a practical level the MoU puts in place formal mechanisms to undertake on-site supervision in the host state.[124]

The utility of MoUs is limited in the light of the fact that information may be prevented from being transferred if it is not in the 'public interest or national security', as is highlighted in most MoUs. Moreover, the MoU makes it quite explicit that it is a 'statement of intent and does not, and is not intended to, create any legally binding obligations on either party'. MoUs are therefore simply administrative arrangements for the dissemination of information between the respective parties. States or courts could block information being transferred if this is perceived not to be in the national interest. However, given the formal support by the international organisations and indeed the Singapore decision explaining how regulators cooperate and share information with each other, the importance of MoUs is considerable as the courts may consider them a 'strong' indication that cooperation is formally recognised by responsible states.

---

119 IMF (1996) *International Capital Markets: Developments, Prospects, and Policy Issues*, Washington, DC, International Monetary Fund, at p. 150.

120 FSA (2003) 'Information Exchange between the OSFI and the FSA: Inclusion of Insurance Organisations within the Scope of the OSFI and FSA Banking Memorandum of Understanding', 11 February.

121 For example, MoU between the FSA and US FRS, FDIC and OCC, 18 May 1998.

122 MoU between the FSA and the China Banking Regulatory Commission, 9 October 2003.

123 Ibid., at p. 1.

124 Ibid., at p. 3.

The US Regulation of the Business of Banks and Safe and Sound Requirements

The business of banking in the USA is primarily interpreted in the light of statute and common law, giving rise to a broad interpretation of its definition. The 'business of banking' articulated in the National Bank Acts of 1863–1865 identified some specific bank activities, such as acceptance of deposits and note issuance, but with the added proviso 'powers... necessary to carry on the business of banking'.[125] In common law the traditional business of banks, while considering receiving deposits to be an 'indispensable'[126] and 'unique'[127] part of banking, includes other business that has come to be associated with banking, namely 'discount bills' and 'loan money on mortgage'.[128] The pursuit of either one was considered sufficient for an institution to be deemed to be undertaking banking business.[129] The statutory definition of banking at a federal level therefore focuses on 'accepting deposits', but refers to a whole host of activities such as 'discounting and negotiating promissory notes' and 'buying and selling exchange'. It consequently provides a broad activity-oriented definition that refers to 'all such incidental powers as shall be necessary to carry on the business of banking'.[130] This provides scope to include activities that may or may not be in the traditional domain of banking business but over time are considered appropriate for banks to pursue under this umbrella.[131] The expansion of activities, according to Bernard Shull, 'reflects a culmination of almost 20 years of debate regarding permissible activities of banking firms'.[132]

The OCC encourages national banks to undertake other financial services to meet the various needs of their customers, provided this does not undermine the safety and soundness of the chartered bank.[133] The OCC in its recent report on permissible activities contends that the 'business of banking is an evolving concept and the permissible activities of national banks similarly evolve over time'.[134] This has led to the inclusion by the OCC of a whole host of financial services, post-GLB, that banks can pursue, categorised as general banking activities, fiduciary activities,

125 12 USC § 24 (seventh). For a historical exposition of US banking see *US v. Philadelphia National Bank et al.*, 374 US 321 (1963). See footnote 5 where a list of 'principal banking products' is provided.

126 *Texas & Pacific Railway Co. v. Pottorff, Receiver No. 128*, 291 US 245 (1934) p. 247.

127 *US v. Philadelphia National Bank*, n. 125 above.

128 *Outlon v. Savings Institution*, 84 US 109; 21 L. Ed. 618 (1873) Lexis 1318; 17 Wall, 109, p. 620.

129 Ibid.

130 12 USC § 24 (seventh).

131 See for example *Nations Bank v. Variable Annuity Life Insurance Co.* 513 US 251 (1995).

132 Shull, B. (2000) 'Financial modernization legislation in the United States: Background and implications', UNCTAD Discussion Paper No. 151, UNCTAD/OSG/DP/151, at p. 8.

133 OCC (2005) *A Guide to the National Banking System*, p. 13. See also OCC (2005) *Activities Permissible for a National Bank.*

134 OCC *Activities Permissible*, ibid., at p. 1.

insurance and annuities activities, securities activities and technology and electronic activities.[135]

Safety and Soundness

Safety and soundness is a central tenet of US banking regulation, supervision and enforcement. The provision was first incorporated in US bank regulation with the enactment of the Banking Act 1933 to act as a benchmark to deal with bank mismanagement.[136] In accordance with USCA 1831p-1, federal agencies have in place measures to fulfil the standard of safety and soundness. The federal agencies can require banks that do not meet the standard of safety and soundness to correct the 'deficiencies' identified by them. In exceptional circumstances a lack of compliance with the safety and soundness provision can give rise to a variety of enforcement sanctions exercised by the federal agencies.[137] The provision is frequently referred to but rarely defined in the statutes, thus reliance is placed on the intent of Congress, the judiciary and the regulators to provide some clarity as to its meaning.

The principle of safety and soundness is purposefully left in an ambiguous state in the statute books in light of the fact that it needs to evolve with the changing expectations of those at the helm of managing banks and their risks. To assist with its evolving nature, particular responsibility for its scope has traditionally been left to the regulators to articulate acts and omissions considered to threaten the safety and soundness of those institutions they charter or confer membership upon. The statutes have occasionally assisted in clarifying the scope of safety and soundness by prescribing certain acts or omissions considered to be associated with it. But the reason for its first appearance on the statute books seems to be rather unclear. The early rationale of the principle was to enable regulators to remove bank directors who failed to comply with their warnings to avoid 'unsafe and unsound' practices. As Holzman explains, the principle was a tool conferred on regulators by Congress to ensure their decisions and warnings were acted upon with the appropriate level of care and attention.[138] Indeed, the subsequent use of the principle to protect the deposit insurance fund adds further weight to the authority of regulators, with the power to withdraw a bank from the insurance scheme if it failed to comply with their directions. According to Schooner, for instance, the safety and soundness standard is a mechanism to 'guard against the threat of bank insolvency'.[139] In addition to it being a term used to direct bank behaviour, the principle of safety and soundness is considered a mechanism to reduce regulatory forbearance by having in place

135 Ibid.

136 Banking Act 1933, § 30.

137 For a critical look at the way regulators examine banks in accordance with the 'safety and soundness' standard see GAO (1993) 'Bank examination quality. FRB examinations and inspections do not fully assess bank safety and soundness', Report to Congressional Committees, GAO/AFMD-93-13, February.

138 Holzman, T. L. (2000) 'Unsafe or unsound practices: Is the current judicial interpretation of the term unsafe and unsound?', *Annual Review of Banking Law*, vol. 19, 428.

139 Schooner, H. M. (1995) 'Fiduciary duties' demanding cousin: Bank director liability for unsafe or unsound banking practices', *George Washington Law Review*, vol. 63, 190.

provisions that assist in articulating what is considered to be under the umbrella of 'safety and soundness' and triggers to initiate regulatory intervention, as with the provisions regarding prompt corrective action. According to Baxter, 'safety and soundness has been a principal concern driving a "cradle to the grave" regime of tight regulation' that has underpinned both federal and state bank regulation.[140]

The principle of safety and soundness has not been formally defined in the statutes, as mentioned above, but it has spawned a considerable level of judicial attention as to its scope and meaning.[141] This attention has tended to rely on the interpretation provided by John Horne in his written memorandum during the debate on the Financial Institutions Supervisory Act 1966.[142] This memorandum is cited in a number of cases by various academics as a generic interpretation of safety and soundness. It refers to the lack of clarity over terms such as fraud and negligence as necessary in order to capture the evolving nature of banking business. But more specifically Horne states that 'an "unsafe or unsound practice" embraces any action, or lack of action... the possible consequences of which, if continued, would be abnormal risk or loss or damage to an institution'.[143] However, as pointed out by Schooner, there is a difference in approach by the various court circuits: some have focused on the safety and soundness issue from the point of view of the banking institution or shareholders, whereas others refer to the potential impact on the deposit insurance scheme as well.[144]

In *Seidman*, the term was interpreted to be a 'flexible concept which gives the administering agency the ability to adapt to changing business problems and practices'.[145] Loans were given to a company called Crestmont Federal Savings and Loans, in which Seidman continued to have an interest during the completion of a real estate project: an interest that was prohibited by Crestmont in accordance with OTS guidelines governing self-dealing. During its investigation into this violation of regulations the OTS considered that Seidman had attempted to obstruct its investigation and so decided to seek to remove him from his office permanently, on the basis that such acts amounted to an unsafe and unsound practice. The court concluded that the evidence regarding the self-dealing claim did not amount to an unsafe and unsound practice in light of the fact that during the completion of the loans Seidman was making attempts to relinquish his links to avoid allegations of self-dealing. However, his conduct during the investigation was considered to be an unsafe and unsound practice, as according to s. 1818 (e) (1) (c) it amounted to a wilful disregard for the safety and soundness of the bank. His failure to cooperate by not disclosing key facts to the regulator amounted to 'personal dishonesty'.

140 Baxter, L. G. (1993) 'The rule of too much law? The new safety/soundness rulemaking: Responsibilities of the federal banking agencies', *Consumer Finance Law Quarterly Report*, vol. 47, 211.

141 For a jurisprudential analysis of safety and soundness and the policy implications of the various interpretations see Holzman, n. 138 above.

142 Horne, J. (1996) Memorandum submitted to the Chairman of the Senate Committee on Banking and Currency, 112 Congress, Record 26.

143 Ibid., at p. 474.

144 Schooner, n. 139 above, at p. 191.

145 *L B Seidman v. Office of Thrift Supervision* 37 F.3d 911 (3d Cir 1994), at pp. 926 927.

The US courts have judged a whole host of acts and omissions as unsafe and unsound practices, legitimising the decision by the federal regulators to initiate enforcement action provided the practice has a 'reasonably direct effect' on the financial soundness of a bank. In the case of Roque de la Fuente II[146] the FDIC sought to prohibit him from acting as director of First International Bank as a result of his violation of Regulation O, the self-dealing regulation prohibiting 'insiders' from lending to companies in which they have interests.[147] The action taken against Roque de la Fuente was legitimised by the court for a number of reasons: Roque de la Fuente sought to benefit from the transactions to the detriment of the depositors of First International Bank, and in light of the fact that the collateral to secure the transactions were of poor quality it was foreseeable that there could be an increased chance of the bank sustaining a loss. The evidence in the appeal against the FDIC's decision showed that he acted dishonestly and in wilful disregard for the safety and soundness of the bank. In addition, his acts and omissions attempted to hinder the progress of the investigation, which in itself constituted unsafe and unsound practice in violation of s. 1818 (e). The court decided that while there was sufficient evidence to justify exercising enforcement sanctions, it was left to the FDIC to decide whether it warranted permanent exclusion.

Risk-based Supervision

The USA introduced a risk-based approach after the 'savings and loans' débâcle of the late 1980s and 1990s.[148] A far-reaching review of regulation and supervision of the banking industry was undertaken to address the factors considered to have caused the failures. A criticism levelled at the regulators was the level of 'forbearance' amongst the authorities towards compliance with the standards and rules that governed thrift and banking business.[149] This resulted in a change to the culture of regulation, with additional checks and balances to restrict the level of discretion exercised by bank regulators.[150] In addition to this move to improve the compliance culture, other measures implemented at the time focused on reducing the burden on the public

146 *Roque de la Fuente II v. Federal Deposit Insurance Corporation* 332 F.3d 1208 (9d Cir. 2003).

147 Ibid., at pp. 1224–1226.

148 Other reasons included the developments discussed above, such as new financial products, risk management techniques and the formation of bank-financial conglomerates. GAO (1998) *Bank and Thrift Examinations: Adoption of Risk-Focused Examination Strategies*, GAO/t-GGD-98-13, Washington, DC, US General Accounting Office. In this report, over the 1980s and 1990s the US Federal Deposit Insurance Fund experienced record payouts as a result of the losses incurred by the failure of 1,300 thrifts and 1,617 federally insured banks, which were closed or received some form of assistance. The total losses experienced by the FDIF were $125 billion. For an examination of the risk-based approach for foreign US banks see Welsh, G. M. (1995) 'The new supervisory regime for foreign banks in the US: The ROCA, combined and SOSA rating systems', *Butterworths Journal of International Banking and Finance Law*, July, 267.

149 GAO, ibid., at p. 4.

150 Ibid.; see also pp. 144–147.

safety net by more periodic examinations.[151] The regulators were also required to focus more attention on the adequacy of internal governance systems in banks as a method of enhancing the supervision of their activities and risk management. This was an area previously given little attention by the regulators, and the move was designed to reduce the likelihood of past disasters reoccurring – a common problem amongst the savings and loans banks that had experienced difficulties.[152]

The adoption of a risk-based approach that centres regulatory efforts on internal governance systems was considered necessary to oversee the ever-growing complexity of banking business.[153] It departed from the previous approach to supervision, which tended to focus on testing transactions for the purpose of determining the value of a bank's assets at a given point in time. According to DeFerrari and Palmer, the 'supervisory process is continuous and is more tuned to market developments' rather than based on a 'single point in time and rarely continuous unless there is a crisis'.[154] Indeed, the move to a risk-based approach to regulation mirrored the risk-based system of management generally adopted in the financial and commercial world to cope with the associated risks of business affairs. One of the benefits highlighted by DeFerrari and Palmer is that decisions made by supervisors are more reflective of best practice in the industry.[155] The GAO also indicates the risk-focused approach enables regulators to account better for their decisions.[156]

The growth of complex financial products and more diverse banking and financial groups requires a more efficient and systematic method of regulating and supervising the risks they undertake in their business. According to Alan Greenspan, a combination of improved risk management and the utilisation of financial derivatives to manage the risk portfolio has enabled banks to calculate risks more efficiently in business, which has resulted to some extent in a reduction of the burden of the banking system on its regulators.[157] The complexity of these risks requires regulators to oversee a variety of risks not generally subjected to monitoring to understand the potential impact they could have on the financial institutions for which regulators are responsible. In addition, the risk-based approach enables regulators to manage their resources according to areas considered to give rise to the most risk. The move to non-bank business required a more sophisticated approach to supervision and examinations so that bank examiners could capture the risks posed by such activities

151 Financial Institutions Reform, Recovery, and Enforcement Act 1989 (FIRREA) and Federal Deposit Insurance Corporation Improvement Act 1991 (FIDICIA) respectively.

152 GAO, n. 148 above.

153 GAO (2000) *Risk-focused Bank Examinations: Regulators of Large Banking Organizations Face Challenges*, Washington, DC, US General Accounting Office.

154 DeFerrari, L. M. and Palmer, D. E. (2001) 'Supervision of large complex banking organizations', *Federal Reserve Bulletin*, February, 51. See also Lichtenstein, C. C. (2006) 'The Fed's new model of supervision for "large complex banking organizations": Co-ordinated risk-based supervision of financial multinationals for international financial stability', Boston College Law School Faculty Paper 129, available at http://lsr.nellco.org/bc/bclsfp/papers/129.

155 DeFerrari and Palmer, ibid., at p. 57.

156 GAO, n. 153 above, at p. 3.

157 Greenspan, A. (2002) 'Banking', *Federal Reserve Bulletin*, 7 October.

by 'testing' the robustness of risk management systems. In many respects the move to the risk-based approach was an attempt to realign bank regulation and supervision with the commercial realities they faced, and involved institutions managing their risks in a more efficient manner to reflect the growth of a broad range of ways to finance business and hedge risks.

The risk-based approach in the USA focuses on both small 'community banks' and 'large banks'.[158] The OCC and the Federal Reserve interpret a 'large bank' to be either a national bank with assets of $1 billion or more, or a national bank with this level of assets but part of a holding company.[159] This general classification also determines the intensity of the supervision. However, given that the US banking system consists of more than one bank regulator at the federal level, the method of risk-based supervision has evolved in distinct ways.[160] It has not been coordinated like other areas of bank supervision, such as the CAMEL rating system, at an interagency level to ensure a higher degree of consistency between the federal regulators. The Federal Reserve and the OCC have formally adopted a risk-based system, albeit with a different slant to their approaches.[161] Nevertheless, as noted by the GAO, similarities do exist between the two approaches. For example, both adopt a more proactive rather than reactive approach to problems that may ensue at banks, and both advocate that this enhances the efficient use of regulatory resources. The risk-based approach builds on the extent to which a risk could adversely affect the safety and soundness of a bank.[162]

The OCC, for example, set out its policy on supervision of national banks in its Comptrollers Handbooks of 1996 and 2001. It takes a rather pragmatic approach in the light of the fact that the financial services industry is a diversified and complex environment where risks are managed in a number of ways. It highlights that the supervisory policy is not one which tries to 'restrict risk-taking'. But the OCC does expect banks to keep up with such risk-taking by having in place the commensurate level of risk management processes to capture those risks.[163] In addition to banks themselves increasing the level of resources to capture risks safely, the OCC sets itself the responsibility to allocate regulatory resources to areas that it considers pose the most risk. It places reliance on a bank being able to manage the risks it faces regardless of whether these are complex.[164] In the examination process particular reliance is placed on internal governance systems, such as the internal audit function. However, as noted by the GAO, weight is only given to the findings of such functions if they are considered reliable.[165]

The OCC produces a risk profile of a bank to enable it to devise an appropriate strategy to oversee its activities. According to the GAO, the risk-based approach is

158 12 USC § 1817 (b) (D).

159 OCC, n. 133 above, at p. 8.

160 GAO, n. 153 above, at p. 16.

161 Ibid., at p. 18.

162 Ibid., at p. 17.

163 OCC (2001) *Large Bank Supervision, Comptrollers Handbook*, at p. 3.

164 Ibid., at p. 5.

165 GAO, n. 153 above, at p. 27.

'more forward looking' than the previous approach.[166] The core assessment criteria enable the OCC to apply a common methodological approach to assess the risk profile of individual group entities to ensure that risks can be measured consistently. The proactive nature of the OCC's approach is evident with the application of a risk assessment system which enables it to gauge how risks will change over the next 12 months. This ultimately determines how the OCC will apportion its resources across the national banking sector to shape the examination processes. For example, the OCC policy document specifically mentions the importance of examiners ensuring that there is a good level of communication between them and the bank to capture all domestic and international activities.[167] But, more importantly, it requires the examiners to set out the programme of supervision on a continuous basis, giving the required resources and budget for the examinations. In the part of the examination entitled 'Corrections' examiners require banks to deal with problems with their risk management processes, thus addressing 'root causes rather than symptoms' found during the examination.[168]

The risk-based approach is not a regulatory panacea, as it continues to rely on trust, honesty and the cooperation of authorised institutions and persons in providing information and reports.[169] All regulatory systems rely on these, and so no form of regulation can eradicate all fraud, but greater emphasis on management responsibilities and internal controls can produce an increase in detection by the firm itself and the regulator in both on-site and off-site supervisory functions. The risk-based approach poses a particular concern that regulatory attention is focused primarily on areas that cause the greatest risk at the expense of the parts of a business deemed to be low risk. The GAO highlights that the success of the approach is very much dependent upon the expertise of supervisors in identifying potential risks.[170] For example, regulators did not fully assess the risks posed by Long-Term Capital Management (LTCM).[171] Too much reliance on management and the information system of the regulated leads to over-reliance on the information and data generated by the risk management systems, resulting in possible underestimation of the risks to the counterparty or market risks by the institution. This can be exacerbated when the regulator is assessing internal models devised and utilised by an authorised institution.[172] According to the GAO, such models require individual attention because they are devised to delineate the risk parameters of an institution rather than to assist regulators.[173] Whether the management systems of an authorised institution are centralised or decentralised is also an issue. It is necessary for a

166 Ibid., at p. 24.

167 OCC, n. 163 above, at p. 22.

168 Ibid., at p. 20.

169 GAO, n. 153 above, at p. 40.

170 Ibid.

171 GAO (1999) *Long-Term Capital Management: Regulators Need to Focus Greater Attention on Systemic Risk*, GAO/GGD-00-3, October, Washington, DC, US General Accounting Office.

172 See the examination of VaR models on pp. 64–65.

173 GAO (1998) *Risk Based Capital: Regulatory and Industry Approaches to Capital and Risk*, GAO/GGD-98-153, July, Washington, DC, US General Accounting Office, at p. 92.

decentralised management system to adopt a consolidated risk-based approach to draw out the inherent limitations that could adversely affect the parent company. In situations where there are multiple authorisations across jurisdictions and business lines, an individualised programme of examination is crucial, but this requires a large regulatory resource. In addition, the fact that large groups of financial services firms undertake business overseen by a whole host of different regulators means that some coordination needs to be clearly in place at that level as well, so that risks in one part of the group do not adversely affect another simply because of a lack of communication.

Conclusion

The risk-based system of regulation and supervision adopted by the FSA takes a top-down approach, and the resources utilised are determined by the likelihood of the risks posed by a firm or sector affecting it achieving its objectives. The key efficiency gain from using a single risk-based approach rather than having a plurality of systems for the various parts of the industry is that the risks posed by individual sectors can be compared against one set of criteria. A single approach does not necessarily mean that all sectors of the industry pose the same kinds of risks, nor will they give rise to the same degree of risk to the individual objectives or principles of regulation; however, a risk-based system places a responsibility on the regulator to give a better account of the decisions it makes.

In the context of this risk-based system there are rules concerning prudential management, with which banks are required to comply to fulfil the threshold conditions to retain permission to undertake banking business. The prudential requirements enable regulators to assess the risks banks are taking, both domestically and internationally. Capital adequacy standards are a central cushion against such risks. The monitoring of large exposures by setting limits on a bank's ability to do business with a particular sector of an economy enables regulators to assess the extent to which a bank is vulnerable to a particular sector or counterparty if it were to experience a downturn.

The US risk-based system primarily focuses on the 'probability that the deposit insurance fund will incur a loss with respect to the institution'.[174] The significance of the US approach is that it focuses on the firm's risk management techniques and the safety and soundness of the bank, whereas the UK attempts to focus on a specific interpretation of risk which links risk and risk-taking to objectives and principles. However, the UK and US approaches are similar in that both try to manage regulatory resources according to the risks posed by the respective institutions. The UK system, in similar fashion to the USA, indicates the importance of being able to oversee the business undertaken by a group and an individual bank to gauge whether activities in the group pose a risk to objectives. Indeed, the UK and US risk assessments consist of similar categories, albeit labelled differently. The work in the USA undertaken by the OCC, unlike its UK counterpart, does not indicate whether it also provides for

174 12 USC 1817(b) (C) (i).

cross-comparisons with other banks in a sector. The different risk-based systems in the banking sectors mean cross-sector comparisons may be difficult, given that the individual regulators would be using different sets of criteria. This issue would be exacerbated if one were to include other financial sectors in the equation.

Chapter 3

Corporate Governance and Banking Supervision

Introduction

Financial regulation and supervision provide an external framework of rights and obligations in which a firm operates so that it can undertake regulated activities in the financial marketplace. To aid compliance with this external framework, formal mechanisms of internal self-regulation are also employed. The purpose of the external and internal regulatory systems is to ensure that risks can be sufficiently managed such that competitiveness and the drive for profitability do not adversely threaten the stability of the firm, investors' interests or market confidence. The caveat is the fact that the regulatory and supervisory framework does not necessarily eliminate the likelihood of loss, failure or fraud. In this respect, financial supervisors have, over a considerable period of time, placed more emphasis on effective corporate governance in regulated firms to reduce the likelihood of risks becoming unmanageable.

The fact that banking is formally regulated by the FSA does not preclude the fact that both the common law, in the form of fiduciary duties and duties of care and skill, and statutory measures, namely the Companies Act 1985, also govern its business affairs. In this chapter the first section will consider the scope of corporate governance and its importance. It will highlight that the corporate legal framework simply focuses on the interests of the company and shareholders as a whole, rather than other stakeholders. The second section will analyse the position of depositors as stakeholders in banks, and delineate the duty the bank has towards them as unsecured creditors and the limited powers depositors have to respond collectively. The third section will focus on the wider stakeholder ideas incorporated in the FSMA 2000 by examining the FSA's work to meet its objectives. The fourth section outlines the FSA's powers governing authorisation and supervision, paying particular attention to the additional responsibilities placed on shareholders to safeguard the interests of depositors. The FSA formally refers to the interests of a whole host of stakeholders in its regulatory regime, namely consumers, regulators and financial intermediaries, as a result of the application of market confidence and integrity requirements. These outweigh the interests of shareholders. The fifth section introduces the Principles for Businesses that govern the internal operations of a regulated firm. It illustrates their application by referring to a number of FSA enforcement decisions. The importance attached to internal controls within the corporate governance debate will also be considered in respect of the internal audit function and audit committee. The point highlighted here is if the regulator wants to ensure management is in compliance with its standards and rules then it needs to establish appropriate guidelines to ensure its objectives are achieved, especially given that the internal audit and audit committee act on behalf of a narrow set of interests, namely the companies and shareholders. The sixth section will then outline the common law and statutory principles that govern the function and duties of the board of directors and senior management as the persons with control. These common law principles are separate sources of obligations from the principles provided in the FSMA 2000, but common features do exist. These will be explored in part in the examination of the 'approved person' regime and the 'fit and proper' criteria. Here the regulatory provisions pertaining to the legal duty to which directors and management of regulated firms are expected to adhere are analysed, as are recent Financial Markets Tribunal decisions. The FSA seems to have adopted the general standard of care and skill in its regulatory regime. However, it has also prescribed a number of provisions to govern the behaviour of banks and their directors in controlled functions much more explicitly. This in many respects reduces the expectations gap between the FSA and regulated firms and individuals as to their obligations when authorised and approved to undertake regulated activities. While a considerable degree of regulation and supervision exists, it is the responsibility of the banks to ensure that they are mindful of the interests of other stakeholders. The seventh section discusses the duty of bank directors in the USA. It will highlight the salient points, such as the move towards a more standardised approach and away from a plurality of high and low standards expected of bank directors at a federal and state level, the minimum being a standard of gross negligence. Finally, the eighth section will provide some concluding points and some comparative observations about the UK and US approach.

Corporate Governance

The importance of effective corporate governance is evident when the history of the international capital markets is reviewed, as it demonstrates that a weak system of governance in, for example, banks increases the likelihood of financial fraud or loss. In an extreme scenario the fallout from these failures may have wider systemic consequences, with a significant risk of contagion in the banking system.[1] Banks as financial intermediaries in capital markets require overall investor and depositor confidence to ensure the soundness of their decisions. Incidents such as large-scale bank failure can occasionally undermine this by calling into question the overall well-being of others in the marketplace, as they can adversely affect investor confidence as a whole. Therefore, appropriate attention needs to be given to effective corporate governance so that the likelihood of corporate failure is reduced.

The notion of corporate governance is an ambiguous term that embraces both the internal and external operations of the company.[2] In the UK the corporate

1 Goodhart, C. A. E. and Illing, G. (2002) *Financial Crises, Contagion, and the Lender of Last Resort: A Reader*, Oxford, Oxford University Press.

2 Committee on Financial Aspects of Corporate Governance (1992) *Report of the Committee on the Financial Aspects of Corporate Governance* (Cadbury Report), London, Gee Publishing; Committee on Corporate Governance (1998) *Report of the Committee on Corporate Governance* (Hampel Report), London, Gee & Co; Shickh, S.

governance debate has generally focused on internal operations as they relate to the direction and control of the company.[3] The idea of direction and control consists of numerous issues: the effectiveness of the board of directors, non-executive directors, shareholder involvement, external auditor independence, the robustness of the internal controls, the audit committee and the internal audit function to name just a few. In the context of direction and control specific emphasis has been placed on maintaining a sustainable entrepreneurial spirit of profit maximisation.[4] This refers to the company ensuring that it takes informed decisions to minimise adverse risks and maximise its performance. The fundamental concern is that the processes of accountability do not hinder or undermine the entrepreneurial spirit of a corporation by placing layers of bureaucracy on its decision-making to reduce its performance in terms of taking risks and profit maximisation. This is reaffirmed in the Hampel Report on corporate governance, which states that governance and accountability should not override the importance of improving shareholder interests.[5] Notwithstanding the importance of an 'entrepreneurial spirit', providing the degree of accountability required to ensure that directors do not have unfettered discretion in the way shareholders' interests are steered remains the main challenge. Indeed, the possibility of a company taking on more risk to improve investment returns needs to be kept in check, given that such decisions may turn out to be improvident.[6]

The Anglo-American legal framework of corporate governance places the interests of the company and shareholders at its centre. The board of directors and managers are required to direct and control the company on behalf of its shareholders; this is generally referred to as the principle of separation of ownership and control.[7] It provides that the company through its board of directors has a primary duty to the interests of the company,[8] which equates to satisfying the interests of shareholders

---

and Rees, W. (1995) *Corporate Governance & Corporate Control*, London, Cavendish; Jones, I. and Pollitt, M. (2004) 'Understanding how the issues in corporate governance develop: Cadbury Report to Higgs Review', *Corporate Governance*, vol. 2, 162. For an examination of some of the definitional issues see Short, H. (1999) 'Corporate governance: Cadbury, Greenbury and Hampel – A review', *Journal of Financial Regulation and Compliance*, vol. 7, 57, at p. 58; Proctor, G. and Miles, L. (2002) *Corporate Governance*, London, Cavendish, at p. 3; for a critical analysis of the Hampel Report see Dignam, A. (1998) 'A principles approach to self-regulation? The report of the Hampel Committee on Corporate Governance', *Company Lawyer*, vol. 19, 140; Barnard, J. W. (1998) 'The Hampel Committee Report: A transatlantic critique', *Company Lawyer*, vol. 19, 111.

3 Cadbury Report, ibid., at para. 2.5.

4 Hampel Report, n. 2 above, at para. 1.1.

5 Ibid., at paras 1.1, 1.16–1.17 and 1.19.

6 It is the accountability of the company and its management which is the primary issue examined in this chapter.

7 Berle, A. A. and Means, G. C. (1997 [1932]) *The Modern Corporation and Private Property*, New Brunswick, NJ, Transaction Publishers, at p. 8; Salacuse, J. W. (2004) 'Corporate governance in the new century', *Company Lawyer*, vol. 25, 69, at p. 70.

8 *Percival v. Wright* [1902] 2 Ch 421; see further *Dawson International plc v. Coats Paton plc* [1989] BCLC 233. Lord Cullen interpreted the position as directors having only 'one master, the company'; see also *Howard Smith Ltd v. Ampol Petrol Ltd* [1974] AC 821, in particular where 'in the interests of the company as whole is interpreted to mean

as a whole,[9] although this principle does not mean the interests of minority shareholders can be simply set aside and ignored.[10] While the boards of directors are responsible for relations with a broad range of stakeholders, they are accountable only to shareholders as a whole.[11] As such, the appointment of external auditors on behalf of the shareholders is to ascertain whether the stewardship of the company is satisfactory and void of any irregularities.[12] The shareholders are then able to gauge whether the company is governed in the appropriate way.

The management and shareholder approach in the legal framework places limits on how other stakeholders of the company can exercise their rights. According to Margaret Blair,[13] corporate governance has a wider ambit than simply the 'agent-principal' model; it also needs to take into account the economic and social contexts within which corporations function. Therefore, governance issues may include the employees, creditors, consumers, markets, governments and regulators. But this perspective of corporate governance is not represented in the legal framework. The legal position remains rather limited, in that the directors have a duty to ensure the success of the company for the collective best interests of the shareholders and stakeholders. For example, in the case of creditors any obligation is limited unless the company is in a position of insolvency, in which case they become of central importance.[14]

The bank-customer relationship of debtor and creditor provides that a bank does not have a continuous obligation to account for its decisions as to how it uses depositors' money. Indeed, a bank can place this at any risk provided it can pay the deposited money on demand. This is explored in the next section.

---

in the interests of the company as a commercial entity', at p. 824; in *Brady v. Brady* [1988] BCLC 20, Nourse LJ referred to 'the interests of the company' to have a meaning relative to the principles which are being considered, at p. 23.

9 *Heron International v. Lord Grade* [1983] BCLC 244, where the decisions taken by directors need only take into account present rather than future shareholders in takeover bids, at p. 244.

10 *Re Smith v. Fawcett* [1942] 1 All ER 116; Davies, P. L. (2003) *Gower & Davies Principles of Modern Company Law*, London, Sweet and Maxwell, at p. 372; Hampel Report, n. 2 above, at para. 1.7.

11 *West Mercia Safetywear Ltd v. Dodd* [1988] BCLC 250; see also Hampel Report, n. 2 above, at para. 1.17. It cautions against expanding directors' obligations to other stakeholders with an interest in the company.

12 See pp. 157.

13 Blair, M. M. (1995) *Ownership and Control: Rethinking Corporate Governance for the Twenty-First Century*, Washington, DC, Brookings Institution, at p. 3.

14 Campbell, A. (2006) 'Bank insolvency and the interests of creditors', *Journal of Banking Regulation*, vol. 7, 133.

The Position of Depositor Creditors

The common law position on the status of bank customers gives a useful basis to delineate the limited protection corporate law provides for their interests.[15] In general, unsecured creditors, such as depositors of a bank, will have very little redress to recover their debts if a company is put into liquidation. The courts will not deal with the question of which class of creditor should have priority over other classes in such circumstances.[16] In the case of banking, it indicates the limited responsibility of a bank towards depositors once the bank has the money put into its account. The principle illustrates that the relationship between the depositor and the bank is not one of principal and agent, where the bank as agent acts on behalf of the principal in their interests. The money deposited in an account is no longer deemed as belonging to the principal but rather to the bank. In this relationship the bank is only contractually accountable for the sum of money paid in. This is the sum of money the bank is required to give back, including any interest accrued. According to Cottenham LC in *Foley v. Hill*:[17]

> The money paid into the banker's is money known by the principal to be placed there for the purpose of being under the control of the banker; it is then the banker's money; he is known to deal with it as his own; he makes what profit of it he can, which profit he retains to himself... The money placed in the custody of a banker is, to all intents and purposes, the money of the banker, to do with it as he pleases; he is guilty of no breach of trust in employing it; he is not answerable to the principal if he puts it into jeopardy, if he engages in a hazardous speculation.[18]

The decision in *Foley* set to rest the ambiguous idea that the relationship between bank and customer is one of agent and principal. According to Smart, the fiduciary obligation was regarded as too onerous a burden for the bank and its business as it would have placed a continuous responsibility on the bank to account for its decisions.[19] The principle also highlights the high degree of discretion the bank has with the way it can use other people's money. The obligation on the bank to

---

15 For a detailed analysis of the duty to creditors see Keay, A. (2003) 'Directors taking into account creditors' interests', *Company Lawyer*, vol. 24, 300; Keay, A. (2001) 'The director's duty to take into account the interests of company creditors: When is it triggered?', *Melbourne University Law Review*, vol. 25, 315; Prentice, D. D. (1990) 'Creditors' interests and directors' duties', *Oxford Journal of Legal Studies*, vol. 10, 265; Sappideen, R. (1991) 'Fiduciary obligations to corporate creditors', *Journal of Business Law*, July, 365.

16 *Space Investments Ltd v. Canadian Imperial Bank of Commerce Trust Co. (Bahamas) Ltd and others* [1986] 1 WLR 1072. Lord Templeman: 'If the bank becomes insolvent the customer can only prove in the liquidation of the bank as unsecured creditor for the amount which was, or ought to have been, credited to the account at the date when the bank went into liquidation', at p. 1074.

17 *Edward Thomas Foley v. Thomas Hill* [1848] II HLC 1002.

18 Ibid., at pp. 1005–1006.

19 Smart, P. E. (1990) *Leading Cases in the Law of Banking*, London, Sweet and Maxwell, at p. 2.

pay on demand the sum placed in the account is obviously a curb on its discretion. Furthermore, depositor activism could provide a force to contend with if the bank went off on a frolic of its own: depositors could wield influence over the decisions of bank management because they have the power to withdraw their deposits on demand. This gives the depositors some leverage in the affairs of the business, to make sure their interests are not undermined. However, this leverage is limited, considering the fact that informational asymmetry regarding the bank's business makes the timing of the decision to withdraw deposits very difficult,[20] thus the question of whether depositors can actually wield any influence on bank management is open to debate. According to Garten,[21] the position of a bank depositor is distinguishable from that of an investor. In the case of depositors the reasons for opening an account with a particular bank are more practical in nature than the reasons of investors, for whom the return associated with the account is more important. Thus the desire to monitor bank risk is generally low, even though a real risk exists of a bank failing and depositors potentially losing their money. Garten contends that depositors have a unique perspective of risk in comparison to investors, giving rise to little incentive to monitor the activities of banks.[22] The limited involvement regarding deposits produces a large group of involuntary 'investors' with relatively inert interest in what the bank is actually doing with their money.

In addition to these general factors, the asymmetry of information surrounding the business of banking places depositors in a vulnerable position. For example, depositors will not know whether their bank has a high or low propensity towards taking risk. This is exacerbated by the fact that banks have no obligation to inform depositors about the risks they are pursuing. The principle governing the bank-customer relationship illustrates the importance of formal prudential regulation to protect the interests of small depositors. It also indicates the unfettered autonomy of the banks, which could threaten the overall stability of the banking system. The conclusion can therefore be inferred from the common law that the interests of the depositor, as a creditor, are secondary to the interests of shareholders as a whole. This inequality of treatment is one reason for some kind of public regulation to mitigate the risks to which depositors are exposed. These risks are different to those associated with investment business, hence bank regulation focuses on the business of accepting deposits and prohibits illegal deposit-taking.[23]

The Financial Services and Markets Act 2000

The FSA is required to undertake its responsibilities in accordance with the objectives and principles set out in the FSMA 2000:[24] market confidence, public awareness,

20 A bank is exposed to the risk of a bank run if it experiences a large number of depositors seeking the money in their accounts. See p. 4.

21 Garten, H. A. (1986) 'Banking on the market: Relying on depositors to control bank risk', *Yale Journal on Regulation*, vol. 4, 129, at p. 134.

22 Ibid., at p. 135.

23 See pp. 54–56.

24 See www.fsa.gov.uk/pages/About/What/Approach/index.shtml.

protection of consumers and reduction of financial crime.[25] These are fleshed out by the FSA in a complex network of handbooks that set out detailed guidance and rules with which regulated firms and approved persons are required to comply in order to protect the interests associated with financial regulation. These are called the Principles for Businesses, Senior Management Arrangements, Systems and Controls, Statements of Principles and Code of Practice for Approved Persons.

The objectives of the FSMA 2000 are not listed in order of priority. Nevertheless, it is fitting that market confidence is first, as it captures a broad range of macro-economic and micro-economic factors to do with the financial system that directly or indirectly relate to the other listed objectives. These objectives and principles provide a foundation for the decisions the FSA takes to fulfil its responsibilities. The financial services industry needs to be mindful of them as being the underlying rationale behind the rules and guidance, governing, *inter alia*, authorisation, supervision and enforcement. The objectives thus provide not only an external but also an internal mechanism to safeguard other stakeholder interests. For example, the second objective (consumer awareness) provides an obligation on the financial services industry as a whole to raise the public's understanding of the industry and its products.[26] The third objective (consumer protection) provides an obligation on regulated firms and approved persons to exercise the appropriate level of care when dealing with customers.[27] The inclusion of the interests of other stakeholders into the broader corporate decision-making process is said to give rise to a more ethical approach to business, which subsequently enhances a company's reputation. The ramifications of failing to take into account the interests of other stakeholders are suggested to be much wider than simply damaging the reputation of the firm: it can also undermine the overall reputation of the financial system.[28] Thus the interests of the firm and the market are not mutually exclusive but are interdependent, giving rise to a responsibility to undertake business without undermining investor or depositor confidence.

The Shareholders' Obligations to Depositor Creditors

Authorisation to undertake deposit-taking business requires shareholder 'controllers' of a bank to be 'fit and proper' before they are allowed to operate.[29] The obligation of shareholder controllers extends beyond simply contributing towards the capital of the company in consideration for the shares issued. The policy of monitoring the controlling interests of a bank was first introduced under the Banking Act 1979, but it was limited only to recognised banks and did not apply to licensed institutions.

25 FSMA 2000, s. 2(2).

26 FSA (1998) *Meeting Our Responsibilities*, August, at p. 17.

27 Ibid.

28 FSA (2002) 'An ethical framework for financial services', Discussion Paper 18, October.

29 FSMA 2000, s. 49.

However, it was extended to all authorised institutions with the repeal of the 1979 Act by the Banking Act 1987.[30]

The FSA monitors very closely the shareholders who constitute 'control' of an authorised body.[31] A person who is proposing to acquire a significant holding is required to notify the FSA of their intention.[32] The FSMA 2000 provides that a person acquires control if, *inter alia*, they hold 10 per cent or more of the shares in an authorised body and are able to exercise significant influence over its management by virtue of powers such as shareholding or voting rights. Shareholders can wield a considerable amount of influence on management to pursue business in a more aggressive manner. While the entrepreneurialism of a bank is not to be dampened down by taking a cautious approach to business and profitability, it certainly needs to be mindful that it must take decisions prudently in the interests of its depositors.

The regulator will first require shareholder controllers to be assessed, to gauge whether they are fit and proper to have such a holding in a bank.[33] This ascertains the financial status of the acquiring person, to determine whether the acquisition could put the bank in jeopardy if those buying it are in a relatively weak financial position. A change in control, whether associated with the parent company or another entity within the group, may require the submission of a 'comfort letter' regardless of the number of controllers that exist.[34] In the case of a bank a comfort letter giving assurances that the acquiring person is fit and proper and the interests of consumers are not threatened is required if they acquire 15 per cent of the bank's voting power. This is to ensure that the shareholder controllers are aware of their obligation to stand behind the bank if concerns regarding its liquidity or solvency arise. The UK position is that a comfort letter is not legally binding like a guarantee or warranty, but does in financial regulation have considerable moral weight attached to it: it is a representation of a moral responsibility extending the obligations of shareholders beyond the return on their investment.[35]

The Principles for Businesses

The Principles for Businesses provide a set of 'fundamental obligations' to which a regulated firm is required to adhere, and build on the FSA's regulatory objectives.[36] The interests of consumers, regulators and other financial intermediaries figure

---

30 'Banking Supervision', Cmnd 9695 (1985), London, HMSO, at p. 27.

31 FSMA 2000, Part XII, ss. 178–192; for guidance see SUP 11: Controllers and Close Links.

32 SUP 11.2G.

33 SUP 11.7.5G(1) (2).

34 Bank Prudential Sourcebook, CL: Section 1 Comfort Letters, June 2001, 22.

35 *Kleinwort Benson v. MMC Metals Ltd* [1989] 1 WLR 379; the Australian decision in *Banque Brussels Lambert v. Australian National Industries* (1989) 21 NSWLR 502, where in a similar set of circumstances a contractual promise was said to exist. But the decision in *Kleinwort Benson* was reaffirmed in subsequent cases, namely by the Court of Appeal in *Re Atlantic Computers Plc* [1995] BCC 696.

36 FSA Principles for Businesses, Chapters 1 and 2 respectively.

largely in them. The Principles for Businesses apply not just to the regulated firm but also across the group and its worldwide activities.[37] These principles provide the context within which regulated business must be undertaken, otherwise the consequences could be intensive supervision, enforcement actions or in the worst-case scenario withdrawal of permission to undertake regulated activities.[38]

A breach of the principles arises on the basis of an objective 'reasonable care' test.[39] The FSA must assess a number of factors on the basis of the reasonable care standard before liability is successfully established. It has to consider whether the act or omission departs from general practice.[40] 'General practice' is interpreted to mean the typical behaviour of a skilled person.[41] The individual is not required to have a high level of skill to avoid liability:[42] the act or omission needs to be judged on whether it departs from 'general practice'.[43] In addition, the FSA will need to determine the probability of loss or damage.[44] It has been held that the mere predictability of harm is not sufficient to identify a breach of duty; one needs to establish whether an act or omission was unreasonable. The FSA also has to consider the likelihood of the risk occurring; this is to determine whether a reasonable person would have attempted to avoid creating the risk in the first place.[45] The FSA must take into account the precautionary measures that a reasonable and prudent person would take in the circumstances,[46] to determine whether the possible precautionary measures would have been apparent to a person of that level of skill. It is also important to assess whether the precautionary steps would have averted the damaging consequences of the acts or omissions. Finally, to establish a breach a balance needs to be struck between taking the necessary precautions and the cost of not taking them.[47]

Principles 1 and 2 govern the way regulated business is undertaken with 'integrity' and 'skill, care and diligence', respectively.[48] For example, Abbey National Asset Managers[49] was fined £320,000 for, *inter alia,* its breach of Principle 2 in not exercising the appropriate level of 'care, skill and diligence' in addressing concerns about the effectiveness of its systems and controls[50] reported by its compliance department. Principle 3 requires a firm to take 'reasonable care' with its management

37 PRIN 1.1.3G, 1.1.5G and 1.1.6G respectively.

38 PRIN 1.1.7G-8G-9G respectively.

39 PRIN 1.1.7G; this is with the exception of honesty, where a subjective test will also need to be applied – see *Royal Brunei Airlines v. Tan* [1995] AC 378, 389.

40 *Kraji v. McGrath* [1986] 1 All ER 54, 61.

41 *Bolam v. Friern Management Committee* [1957] 2 All ER 118, 122.

42 *Corporation of Glasgow v. Muir* [1943] 2 All ER 44, 47.

43 *Bolam*, n. 41 above, at p. 122.

44 *Bolton v. Stone and Others* [1951] 1 All ER 1078, 1081.

45 Ibid., p. 1083.

46 *Latimer v. AEC Ltd* [1952] 1 All ER 1302, 1305.

47 Ibid., at p. 1306.

48 PRIN 2.1.1R.

49 FSA (2003) 'Final Notice: Abbey National Asset Managers Ltd', 9 December.

50 PRIN 2: 2.1.1R.

and control.[51] The FSA fined City Index[52] for a breach of Principle 3 because its risk management controls failed to spot that the risk warnings were too small on their financial promotions, thereby preventing customers from fully appreciating the risks associated with its products. Citigroup Global Markets[53] was required by the FSA to give up profits in the region of £9 million and pay a fine of £4 million for its failure to adhere to Principles 2 and 3 as a result of execution of a trading strategy in the bond market that manipulated the trading system within which the bonds are bought and sold. The FSA decided that the firm failed to take due care in its strategy. Principle 4 requires a firm to 'maintain adequate financial resources'.[54] Principle 5 requires a firm to maintain 'proper standards of market conduct'.[55] Principles 6, 7 and 8 require respectively a firm to safeguard the interests of its customers by treating them fairly; 'pay due regard to their communication' needs and avoid misleading them; and 'manage conflicts of interest fairly'.[56] The FSA imposed a fine of £800,000 on Abbey National plc[57] for failing to treat customers fairly in its mishandling of the complaints process emanating from endowment mortgage mis-selling. It considered that Abbey National breached Principle 6 as a result of its failure to comply with the regulatory requirements at the time to assess the complaints made by its customers. Principles 9 and 10 require the firm to ensure that the advice it gives to customers is suitable and their assets are adequately protected.[58] Principle 11 requires the regulated firm to 'deal with its regulators in an open and cooperative way'.[59] A firm can breach Principle 11 by persistently failing to submit annual accounts despite being asked to do so.[60] The UK FSA fined Credit Suisse First Boston[61] £4 million for deliberately misleading its regulatory counterparts in Japan about its derivatives business. According to Carol Sergeant (former managing director at the FSA), the fine was imposed as a signal to others that misleading regulators was considered a very serious offence which undermines the credibility of the financial markets.[62]

Senior Management Arrangements, Systems and Controls

The FSA expands on Principle 3 of the Principles for Businesses in its Senior Management Arrangements, Systems and Controls (SYSC).[63] These require a

51 Ibid.
52 FSA (2005) 'Final Notice: City Index Ltd', 22 March.
53 FSA (2005) 'Final Notice: Citigroup Global Markets Ltd', 28 June.
54 PRIN 2: 2.1.1R.
55 Ibid.
56 Ibid.
57 FSA (2005) 'Final Notice: Abbey National Plc', 25 May.
58 PRIN 2: 2.1.1R.
59 Ibid. Chapter 3, Rules about Application PRIN 3.3.1R and Table – Territorial Application of the Principles, at pp. 4–5.
60 FSA (2005) 'Final Notice: India Buildings Friendly Society', 7 October.
61 FSA (2002) 'Final Notice: Credit Suisse First Boston International', 11 December.
62 FSA (2002) 'FSA fines Credit Suisse First Boston International £4 million', press release, FSA/PN/124, 19 December, available at www.fsa.gov.uk/pubs/press/2002.
63 FSA, Senior Management Arrangements, Systems and Controls, Chapters 1 3, SYSC1–3.

regulated firm to exercise 'reasonable care' over its business by having in place an 'adequate risk management system'.[64] This highlights the importance of making sure that responsibility for day-to-day management of the company is clearly set out so that delegated activities can be monitored and controlled to avoid individuals for instance perpetrating fraud. In respect to fulfilling these requirements the FSA is more mindful of confidence in the financial system and consumer interests rather than risks that threaten the owners of the financial business, unless they pose a wider problem.[65] This again demonstrates how regulation is not simply concerned with the success of the firm, but looks beyond that to ensure the objectives of regulation are fulfilled.

The SYSC require a regulated firm to apportion management responsibility clearly so that the firm is able to monitor and control its business affairs with reasonable care.[66] For instance, in the prudential context this responsibility extends to wherever the regulated firm undertakes its business. The senior management guidance indicates that responsibilities in a regulated firm need to be apportioned to the chief executive officer, a director or a senior manager.[67] Responsibility is firmly placed on the regulated firm to apportion functions appropriately, and ultimately resides with the board of directors. Moreover, the apportionment of responsibilities needs to conform to good corporate governance, which requires a number of responsibilities to be delegated to specific committees within the regulated firm. The guidance focuses on day-to-day management of the regulated firm rather than the 'direction' of the company.

The FSA requires a regulated firm in accordance with the SYSC to take reasonable care to establish and maintain such systems and controls as are appropriate to its business.[68] This is interpreted to mean the systems and controls need to be commensurate to the size and complexity of the business activities. If responsibilities for systems and controls are delegated, the regulated firm is required to ensure that they are supervised and monitored within the organisation appropriately.[69] In the final penalty of £320,000 imposed on Abbey National Asset Managers it was said to have breached SYSC 3.1.1 as it failed to have in place the appropriate systems and controls for its business. This included an inadequate compliance division to oversee its investment management business. The penalty was significantly large because, *inter alia*, the company did not assess the status of its systems and controls to satisfy that it complied with the SYSC rules for up to nine months.[70]

A regulated firm is obliged to have in place systems and controls to counter the risk of financial crime.[71] The FSA fined the Bank of Ireland £375,000 for breach of SYSC 3.2.6 as it failed to take reasonable care to counter the risk of its bank-

64 SYSC 1.2.1G.

65 SYSC 1.2.2G.

66 SYSC 2.1.1R and 3.1.1R.

67 SYSC 2.1.1R, 2.1.3R and 2.1.5G; Table – 'Frequently asked questions about allocation of functions'.

68 SYSC 3.1.1R.

69 SYSC 3.2.3G.

70 FSA, n. 49 above, at p. 3.

71 SYSC 3.2.6G.

draft facility being used as a channel for financial crime and thus it was particularly exposed to money-laundering activities.[72] The bank risked its facilities being used for money laundering at one of its branches that issued bank drafts with the identity of the beneficiary being disguised.[73]

The systems and controls requirement set out in the SYSC also refers to the work of the audit committee and internal auditor.[74] These are considered in more detail below. The broader corporate governance literature is used to analyse the utility of these functions and the extent to which regulators can rely on their findings. What is clearly established is that they are no panacea for overseeing the management of a firm, so reliance on them needs to be placed with a degree of scepticism and vigilance. Indeed, it is evident that the FSA has not entirely set out guidance for these functions, which creates problems if their objectives are not appropriate to achieve regulatory objectives and principles. Therefore the constitution of both functions needs to be scrutinised to ensure public objectives are clearly articulated in them.

The Role of the Internal Auditor

The FSA has incorporated the internal audit into its SYSC,[75] and also articulates it as a controlled function in its approved person regime.[76] The FSA has highlighted the importance of an appropriately resourced internal audit function that is able to report to the audit committee and senior management, but has not defined it or provided any guidance.[77] The most recent definition of internal audit is provided in the code of ethics and international standards for the internal auditing profession.[78] The code is accepted as the benchmark for best practice in the UK, and attempts to delineate a clear set of criteria to evaluate the services provided by an internal auditor. More importantly, it heightens the expectations of the function to reduce the likelihood of corporate failure. The code provides the accepted industry definition:

> Internal auditing is an independent, objective assurance and consulting activity designed to add value and improve an organisation's operations. It helps an organisation accomplish its objectives by bringing a systematic, disciplined approach to evaluate and improve the effectiveness of risk management, control, and governance processes.[79]

---

72 FSA (2004) 'Final Notice: The Governor and Company of the Bank of Ireland', 31 August.

73 Ibid., para. 2.2(2).

74 SYSC 3.2.15G and 3.2.15G respectively.

75 Ibid.

76 SUP 10.4.5R, CF 15.

77 This move is also evident in the general governance debate and gets formal recognition in the Combined Code on Corporate Governance, July 2003, available at www.fsa.gov.uk/pubs/ukla/lr_comcode2003.pdf.

78 Institute of Internal Auditing – UK and Ireland (2004) *Code of Ethics and International Standards for the Professional Practice of Internal Auditing*, 1 January, available at www.theiia.org/?doc_id=1499.

79 Ibid., Introduction.

This definition points out the importance of independence and objectivity in internal auditing work, which is developed through an ethical framework. For instance, the internal audit is required to comply with certain principles whilst undertaking its work: integrity in its decision-making; objectivity in its assessment; confidentiality of information; and finally competence to undertake the task. These principles are then fleshed out with further guidance to ensure the standards are achieved.

The standards first set out that the organisation must define the purpose and authority of the internal audit by providing a charter for its role.[80] This is to give the internal audit the 'assurance' that its work has a high degree of importance in the organisation.[81] In order to achieve its purpose it is required to undertake its work with independence and objectivity.[82] The internal auditor must establish an effective system to maintain and enhance quality assurance within an organisation to improve its internal operations.[83] The fulfilment of these functions requires the internal auditors to plan their programme of activities to achieve their objectives and add value to the organisation.[84] Finally, and somewhat more controversially, the internal auditors must be able to communicate their findings to those who can act upon their conclusions and recommendations within the organisation.[85] This provides a gateway to the board of directors if need be to ensure that audit findings and recommendations are given due attention and consideration.

However, a tension can exist between management and the internal audit function: cooperation from senior management may not always be forthcoming or the findings of the internal audit may not be implemented.[86] This part of the audit role has given rise to a perception of the internal audit as being the 'insider' that can act as a 'policeman' within an organisation.[87] Thus it comes as no surprise that the utility of the internal auditor has generated a lot of interest, especially among public regulators seeking to place responsibilities on them to ensure regulatory rules and standards are complied with by a firm: the internal auditor is seen to complement the functions of the supervisor and external auditor with the potential to identify and resolve matters by utilising company resources rather than public resources. Work in this area by the FSA and the Basel Committee brings to the fore the internal

---

80 Ibid., at para. n. 1000.

81 Ibid., at para. n. 1000.A1.

82 Ibid., at para. n. 1110.

83 Ibid., at para. n. 2000.

84 Ibid., at para. n. 2010.

85 Ibid., at para. n. 2020.

86 This was clearly a failure in the Barings débâcle, where the internal audit review of the operations relating to Leeson's activities raised a number of concerns but were not acted on by senior management. See also GAO (1997) 'Foreign banks: Internal control and audit weaknesses in US branches', GAO/GGD-97-181, at p. 31.

87 Morgan, G. (1979) 'Internal audit role conflict: A pluralist view', *Managerial Finance*, vol. 5, 160; Power, M. (1999) 'Regulating organisations from inside: Turnbull and the rise of the internal auditor', paper presented at Best Practice Corporate Governance Conference, 4 October, cited in Spira, L. F. and Page, M. (2002) 'Risk management: The reinvention of internal control and the changing role of internal audit', *Accounting, Auditing & Accountability Journal*, vol. 16, 640.

auditors quasi-regulatory function, which is separate from management. This has the advantage that an organisation can use its own resources to correct its deficiencies as and when they are identified rather than have them pointed out through the examination process undertaken by an external regulator.

The Bank of England post-Barings explored the idea of a direct reporting line between the internal auditor and itself.[88] However, this move was not successful, and holding general dialogue between the Bank and the internal auditor during visits still remains the case today. A survey carried out by the Basel Committee on Banking Supervision[89] indicates a reluctance to move in the direction of making the internal auditor a formal whistleblower.[90] It is suggested that such a move would undermine the auditor's position within the organisation rather than enhance it by conferring this obligation on the role. The general conclusion from the survey was that this responsibility lay on the shoulders of the directors and audit committee.

Apart from incorporating the function of internal audit into financial regulation, the FSA has not sought to provide guidance to flesh out what the internal audit should look like and do. Thus it should come as no surprise that a number of inconsistencies in terms of practice among firms regulated in the UK have arisen. In a recent FSA review of internal audit functions in banks and building societies the utility of audit work was considered high.[91] However, not surprisingly, the size of the institution very much determined the size of the audit function. This had an impact on its effectiveness as it determined the amount of technical expertise it had at hand to deal with areas such as information technology. In addition, a number of audit functions were partly or fully outsourced for cost reasons. In these circumstances the FSA simply reminded institutions that it was their responsibility to ensure the outsourced function was monitored closely so it complied with FSA standards and rules. A significant finding was that the internal audit function was not always as risk-focused as it thought it was, so compromising findings. Moreover, the function of tracking unresolved issues was in place, but inconsistencies arose and the rigour differed across the firms visited. The effectiveness of the internal audit function is severely undermined if problems it identifies are not then rectified, as was the case with Barings Bank.

The Role of the Audit Committee

The FSA encourages regulated firms to form an audit committee as part of the senior management arrangement to ensure the effectiveness of internal control systems.[92] The guidance suggests a much wider role for the audit committee to focus on

88 Bank of England (1997) *Banks' Internal Controls and the Section 39 Process: A Consultative Paper by the Bank of England*, February, at p. 14.

89 Basel Committee on Banking Supervision (2002) 'Internal audit in banks and the supervisor's relationship auditors: A survey', August.

90 Ibid., at p. 3.

91 FSA (2004) 'Review of internal audit and quality of prudential reporting at DTD banks and building societies', letter to CEOs, 31 March, available at www.fsa.gov.uk/pubs/ceo/ceo_letter_31mar04.pdf.

92 SYSC 3.2.15G.

systems and controls and assess a firm's compliance with the regulatory regime. It is interesting to note the priority the guidance places on ensuring the independence of external auditors is lowest, though this is considered to be primarily its traditional responsibility. The utility of audit committees has long had support from regulators. For example, a government white paper in 1985 regarding the subsequent Banking Act 1987 (now repealed) highlighted the importance attached to the wider role of non-executive directors and audit committees.[93] In the former case it pointed to the contribution they could make to a bank's business by having an input into the overall quality of lending and risk. In the latter case the audit committee was encouraged to play a wider role, not simply focused on the annual accounts, but overseeing the bank's systems of internal controls and the work carried out by both internal and external auditors in this area.

The use of the audit committee in financial services has mirrored in some respects the wider move in the business world to reduce corporate fraud and failure by improving external auditor independence and vigilance with its presence. This has led to the audit committee being an established part of the governance of listed companies in the UK for some time.[94] This move in the UK came about with the decision in 1978 by the New York Stock Exchange that an audit committee should be a listing requirement. However, the initial endorsement for the establishment of audit committees came much earlier, as a result of the Securities and Exchange Commission (SEC) investigation into the affairs of McKesson and Robbins.[95] This decision noted that to protect the independence of the auditor a 'special committee of the board composed of directors who are not officers of the company appears desirable'.[96] Building on this, the SEC recommended that such committees should also arrange the audit engagement.[97] In the UK there was a similar approach to the evaluation of the audit engagement, but its scope was limited to determining whether directors discharge their statutory duty in the matter of financial statements.[98] The traditional practice is that an audit committee acts on behalf of a board of directors relating to matters to do with the company's financial reports. The committee also assists in the review of internal controls, internal audit programmes and the results of audit assignments. According to Wolnizer, the encouragement to form audit

---

93 'Report of the committee set up to consider the system of banking supervision', Cmnd 9550, June 1985, at p. 7.

94 Verschoor, C. C. (1993) 'UK expands role of audit committees: Echoing Treadway Commission recommendations, the British issue a code of best practice', *Management Accounting*, December, 44; Buckley, R. (1979) *Audit Committees: Their Role in UK Companies*, London, Auditing Practices Committee of the Consultative Committee of Accountancy Bodies; Institute of Internal Auditors UK (1994) *Audit Committees of the Board, Professional Briefing Note Four*, London, IIA UK.

95 Securities and Exchange Commission (1940) *In Matter of McKesson and Robbins Inc*, Commerce Clearing House, Release No. 19, 5 December.

96 See also GAO (1996) *The Accountancy Profession: Major Issues: Progress and Concerns*, GAO/AIMD-96-98, September.

97 Accountants International Study Group (1997) *Audit Committees*, AISG, at paras 12 13.

98 Ibid., at paras 19–21 and 24.

committees to raise the standards of accounting practice is rather a 'red herring', distracting attention away from the real need to try to authenticate the evidence provided in financial statements with evidence in the public domain.[99]

The recent initiatives post-Enron governing the audit committee have attempted to give it a new will to undertake its work with a greater degree of vigilance. The Smith Report[100] provides guidance that sets out broad provisions rather than taking a 'one-size-fits-all' approach. The audit committee is required to work with the board of directors in a 'frank and open' and robust manner,[101] with management proactively providing the information it needs.[102] This position is given emphasis by reasserting the common law duty of directors to provide information to fulfil their duties to the company.[103] The report provides a far more burdensome responsibility on the audit committee, asserting that it will be 'time consuming' and 'intensive' and thus requires monetary and training resources so it can fulfil its responsibilities effectively.[104]

The audit committee is required, *inter alia*, to monitor the integrity of financial statements;[105] review internal financial controls and, in some cases, management systems; monitor and review the internal audit function;[106] assist in the appointment of external auditors and their remuneration package;[107] monitor and review the independence, objectivity and effectiveness of external auditors;[108] and devise and implement a policy to govern non-audit work provided by the external auditor.[109]

The membership of the audit committee should consist of at least three independent non-executive directors, and should not include the chairman of the company.[110] The audit committee is given a far more significant role of overseeing the affairs of a company; it is required to meet at a minimum three times a year,[111] but it is anticipated it will meet more frequently.[112] This is notwithstanding the fact that these opportunities may not be sufficient to deal with all the issues raised at the company. The report therefore envisages the chair of the committee liaising continuously with key individuals in the company, such as the chairman, finance director, the lead partner of the audit and the internal auditor.[113] In order to undertake

99 Wolnizer, P. W. (1995) 'Are audit committees red herrings?', *Abacus*, vol. 31, 45.

100 Smith, R. (2003) *Audit Committees Combined Code Guidance Report and Proposed Guidance* (Smith Report), report by FRC-appointed group chaired by Sir Robert Smith; available at www.frc.org.uk/images/uploaded/documents/ACReport.pdf.

101 Ibid., at para 1.8.

102 Ibid., at para 1.9.

103 Ibid.

104 Ibid., at para. 1.12.

105 Ibid., at para. 2.1.

106 Ibid.

107 Ibid.

108 Ibid.

109 Ibid., at p. 6.

110 Ibid., at paras 3.1 and 3.2 respectively.

111 Ibid., at para. 3.5.

112 Ibid., at para. 3.9.

113 Ibid., at paras 3.5 3.9.

these responsibilities efficiently the report highlights the resources the company needs to provide, such as funds to enable the committee to seek independent legal and accounting advice to assist with its decision-making.[114] The remuneration package of the audit committee needs to be commensurate with the time needed to undertake its duties.[115] The skills brought to the committee need to reflect the demands placed on it, and it is envisaged that members will have a background in financial matters.[116] The company needs to induct new members of the committee formally with what is expected of them, including training where necessary to acquire the knowledge required to discharge their responsibilities.[117]

These support mechanisms provide the audit committee with the foundations to review and monitor the financial affairs of a company; to assess whether it will be effective remains to be seen.[118] The audit committee needs to monitor and review the standards and rules governing financial statements so that it can form a judgement as to whether appropriate accounting policies have been complied with by management and the external auditor.[119] In addition the work entails a review of, *inter alia*, the corporate governance statement of the company and, more significantly, financial returns to regulators.[120] The company's internal controls and risk management systems are also under the purview of the audit committee, so to undertake this responsibility sufficiently it needs to determine whether the review of internal controls has been acted upon by management, the internal auditor or the external auditor.[121] The penultimate responsibility is to overlook the role of the internal audit to gauge whether it has sufficient resources to undertake its responsibilities, and the appropriate standing within the organisation to judge its work and the response to its recommendations.[122] Finally, the audit committee needs to oversee and review the appointment and work of the external auditors,[123] and assess their independence on an annual basis. This is undertaken by first drawing up the terms of the engagement, and then monitoring the non-audit work provided to ascertain whether it undermines the auditors' judgement.[124] The audit committee must have in place a formal policy to assess the level of non-audit work undertaken by the external auditors.[125]

The general literature provides numerous accounts of what a good audit committee should look like, and warns against overburdening it with high levels of detail and voluminous reports. But the Smith Report did not heed this and has certainly placed a considerable burden of work on the audit committee, which it may not be able to fulfil. For example, the limited time an audit committee spends sitting evidences

114 Ibid., at paras 3.11–3.14.
115 Ibid., at para. 3.15.
116 Ibid., at para. 3.16.
117 Ibid., at para. 3.19.
118 Ibid., at para. 5.1.
119 Ibid., at para. 5.2.
120 Ibid., at para. 5.3.
121 Ibid., at paras 5.5–5.8.
122 Ibid., at paras 5.10–5.13.
123 Ibid., at paras 5.14–5.18.
124 Ibid., at para. 5.22.
125 Ibid., at paras 5.26–5.29.

the practical constraints on what it can and cannot do.[126] Consequently, a significant expectations gap has developed regarding the work of the audit committee.

A large amount of empirical work has investigated the effectiveness of audit committees; the findings are inconclusive. Yet there are a number of reasons for forming audit committees, and reasons for the voluntary formation of audit committees differ from jurisdiction to jurisdiction.[127] According to Menon and Williams, the greater the proportion of non-executive directors on a board of directors the more frequently the audit committee meets, and consequently there is increased reliance on the committee.[128] The frequency with which audit committees meet seems to be important in determining whether reliance is placed on their work, because it shows that the committee intends to be informed and vigilant about a company's affairs.[129] More importantly, McMullen suggested that the existence of audit committees reduces incidences of error, irregularity and other accidents that produce unreliable financial reporting.[130] This study shows that where there is an audit committee there are fewer lawsuits by shareholders alleging fraud. While the general purpose of an audit committee may seem to be a panacea against incompetence, it is only as effective as the reliance placed on it in an organisation. The existence of an audit committee does not mean the end of financial reporting crises, and it is important to look at the substance rather than the form its work takes. Moreover, the literature on audit committees is rather vague when it comes to their effectiveness in avoiding corporate failures. Due to the various 'shapes and sizes' committees come in and the varying reliance placed on them, it is no surprise that their effectiveness is difficult to assess; Spira also highlights the practical problems of the 'high degree of confidentiality' surrounding the meetings, making it difficult to research their actual effectiveness.[131]

Financial regulators require regulated firms that need an audit committee to do much more than 'simply' overlook the relationship between the company and the external auditor. The audit committee must consist of individuals who are familiar

---

126 Spira, L. (2003) 'Audit committees: Begging the question?', *Corporate Governance*, vol. 11, 180.

127 Bradbury, M. E. (1990) 'The incentives for voluntary audit committee formation', *Journal of Accounting and Public Policy*, vol. 19, 9; Pincus, K. (1989) 'Voluntary formation of corporate audit committees among NASDAQ firms', *Journal of Accounting and Public Policy*, vol. 18, 239.

128 Menon, K. and Williams, J. D. (1994) 'The use of audit committees for monitoring', *Journal of Accounting and Public Policy*, vol. 13, 121; Eichenseher, J. W. and Shields, D. (1985) 'Corporate director liability and monitoring preferences', *Journal of Accounting and Public Policy*, vol. 4, 13; Scarbrough, D. P. (1998) 'Audit committee composition and interaction with internal auditing: Canadian evidence', *Accounting Horizons*, vol. 12, 51.

129 McMullen, D. A. (1996) 'Enhancing audit committee effectiveness', *Journal of Accountancy*, August, 79.

130 McMullen, D. A. (1996) 'Audit committee performance: An investigation of the consequences associated with audit committees', *Auditing*, vol. 15, 87.

131 Spira, L. (1998) 'An evolutionary perspective on audit committee effectiveness', *Corporate Governance*, vol. 6, 33.

with the regulation and supervision requirements governing the business. In this respect the traditional limits of what an audit committee can and cannot do could be stretched by the additional responsibilities of being conversant with the requirements of financial services regulators. The addition of financial services regulation means the audit committee would be dealing with the directors, internal audit, external audit and the regulator, giving rise to the possibility of competing needs between private and public interests. For example, the issue of market confidence and consumer interest confers unique obligations that may conflict with the interests of shareholders, which are central to the relationship between the company, the external auditor and the audit committee.[132] Indeed, the interests of consumers outweigh the interests of shareholders, if one refers to the additional responsibilities attached to their holdings.

The Common Law Position of the Directors and the Senior Management Role

The Companies Act 1985 provides that the responsibility for management of a company is most commonly conferred on the board of directors.[133] The board has the authority to delegate responsibilities within the firm, and can delegate part or all of its powers to an individual director to exercise,[134] so devolving responsibility for day-to-day management of the company on an executive or managing director as the board sees fit.[135] The courts have provided that the role of 'managing director' is distinct from an ordinary directorship given that special powers are vested in this office; normally these powers will be to oversee day-to-day management.[136] However, the courts have avoided attributing specific responsibilities to a managing director, preferring to indicate the distinction in form rather than substance.

The directors of the company are individually responsible for its governance.[137] Indeed, for the purpose of criminal liability individual directors are said to constitute the 'directing mind' and will of the company.[138] In an agency relationship, whereby the director is the agent of the company (the principal), acts and omissions of the director would be deemed to be those of the company according to the principle of attribution of knowledge. The directing mind may be delegable to others in the company, such as senior management, and thus their acts are considered to be an 'act of the company'.[139] A company may also be deemed vicariously liable for

132 Smith Report, n. 100 above, at para. 1.5.

133 Companies Act 1985, Table A, Art. 70.

134 Ibid., Art. 72.

135 *Harold Holdsworth & Co. (Wakefield) Ltd v. Caddies* [1955] 1 WLR 352; *Re Newspaper Proprietary Syndicate Ltd* [1900] 2 Ch 349, 350.

136 *Newspaper Proprietary Syndicate*, ibid., at p. 350.

137 Companies Act 1985, s. 741(1).

138 *Bolton Engineering Co. Ltd v. T J Graham & Sons Ltd* [1957] 1 QB 159, 172.

139 *Tesco Supermarkets Ltd v. Nattrass* [1972] AC 153; see also *Meridian Global Funds Management Asia Ltd v. Securities Commission* [1995] BCC 942. The latter decision has come under particular criticism for failing to attribute responsibility by using the agency and principle rule – see Bartlett, A. (1998) 'Attribution of contributory negligence:

the tortuous acts of an employee. In terms of vicarious liability, the courts look at whether there is sufficient 'proximity' between the employee's wrong and the class of acts he/she is required to perform before deciding whether to hold an employer vicariously liable.[140]

The directors are required to act in good faith and with reasonable care in the interests of the company.[141] The standard of care and skill required of a director is a difficult issue to address, given the nature of the general office. In modern times assistance is provided by the application of s. 214(4) of the Insolvency Act 1986.[142] This statutory provision gives both an objective and a subjective test of care, skill and diligence required by directors in the execution of their duties. The standard of care is more demanding than its predecessors, which contained a subjective test equivalent to recklessness.[143] While the test emanated from the context of the failure of a company, the standard is applicable during the life of the company as well. In the decision of *Theodore Goddard*, s. 214(4) of the Insolvency Act was considered to contain the relevant standard of care expected of directors.[144] The standard consists of an objective and a subjective element.[145]

The first test to be satisfied is whether the director has acted as a reasonable person would have in the circumstances. The subjective element refers to the individual level of knowledge and skill the director professes to have: the act or omission will be judged according to the director's own attributes. The courts will normally apply the objective test to ascertain whether the individual has acted as a reasonably diligent man would have in the circumstances regardless of the fact that he thought he acted honestly. The application of the standard of care is relative to the facts of each individual case and so must be applied accordingly. Mere errors of judgement do not constitute a breach of the duty of care.[146] In *D'Jan*[147] a director was considered negligent when he did not complete an insurance proposal properly by not disclosing the fact that he was a once a director of a company that went into liquidation. In *Theodore Goddard* a director acted reasonably in accordance with s. 214(4) by trusting the decisions made by others in the company at a time when there was no evidence to do otherwise. But in *Dorchester Finance* the court placed particular emphasis on the fact that the two directors were chartered accountants with

---

Agents, company directors and fraudsters', *Law Quarterly Review*, vol. 114, 460, at p. 473.

140 *Dubai Aluminium v. Salaam* [2002] 3 WLR 1913.

141 *Dorchester Finance v. Stebbing* [1989] BCLC 498, p. 501.

142 This provision is applied in an insolvency case to determine wrongful trading.

143 *Re City Equitable Fire Insurance Co. Ltd* [1925] Ch 407.

144 *Norman and another v. Theodore Goddard (a firm) and others (Quirk third party)* [1991] BCLC 1028, p. 1031.

145 *Re D'Jan of London Ltd Copp v. D'Jan* [1994] BCLC 561, 563; Hicks, A. (1994) 'Directors' liability for management errors', *Law Quarterly Review*, vol. 110, 390.

146 *Marshall v. Osmond* [1983] QB 1034, 1038; *Whitehouse v. Jordan* [1981] WLR 246, 263. It establishes a narrower rule: it is not negligence if it is an error that a man, acting with ordinary care, might have made.

147 *Re D'Jan*, n. 145 above.

a significant amount of experience.[148] The court decided they were both negligent in signing blank cheques for another director simply to do as he pleased with the money drawn on the cheques. The latter was held to be grossly negligent in the misapplication of the money.

In addition to the objective and subjective tests articulated in s. 214(4), other factors are relevant when considering the act or omission of a director: the complexity of the business; judging like with like; not comparing directors in different departments with each other; not comparing directors of a large company with those of a small company; the way the work in a company is distributed; and the distrust of co-directors.[149] More recently additional 'propositions' have been widely regarded as capable of importation in the general description of directors' duty: directors have a continuous obligation to keep themselves informed about the nature of the business; and have an obligation to ensure those to whom responsibilities are delegated are supervised on a continuous basis.[150]

The FSMA 2000 Approved Persons Regime

In its statutory provisions and handbooks the FSA has built on the common law principles that govern directors', senior management's and indeed employees' responsibilities with additional rules to address the idiosyncratic features of the financial services industry. The common law provisions prescribe not only what standard of care is expected of directors and senior management but also the kinds of acts or omissions that have resulted in liability; they also prescribe how the acts or omissions of directors, senior management and employees can give rise to liability through the principle of attribution of knowledge. The FSA has extended those ideas beyond the jurisdiction of incorporation to take into account the way business operations are undertaken and managed by organisations, as highlighted in the Barings case. The decision in *Barings (unreported)*[151] outlines how in a matrix management system of control and direction the directing mind and will could be located in a sister company in another jurisdiction. In this instance the matrix management system overseeing parts of Barings' business included activities in other jurisdictions, namely Japan, London and Singapore where Leeson undertook trading activities on behalf of Barings Group in the UK.

The FSA has articulated the principles emanating from the common law into rules specifically designed for regulating and supervising activities within the financial system. For instance, the standard of care expected is that of reasonable care. In addition the FSA has extended the scope of its rules so that the interests of consumers and regulators are given equal prominence, beyond the interests of

148 *Dorchester Finance*, n. 141 above.

149 *Re City Equitable Fire*, n. 143 above, at p. 408.

150 *Re Barings Plc (No. 5), Secretary of State for Trade and Industry v. Baker and others (No. 5)* Ch D [1999] 1 BCLC 433.

151 *Barings Plc v. Coopers & Lybrand* [2003] EWHC 1319 (Ch) 11 June 2003 (unreported), at para. 899 and further para. 945.

the company *per se*. Indeed, there is a common thread running through the FSA guidelines that mirrors the common law.

The FSA regime not only governs who can undertake regulated activities at a institutional level but also those who are responsible for discharging a firm's responsibilities on its behalf.[152] Whether or not an individual requires approval by the FSA depends on the role they perform; that is, whether they perform a 'controlled function'.[153] The functions designated as controlled are those that 'add value' to the regulatory process and assist the FSA to fulfil its regulatory objectives.[154] Therefore no person can exercise a controlled function unless the individual is approved by the FSA under s. 59 of the FSMA 2000.[155] In accordance with the FSMA 2000 those approved have to meet the FSA's 'fit and proper' criteria before they can take up their positions.[156] It is the responsibility of the regulated firm to exercise reasonable care when appointing individuals to undertake a controlled function to ensure they are appropriate for the position. The FSA has responsibility for establishing whether a breach of the rules has occurred. An individual who is refused approval on the basis that they are not 'fit and proper' does have a right to have the case heard again by the Financial Services and Markets Tribunal. Indeed, a number of cases have been heard which have shed further light on the decision as to whether someone is fit and proper to undertake a controlled function. The role of the tribunal in these matters is to consider the case 'afresh in the light of all the evidence made available', which includes evidence that was not previously available to the FSA. The tribunal acts as a court of first instance rather than an appeal court. Therefore a decision by the FSA to withdraw approval on the basis that the individual is not fit and proper would have to be reviewed in light of the tribunal's decision.[157] The lack of an appeals process has led to criticism by practitioners because the only route for them to change the decision would be judicial review.[158]

The idea of a controlled function is not simply confined to the higher levels of directors and senior management of a regulated firm, but includes those with positions at the customer interface as well.[159] It includes employees who have contact with customers, whether in an advisory capacity or to organise or undertake transactions on their behalf. A function is 'controlled' when it fulfils the general conditions of s. 59(5)–(7) of the FSMA 2000. The controlled functions are separated into three categories: s. 59(5), where the individual has significant influence over the conduct of the approved person; s. 59(6), where the individual deals with customers; and s. 59(7), where the individual deals with the property of customers. The FSA has listed the functions that require prior approval: there are currently 27 controlled functions. The first 20 are deemed functions of significant influence: 1–7 relate to

152 AUTH 6 and exceptions, see AUTH 6.5.1G. See also TC 1 training and competency rules apply to employees responsible for regulated activities. SUP 10: Approved Persons.

153 SUP 10.4.5R Controlled Functions.

154 APER 4.4.1G-9E.

155 SUP 10.2.1G.

156 The Fit and Proper Test for Approved Persons, Chapters 1 and 2.

157 FSMA 2000, s. 133(5).

158 See pp. 139–140.

159 SUP 10.4.5R.

the governing body (directors, chief executive officer and non-executive directors); 8–12 govern 'required functions' (money-laundering officer); 13–15 govern systems and control functions; and 16–20 govern significant management functions (internal auditor). Items 21–27 govern customer functions.[160]

The Fit and Proper Test for Approved Persons

Individuals performing a controlled function are required to be a fit and proper person.[161] The FSA sets out a number of factors that need to be considered, such as 'honesty', 'integrity', 'reputation', 'competence', 'capability' and 'financial soundness'.[162] In general terms, to be 'fit and proper' a person must be suitable to 'hold a licence' and undertake the business of the licence-holder.[163] This requires an assessment of the individual's character and the nature and complexity of the business undertaken by the regulated firm. In this respect it is the responsibility of the individual to satisfy the FSA that they are 'fit and proper' to undertake a controlled function rather than for the FSA to show that they are not. The FSA has the authority to withdraw approval of a person if it considers them not to be fit and proper for the controlled function for which they have sought approval.[164] The FSA takes a cumulative as well as an individual approach towards regulatory failures rather than taking action against individual incidents of minor indiscretion that would not necessarily always lead to holding a person unfit. This policy concurs with the views of Nicholls V-C in *Re Swift 736 Ltd*, where he strongly emphasised the importance of condemning a blatant disregard of not fulfilling reporting requirements. The V-C suggested that attitudes such as these need to be corrected.[165] The essential ingredient in this form of non-compliance is blatant disregard of such requirements rather than an element of dishonesty. Provisions like these ensure accountability; thus an accumulation of 'administrative' failures suggests a lack of rigour or discipline. For example, the FSA took action against a firm called India Buildings Friendly Society for repeated failure to submit annual accounts, which called into question its compliance with the threshold conditions and its willingness to cooperate with its regulator.[166]

The probity of an individual is very important for the purposes of the FSA. Probity refers to an individual's uprightness and honesty. For example, the FSA prohibited John Edward Rourke[167] from performing any function in relation to a regulated activity because he had been convicted of several counts of illegal deposit-taking, resulting in him getting a custodial sentence. The evidence in the case went to the very core of his honesty and integrity, demonstrating he was not fit and proper.

160 Ibid.

161 FIT 1.1.2G.

162 FIT 1.3.1G.

163 *R v. Hyde JJ* (1912) *The Times Law Reports*, vol. 106, 152, 158.

164 FIT 1.2.3G.

165 *Secretary of State v. Ettinger, Re Swift 736 Ltd* [1993] BCLC 896, 900.

166 FSA, n. 60 above.

167 FSA (2004) 'Final Notice: John Edward Rourke', 18 November.

A person's probity is an important characteristic; this is called into question in whatever position the individual holds in a regulated firm when breach of trust and level of culpability need to be ascertained. Gowan J generally interprets honesty as equating to acting in good faith.[168] The FSA takes into account a person's reputation and whether the person has a criminal record or has contravened any regulatory requirements, and also non-compliance with non-statutory codes of conduct governing the capital markets. According to Mayo J, reputation is a summation of all the beliefs popularly held about the individual in a community, whether positive or negative.[169] Consequently, the FSA has the discretion in many respects to delve further than formal records about the individual.

The competency of an individual is also important when judging whether a person is fit and proper. This is generally interpreted by Winn J to mean a person, on a fair assessment, able to perform a particular function in the light of the problems to study and the degree of risk associated with the task.[170] This interpretation of 'competency' can be complemented by the definition provided by Cantley J, who suggests that it is the virtue of a practical and reasonable man who can look and recognise what to look for.[171] These interpretations focus on an individual's experience and knowledge in identifying relevant issues and dealing with them accordingly to contain the possible adverse consequences that may arise.

In the standard of care required of an individual, skill is referred to widely. The traditional approach adopted by the English courts is that a director needs no special qualifications for that office.[172] However, this is based on the proviso that if a director does have specialist knowledge then he is bound to bring that knowledge to his office. According to Clarke and Sheller JJA, skill is a special level of competency that is distinct from that possessed by a reasonable man, is gained by special training and experience and is determined by the level of care reasonably expected of a person undertaking particular work.[173] This definition clearly highlights that particular qualities are required and that they are additional to those an 'ordinary man' would profess to have. The FSA recognises that a director's responsibilities are relative to the department and the position held. According to the FSA, a person could be fit and proper for one position but not for another because it involves different responsibilities and duties.[174]

Withdrawal of Approval

The FSA has the authority to withdraw approval if it considers an individual not fit and proper to take up the controlled function indicated with a regulated firm. The

168 *Marchesi v. Barnes* [1970] VR 434, 438.

169 *Dias v. O'Sullivan* [1949] ALR 586, 591.

170 *Brazier v. Skipton Rock Co., Ltd* [1962] 1 All ER 955, 957.

171 *Gibson v. Skibs A/S Marina and Orkla Grobe A/B and Smith Coggins, Ltd* [1966] 2 All ER 476, 478.

172 *Re Brazilian Rubber Plantations and Estates Ltd* [1911] 1 Ch 425, 437.

173 *Daniels v. Anderson* 16 ACSR [1995] 607, 667.

174 SUP 10.13.1G

reasons for withdrawal would be a failure to satisfy the criteria set out for approval to be granted. In respect to an approval decision it is important to assess whether the individual poses a significant risk to consumers and confidence in the financial system. However, whatever decision the FSA reaches it must be proportionate to the risks an individual poses.

The most important factors to be taken into account are the honesty, integrity, competence and capability of an individual. In addition, the withdrawal of approval needs to comply with the enforcement guidelines, which refer, *inter alia*, to issues of honesty, integrity and reputation; the individual's openness in dealing with the industry, consumers and regulators (present and past); competence and capability to carry out the controlled function; whether the individual has failed to comply with the Statement of Principles; the relevance and materiality of the incident and the time that has elapsed since it occurred; the severity of the risk the individual poses to consumers and confidence in the financial system; and finally the individual's previous disciplinary record. In order to decide whether an individual is not fit and proper the standard of proof required is one of balance of probabilities. A decision to reject an application for approval for a controlled function has to be based on material significance.

In the decision of *Cox v. the FSA*[175] an application for approval was refused on the basis of Ian Douglas Cox's previous conduct of trying dishonestly to surrender a pension, which resulted in two insurance companies and the Inland Revenue being defrauded. The tribunal's decision was to dismiss his application on the grounds that while it was a single one-off incident, the matter was not completely resolved as the Inland Revenue was not given the opportunity to seek reparations and hold him to account for the dishonesty he had perpetrated. The decision highlights the fact that an individual could be considered fit and proper to hold a controlled function if a sufficient length of time has elapsed between the incident and seeking approval, and if approval were granted the individual would be appropriately supervised. However, in this instance Cox did not satisfy the tribunal that that was the case.

In *Hoodless and Blackwell v. the FSA*[176] the issue was an incorrect announcement relating to the placement of a share issue. In this case the tribunal rejected the FSA's decision simply to withdraw approval on the basis that the individuals were not fit and proper. Indeed, it rejected the FSA's claims that their behaviour was dishonest, and that they failed to cooperate with regulators and put in detriment the interests of consumers and confidence in the financial system. The tribunal followed the test in *Ghosh* to ascertain whether dishonesty existed in the case.[177] Here it was said an individual was dishonest if he must have realised that what he was doing was dishonest by the ordinary standards of reasonable and honest people. In this case the evidence pointed to limited failures rather than a general failure: for instance, a lack

175 *Ian Douglas Cox v. Financial Services Authority*, 12 May 2003, available at www.financeandtaxtribunals.gov.uk/decisions/seldecisions/financialservices.htm.

176 *Geoffrey Alan Hoodless & Sean Michael Blackwell v. Financial Services Authority*, 3 October 2003, available at www.financeandtaxtribunals.gov.uk/decisions/seldecisions/financialservices.htm.

177 Ibid., p. 2.

of volunteering information to regulators was not evidence of improper motive or lack of integrity. Moreover, an isolated lack of candour did not automatically amount to evidence of dishonesty. Therefore, in the case of Hoodless the tribunal considered him to be fit and proper as it did not consider him to pose any threat to consumers or to confidence in the financial system.

The Assessment Criteria

The approved persons regime is governed by a number of principles that delineate the standards expected of persons who undertake controlled functions. In line with the obligation to provide principles, the FSA also provides a code of practice to assist in their interpretation. The code highlights the kinds of acts or omissions that may give rise to an approval being called into question because it fails to comply with the principles.[178] In order to ascertain whether a person has breached the principles the FSA will look at the person's acts or omissions to try to assess the degree of culpability.[179]

Principle 1 focuses on carrying out approved functions with 'integrity'.[180] Principle 2 requires that those exercising such functions should act with due skill, care and diligence.[181] Principle 3 requires observation of proper standards of market conduct.[182] Principle 4 requires the approved person to cooperate with the FSA openly.[183] Principles 5–7 relate specifically to those in senior management and performing controlled functions; they are not necessarily more draconian than the other principles, but recognise that those in senior management have an additional responsibility regarding the affairs of the business. Principle 5 requires senior management to organise the business so that it can be controlled effectively with reasonable care.[184] Principle 6 requires an approved person to exercise due skill, care and diligence in their management responsibility.[185] Principle 7 requires an approved person to ensure that the firm for which they are responsible complies with the regulatory requirements.[186]

The code of practice highlights the kind of acts or omissions that can result in a breach of the principles. It not only articulates conduct that could be deemed negligent, but also highlights acts that could give rise to criminal charges. In addition to these kinds of serious offences there are other offences which, although less serious, would entail a breach of the principles. In relation to Principle 1, acts or omissions that evidence, *inter alia*, falsifying information and misleading clients or a firm can give rise to serious questions about an individual's integrity. These acts and omissions are of a very serious nature and could lead to criminal charges; they are at

178 Statement of Principles and Code of Practice for Approved Persons, APER 1.
179 APER 2, 2.1.2; Ch. 3, APER 3, 3.1.4G (1); Ch. 4, APER 4.
180 APER 4.1.1G.
181 APER 4.2.1G.
182 APER 4.3.1G.
183 APER 4.4.1G.
184 APER 4.5.1G.
185 APER 4.6.1G.
186 APER 4.7.1G.

the least evidence of gross negligence. A failure to inform a client about the nature of a financial product or risks associated with it could call into question Principle 2: whether an approved person has exercised the appropriate level of due skill, care and diligence in carrying out their functions. A failure to comply with the necessary market conduct rules could result in evidence that the approved person has breached Principle 3. In relation to Principle 4, failure to cooperate with the regulator, or if the approved person responsible for reporting to the FSA information they have that may be of material significance fails to disclose it, could amount to a breach.

Principles 5–7 specifically relate to those individuals who are approved to undertake controlled functions which are of significant influence. A breach of Principle 5 can arise if, for instance, an approved person fails to organise the business with reasonable care so that responsibilities within the organisation are not apportioned or delegated properly. An approved person could breach Principle 6 if they fail to exercise due skill, care and diligence in managing the business of the firm. This could arise were they to fail to take reasonable care to inform themselves adequately about the affairs and/or risks associated with the business they are undertaking. Failure to take reasonable care to ensure that the firm undertakes its business in accordance with the relevant requirements and standards of the regulatory system could amount to a breach of Principle 7.

The FSA prohibited Michael Harding[187] from performing a controlled function on the basis that it was not satisfied he was fit and proper after he had failed to undertake a review of the pensions sold by his firm as required by the Personal Investment Authority. Harding had failed to be 'fit and proper' by not acting with the necessary level of honesty, integrity and competence. The FSA held that he breached Principle 1 by falsifying information about the firm's pensions review quarterly returns; providing inaccurate information to the firm; submitting misleading information to the FSA; and failing to treat his customers fairly. A breach of Principle 2 was also evidenced by the fact that he failed to inform his partner correctly about the progress of the pensions review. The FSA considered Harding to be in breach of Principle 4 as a result of his failure to report accurately the actual progress made with the review.

The US Position on the Bank Director

The role of the bank director in the USA is governed by common law, company by-laws of association, statute and regulatory rules. The law governs the relationship between the bank and its shareholders and a broad range of other stakeholders, namely creditors, depositors and regulators.[188] The wider stakeholder agenda is articulated in the guidance provided to, for instance, national and state bank directors. It highlights the importance attached to the position of a bank director and how integral this role is to the local economy and community.[189] While the responsibilities of bank directors are to take account of a number of wider stakeholders, it is the interests of

187 FSA (2005) 'Final Notice: Michael Harding', 21 January.

188 *Marine Bank v. Fulton Bank*, 69 US 252 (1864).

189 OCC (1997) *The Role of a National Bank Director: The Director's Book*, at p. 3; FDIC *Manual of Examination Policies, Management/Administration II, Directors*, available

the bank and shareholders that need to be the main concern in light of their common law fiduciary duties; however, the interests of creditors are of paramount importance when an insolvency situation arises, as in this respect the fiduciary duty reverses to protect the interests of creditors.[190] Directors owe a general duty of care and fiduciary duty to the corporation in common law. Notwithstanding this, it is the interests of the bank and the duty owed by directors to it that are of concern in this section. The standard of care that governs bank directors is specifically considered.

The law governing directors' duties has certainly created a lot of concern due to the complexity of the prudential regulation and supervision that exists in the USA.[191] It is thus not surprising that the standard of care expected of bank directors is a complex affair, as it can emanate from common law rules and statutory rules on a federal and a state level and is often cited as a 'muddle'.[192] The common law and statutory sources governing this standard of care are somewhat different. For example, the common law principles are broad and ambiguous whereas the statutory provisions give more precise sanctions for acts and omissions that arise from safety and soundness problems. The statutory duty and the common law duty of care can be applied individually or concomitantly in different circumstances.[193] For example, shareholders, creditors and depositors of a bank could sue a bank director in the same petition because his fiduciary obligations to them emanate from both common law and statute law. In addition to these two sources of law, the regulators have a number of administrative sanctions that they can apply in circumstances where the bank has not been placed in administration or insolvency.[194]

The federal common law standard of care is generally said to be one of simple negligence, but with the application of the business judgement rule it equates more

---

at www.fdic.gov/regulations/safety/manual/Section4-1.html; FRB Commercial Bank Examination Manual, Section 5000.1.

190 Sjovall, J. M. (2001) 'What duty do company directors owe to banks and other creditors?', *Banking Law Journal*, vol. 118, 4.

191 Schooner, H. (1995) 'Fiduciary duties' demanding cousin: Bank director liability for unsafe or unsound banking practices', *George Washington Law Review*, vol. 63, 175; Stevens, R. W. and Nielson, B. H. (1994) 'The standard of care for directors and officers of federally chartered depository institutions: It's gross negligence regardless of whether section 1821 (K) preempts federal common law', *Annual Review of Banking Law*, vol. 16, 169; Lowry, P. A. (1997) 'The director liability provision of the Financial Institutions Reform, Recovery and Enforcement Act: What does it do?', *Annual Review of Banking Law*, vol. 16, 355; Weinstock, P. G. (1989) 'Directors and officers of filing banks: Pitfalls and precautions', *Banking Law Journal*, vol. 106, 434; Galbraith, C. and Seidel, J. (1987) 'FDIC vs imprudent banking officials: The enforcement apparatus', *Banking Law Journal*, vol. 104, 92; Mills, L. C. (1997) 'Director and officer liability/fiduciary liability', *Annual Review of Banking Law*, vol. 16, 18; Shepherd, J. (1992) 'The liability of officers and directors under the Financial Institutions Reform, Recovery and Enforcement Act of 1989', *Michigan Law Review*, vol. 90, 1119.

192 Stevens and Neilson, ibid., at p. 169, citing Soderquist, L. D. (1990) 'The proper standard for directors' negligence liability', *Notre Dame Law Review*, vol. 66, 37.

193 *Bowerman v. Hamner*, 250 US 504 (1919), at p. 511–512.

194 For a comparison of the standards of care that exist within the various sources see Schooner, n. 191 above, at p. 214.

to a standard of gross negligence rather than ordinary negligence. The position at state level was in a number of instances different, and so gave rise to more than one standard of care pertaining to bank directors' duty of care. In fact some states prescribed a higher threshold of evidence to be satisfied, equivalent to intentional or wilful misbehaviour, before directors and officers could be successfully sued in tort of negligence. In some states 'wilful neglect' and in others a simple 'neglect standard of care' is provided before a breach of duty is deemed to have occurred.[195] According to Macey and O'Hara a pattern arose: 'the history of banking directors' duty of care cases follows a cyclical pattern. During or immediately following a period of high bank failure, courts have traditionally raised the standard of care required of bank directors.'[196] However, they also note the reluctance of states to follow suit; indeed, states had in some instances raised the standard to 'wilful or wanton neglect' to safeguard directors from such legal actions.[197]

The Directors' Duties

The federal regulators articulate the practical responsibilities and duties of directors to ensure compliance with their fiduciary duties. The board of directors of a national or state member bank is required to have at least five and no more than 25 members to be properly constituted.[198] A bank director has the responsibility of both directing the bank strategically in its affairs and overseeing its management as they undertake their work. Indeed, the FDIC, for example, contends that the board of directors is 'the source of all authority and responsibility'.[199] It is the board's responsibility to appointment and remove executive officers and managers, and hence it is the board's responsibility to ensure that appointees are suitable for their positions. Therefore, boards of directors have the ultimate responsibility to ensure the bank's safety and soundness. In the execution of these responsibilities the directors are required to exercise diligence and loyalty towards the bank's interests. In order to ascertain whether a director has exercised diligence a number of factors have been noted as being significant: attending meetings, reviewing information about the bank's activities, acting with independent judgement and reviewing audit and supervisory reports. These factors evidence the extent to which a director is actively participating

195 For a survey of the standard of care in the states see Stevens and Neilson. n. 191 above, at pp. 194–231.

196 Macey, J. R. and O'Hara, M. (2003) 'The corporate governance of banks', *Federal Reserve Bank of New York Economic Policy Review*, vol. 91, 100, available at www.newyorkfed.org/publications.

197 Ibid., at p. 101; for an examination of the various standards of care adopted by states see for example *FDIC v. Wheat J D et al.*, 970 F. 2d 124 (5d Cir.1992); *RTC v. Gibson J M et al.* 829 F Supp 1110 (W.D MO. 1993); *FDIC v. Russell* 739 F Supp 450 (D.C. IL. 1993); *FDIC v. Healey F*, 991 F Supp 53 (D.C. Ct.1998).

198 National Bank Act 1863, s. 71; Banking Act 1933, s. 31.

199 FDIC, n. 189 above, at p. 1; see also *Rankin v. Cooper et al.* 149 F 1010(C.C. AR. 1907).

within the decision-making process, and in particular the level of scrutiny a diligent director would show.[200]

The Common Law Standard

The US Supreme Court articulated the broad federal common law duty of care owed by bank directors in its decision in *Briggs v. Spaulding*.[201] In this case Spaulding and others were directors of First National Bank of Buffalo, which was placed into receivership after having sustained considerable losses through mismanagement and alleged failure to supervise the bank's activities appropriately. However, it was held that the directors, namely Spaulding, were not liable in negligence for not discovering the losses or preventing their occurrence.[202] The case articulated a standard of care based on what an ordinary prudent and diligent man would exercise under similar circumstances. The decision highlights that the question of negligence is relative, therefore each case needs to be assessed on its own facts.[203] The decision by the court recognised the balance that needs to be struck between an over-stringent standard of care and putting inappropriate individuals off from acting as directors of banks.

The facts of this case suggest that gross negligence was needed before the directors of the bank were culpable, rather than simple negligence. This is contended on the basis that the court applied the simple negligence test with 'something more than officiating as figureheads', suggesting that a gross negligence test was more suitable. Furthermore, the opinions of the dissenting judges contend that a significant proportion of the losses could have been avoided if directors such as Spaulding had showed the appropriate level of care commensurate to that expected of ordinary diligent directors over their own business affairs. The lack of attention the directors showed in overseeing the activities of the executive officers was not considered sufficient. Justice Hughes notes the leniency shown by the Supreme Court in *Briggs v. Spaulding* in *Robinson v. Hall*,[204] and the difficult position the state courts are in to act in the necessary manner against miscreant directors. Moreover, in the decision of *Washington Bancorporation*[205] the court contended that the simple negligence standard should apply in specific circumstances, whereas the gross negligence standard should apply to more routine 'transactions and actions'.[206] Indeed, the court also contended that the standard of care applied in *Briggs* equated more with a gross negligence standard of care than a simple negligence test.[207] According to Stevens and Neilson, in most cases courts have found directors liable only when there is evidence of a gross dereliction of duty, whether that is evidenced by, *inter alia*, fraud or a conflict of interest.[208]

200 OCC, n. 189 above, at pp. 69–76.

201 *Briggs v. Spaulding*, 141 US 132 (1891).

202 Ibid., at p. 7.

203 Ibid., at p. 14.

204 *Robinson v. Hall et al.*, 63 F. 222 (4d Cir. 1894), at pp. 227–228.

205 *Washington Bancorporation v. Wafic R Said* et al., 812 F Supp 1256 (D.C. DC.1993).

206 Ibid., at p. 1266.

207 Ibid.

208 Stevens and Neilson, n. 191 above, at p. 186.

The Statutory Position

The liability of bank directors became a particularly prominent issue in the 1980s with the huge number of bank and thrift failures. The savings and loans failures led to the introduction of the Financial Institutions Reform, Recovery and Enforcement Act 1989 (FIRREA).[209] The FIRREA gives the bank regulators new powers to 'disapprove' of individuals who seek appointment at a director and senior management level on the basis that they do not have the appropriate 'background, qualifications, experience, and integrity'.[210] Section 212(a) incorporates § 1812(k) of the FDIA, which confers a federal statutory standard of care on bank directors and officers. Section 1812(k) enunciates a gross negligence standard as the minimum degree of negligence that needs to be evident before directors and officers of a federally insured depository bank can be held liable for personal damages.[211] The main point of contention with the introduction of the standardised approach in the FIRREA is the position regarding the standard of care prescribed by federal common law and standards espoused by individual states. Section 1812(k) provides a gross negligence ceiling on the matter of the standard of care expected of directors; thus it prevents states from exceeding that with the adoption of standards equivalent to wilful neglect.

This point was articulated in the Supreme Court decision of *Atherton v. FDIC*.[212] In this case City Federal Savings Bank was placed into receivership by the Resolution Trust Corporation (RTC), which brought an action against its officers and directors due to various bad loans the bank had made. The court examined the interrelationship of federal and state banking law to determine the scope of s. 1812(k) and the applicable standard of care. It held that s. 1812(k) provides the minimum level of liability of gross negligence when a state has adopted a more restrictive duty of care. It also held that s. 1812(k) does not prevent states from adopting a higher standard of care equivalent to simple negligence. The rationale of the decision was to prevent states adopting a restrictive liability standard by placing a floor on what could be applied to federally chartered banks.[213]

---

209 Public Law 101-73: Financial Institutions Reform, Recovery, and Enforcement Act 1989 ('To reform, recapitalize, and consolidate the federal deposit insurance system, to enhance the regulatory and enforcement powers of Federal financial institutions regulatory agencies, and for other purposes').

210 Ibid., s. 28(e) 'Agency disapproval of directors and senior executive officers of insured financial institutions or financial institution holding companies', see specifically 12 USC § 1831i(e).

211 Shepherd, n. 191 above, at p. 1119; Lowry, n. 191 above, at p. 355; Stevens and Nielson, n. 191 above, at p. 169.

212 *J W Atherton v. FDIC*, 519 US 213 (1997); see also Plotkin, W. (1999) 'Director and officer liability', *Annual Review of Banking Law*, vol. 18, 46.

213 *Atherton*, ibid., at pp. 228 229.

The Business Judgement Rule

The courts have generally refrained from ordering damages where simple negligence is evident and directors and officers acted in good faith in the decisions they made even though in hindsight they were wrong. This is based on the concern that an over-litigious corporate environment could deter appropriate candidates from applying for positions in which they operate to take risks and make profits. In the light of this the business judgement rule has been adopted in a variety of forms to preclude liability if the decision made by the director is taken with reasonable care and void of conflicts of interest. In *Bancorporation* four presumptions are put forward. First, that the director is in a position of 'disinterestedness or independence'. Secondly, no allegation of fraud exists. Thirdly, the director acted in good faith, in the best interests of the corporation. Fourthly, that there is no abuse of discretionary powers.[214] The effect of adopting the business judgement rule is that directors will not be liable for their business decisions provided these decisions in the literal sense do not involve fraud, bad faith, conflict of interest, self-dealing or gross negligence. In order to apply the business judgement rule successfully the director would have to establish that the decision was reached in an informed manner and according to the relevant procedures prescribed by the corporation. The consequence of the rule is that the acts and omissions of directors are no longer judged according to the simple negligence standard prescribed by *Briggs* but rather a gross negligence standard, even in states that have adopted the former rather than the latter standard of care.

Conclusion

This chapter has sought to analyse the interplay between general corporate law and banking regulation and supervision. It is important to highlight how corporate law provides limited safeguards to protect the interests of depositors, giving rise to the necessity for some form of public regulation. In general terms corporate law is designed to maximise shareholder wealth – the interests of creditors are only considered to a limited extent during the existence of a company. Reports on corporate governance have preserved the importance of 'entrepreneurial spirit', and have avoided putting in place layers of accountability that may hinder this.

In the banking context the interests of depositors and shareholders, depending on whether one is looking at it from a corporate law or bank regulation perspective, can compete with one another. Therefore, from a bank regulation perspective, for the purposes of depositor protection additional responsibilities are placed on shareholders to ensure they are fit and proper to hold a controlling position in a bank. The criteria require shareholder controllers to be mindful of the interests of depositors and to stand behind a bank if need arises. While bank regulation and supervision do not advocate pulling back the 'entrepreneurial spirit', they have certainly reconfigured the general corporate law position so that banks are mindful of the interests of other stakeholders in their decision-making processes. Regulators have thus mirrored

214 *Washington Bancorporation*, n. 205 above, at pp. 1268–1269.

commercial practice, and enshrined the idea that 'entrepreneurial spirit' is secure provided it satisfies supervisory objectives.

The FSA has brought to the fore the interests of a number of other stakeholders of which banks need to be mindful, including regulators. In addition, the importance of maintaining market confidence, integrity and reputation gives rise to the possibility of the FSA taking enforcement action if these are undermined or damaged by a bank's actions. The FSA has formalised rules and principles to govern regulated firms at institutional and individual levels. These principles and rules have a number of features in common with the standard of care expected in common law. The standard of reasonable care is, however, fleshed out with additional rules and guidance to ensure more certainty and precision in its application. The way in which the principles have been enforced at institutional and individual levels indicates that the FSA has tried to realign the interests of consumers and practitioners through their enforcement.

The USA has also incorporated a wider number of stakeholders, such as depositors and regulators, into its system of regulation. These stakeholder interests need to be considered on a continuous basis, failing which a bank could be considered in breach of the safe and sound principle. As in UK common law, the relationship between a bank and a depositor is one of debtor and creditor, so the implications of this relationship and the importance of supervision are similar.

The common law position on bank directors' duties in the USA has given rise to much concern as a result of its complexity as well as the low standard of care exacted of directors. A policy concern for federal legislators was some states trying to apply an extremely low standard of care to avoid directors being liable for personal damages. Federal legislation has tried to create more consistency by placing a limit equivalent to 'gross negligence' as the lowest standard of care that can be set; and some states in the USA have opted to have the standard of care expected of bank directors set at a much higher level, equivalent to simple negligence, and where a dispute arises the latter is said to apply. The federal standard of care is much lower than the standard of care expected of directors in the UK. However, it would be a significant misconception to think that the administrative sanctions federal bank regulators can impose also comply with such a low standard – for such sanctions simple negligence is the standard of care applied, as will be shown in the next chapter.

Chapter 4

Enforcement Powers and Banking Supervision

Introduction

The way rules are enforced in financial regulation and supervision is crucial to maintain the appropriate degree of investor and depositor confidence in the marketplace. In equal measure the intermediaries in the financial services industry need to recognise the importance of ensuring that they comply with the obligations conferred on them to undertake banking business. In order to achieve some kind of equilibrium between the interests of the regulator and the regulated firms and individuals in such matters, a single enforcement strategy, whether a compliance- or a deterrence-based approach, is not appropriate but rather a combination of both is necessary. A compliance-based approach should be the first method, to be used to deal with compliance issues, and a deterrence-based approach should only be adopted when non-compliance gives rise to a serious degree of culpability. This is asserted on the basis that the majority of regulated firms will comply and may require the support of the regulator to ensure they continue to comply.

This chapter will analyse the policy behind enforcement decisions in banking regulation and supervision. The first section analyses the two fundamental approaches to enforcement: compliance- and deterrence-based mechanisms. It highlights that the most appropriate enforcement approach to govern a sophisticated industry like financial services is one that uses a mix of both compliance- and deterrence-based measures. Indeed, a mix-based approach is warranted when the regulated are not a cohesive whole but a collection of disparate groups. The second section looks at the sanctions used to deter non-compliance. It suggests that a narrow range of punitive sanctions does not achieve the best possible level of compliance. The third section provides an account of the style of enforcement adopted by the Bank, highlighting that under the previous system enforcement decisions were not routinely disclosed and rather more emphasis was placed on seeking remedies behind closed doors. The fourth section covers the FSA's approach with the introduction of the FMSA 2000 in the light of its regulatory objectives and principles. The fifth section introduces the enforcement powers the FSA has at its disposal, illustrated where necessary with case examples. The broad range of enforcement powers is outlined, given that banks can potentially be exposed to them. It particularly focuses on publicity and fines and the rationale of using them. The FSA's approach to cooperating with overseas regulators in enforcement matters is also discussed, given the transnational nature of banking business. The influence of the Human Rights Act 1998 is considered, given the potential punitive and retributive effect civil sanctions such as prohibitions and fines can have on regulated firms or individuals. The sixth section reflects on the enforcement approach of the FSA. It highlights that although the FSA has taken a more proactive approach to enforcement decisions it has failed somewhat in retaining the confidence of the industry, as it is perceived to be rather punitive and retributive, and in favour of safeguarding the interests of consumers. The seventh section introduces the enforcement powers of US regulators. It establishes that the US enforcement approach has not moved away from the remedial-based approach like the FSA, which is more like an 'adjudicator'. Yet it still imposes very severe sanctions to ensure that banks adhere to the importance of acting in a 'safe and sound manner'. Finally, the eighth section will provide some concluding points and comparative observations about the UK and US approach.

The Enforcement Strategy

To ensure rules are observed two forms of enforcement method are generally encouraged: the compliance- and the deterrence-based approaches.[1] The compliance-based approach refers to making sure rules and standards are observed through dialogue between the regulator and regulated without resorting to the use of administrative, civil or criminal sanctions. The deterrence-based approach, on the other hand, refers to the use of sanction to punish non-compliance with the requisite rules and standards of behaviour. The two enforcement methods have been interpreted to be opposite poles of a compliance continuum.[2] In this continuum the compliance and deterrence methods of enforcement provide a mechanism of 'control', albeit using different approaches.[3] Indeed, the complexity of modern society and those participating in it requires a more sophisticated approach to enforcement that captures the idiosyncratic nature of how individuals and corporations abide by rules.[4] Ultimately the regulatory

---

1 See specifically Scholz, J. T. (1984) 'Cooperation, deterrence, and the ecology of regulatory enforcement', *Law and Society Review*, vol. 18, 179; Brown, R. (1994) 'Theory and practice of regulatory enforcement: Occupational health and safety regulation in British Columbia', *Law and Policy*, vol. 16, 63; Makki, T. and Braithwaite, J. (1993) 'Praise, pride and corporate compliance', *International Journal of the Sociology of Law*, vol. 21, 73; Hutter, B. M. (1989) 'Variations in regulatory enforcement styles', *Law and Policy*, vol. 11, 153; May, P. J. and Burby, R. J. (1998) 'Making sense out of regulatory enforcement', *Law and Policy*, vol. 20, 157; Hutter, B. M. (1988) *The Reasonable Arm of the Law? The Law Enforcement Procedures of Environmental Health Officers*, Oxford, Clarendon Press; Cook, D. (1989) *Rich Law, Poor Law: Differential Response to Tax and Supplementary Benefit Fraud*, Milton Keynes, Open University Press, at p. 104; Hopkins, A. (1994) 'Compliance with what? The fundamental regulatory question', *British Journal of Criminology*, vol. 34, 431.

2 Gunningham, N. (1987) 'Negotiated non-compliance: A case study of regulatory failure', *Law and Policy*, vol. 9, 69, at p. 70.

3 Cotterell, R. (1992) *The Sociology of Law: An Introduction*, London, Butterworths, at p. 245.

4 Reiss, A. J. Jr (1984) 'Selecting strategies of social control over organizational life', in Hawkins, K. and Thomas, J. (eds) *Enforcing Regulation*, Boston, MA, Kluwer Nijhoff, at p. 32.

cost associated with both of these approaches is another important consideration, as it is generally the case that a deterrence-based approach is a more costly route than a compliance-based approach.[5]

The compliance-based approach focuses on the importance of the regulator and the regulated interacting with one another to ensure rules are obeyed. This approach attempts to provide a two-way process to resolve problems that may arise in regulation. The first aspect may be for the regulator to highlight the rationale of the rules that need to be observed. The second aspect may be the regulated highlighting the possible issues that arise by complying with the rules as the regulator suggests. This interaction to determine how to comply results in a more pragmatic approach to ensure the best outcome is achieved by all parties. The regulator will ultimately want to ensure no adverse risks ensue from the way the regulated seek to comply with the rules. The regulated may want to ascertain whether compliance with the rules does not needlessly increase the cost of compliance for little benefit to either the industry or consumers as a whole. A considerable level of tension can arise here between regulator and regulated, leading to a lack of confidence in one another. Ultimately the weight of the bargaining power between the two parties rests with the regulator rather than the regulated, given that the regulator has a considerable range of sanctions at its disposal to force compliance. Indeed, the regulator will have powers to control entry to and exit from the market. The risk here is that the perception of the regulator as being unsympathetic to the issues highlighted by the regulated can lead to needless confrontation, so problems that could be resolved through dialogue are simply brushed under the carpet by the regulated. This is not to suggest that the regulated lack bargaining power, as they can simply decide to undertake their business in another jurisdiction. This is exacerbated by the rivalry between countries for business, which means the cost of regulation and the quality of compliance required are in themselves a barrier to entry.

Education and Incentives

The ideas behind a compliance-based approach include further subdivisions. Consultation and education are important components within this approach, as they enhance communication and provide the regulated with an environment in which they can influence the way regulation is designed to operate in the marketplace.[6] In such circumstances the regulator would depend on the regulated to provide it with the knowledge so as best to regulate the activities within its mandate. This process is especially utilised when 'rules' are being negotiated and forums and committees are set up to gather and disseminate best practice and provide mutually acceptable 'rules' to govern such activities. Whilst such a relationship could raise the concern

5 According to Scholz, J. T. (1984) 'Voluntary compliance and regulatory enforcement', *Law and Policy*, vol. 6, 385, at p. 392; Ayres, I. and Braithwaite, J. (1992) *Responsive Regulation: Transcending the Deregulation Debate*, Oxford, Oxford University Press, at p. 26.

6 Kagan, R. A. and Scholz, J.T. 'The criminology of the corporation and regulatory enforcement strategies' in Hawkins and Thomas (1984) n. 4 above, at p. 82.

of regulatory capture because of the bargaining power wielded by the regulated, the process provides an environment of mutual responsibility which can, on the majority of occasions, outweigh such concerns.

The compliance-based approach includes another facet: the use of incentives by regulatory bodies to ensure control. Grabosky gives cautious encouragement to the use of incentives even though they could reduce the burden of regulation.[7] Incentives generally provide positive inducements to cooperate with the regulator rather than negative penalties such as disqualification or market disclosure.[8] For example, incentives range from grants and subsidies to favourable administrative considerations.[9] Regulatory holidays are another incentive, whereby an organisation is relieved from inspections because of its 'good track record' in compliance with regulatory requirements.

A further aspect of incentive schemes is to 'come clean' with compliance failures which have been identified by the institution itself. This type of action maintains the trust relationship between regulator and regulated. It also supports the view that most firms do accept regulation and supervision as a form of financial control where the reputation of the institution could be adversely affected if non-compliance is publicised. Furthermore, it highlights the importance of self-regulation in an environment where even the most compliant institutions can get it wrong. Ultimately disclosing non-compliance provides the regulated with the possibility of a lesser sanction or, in some cases, no punishment at all, because there is no evidence of complacency or dishonesty.

The Regulated and Choice of Regulatory Enforcement Strategy

The question of whether a compliance or a deterrence style of enforcement is taken is ultimately dependent on the view the regulator has of the regulated firm or individual. The risk of a single enforcement approach is that it would generally assume that the regulated act in a single way and are driven by similar factors as if they were one cohesive body. Ayres and Braithwaite suggest the regulated industry must be seen in a way which recognises the fact that the regulated are driven by both 'rational' and 'irrational' motives.[10] Therefore it is the regulator's responsibility to recognise the existence of both and ensure that there are appropriate sanctions to oblige both the 'rational' and the 'irrational' to comply.

This highlights the need for the regulator to exercise judgement on a case-by-case basis in view of the circumstances and facts before it, so that the appropriate

---

7 Grabosky, P. N. (1995) 'Regulation by reward: On the use of incentives as regulatory instruments', *Law and Policy*, vol. 17, 257.

8 Hawkesby, C. (2000) 'New Zealand's approach to banking supervision: An emphasis on market incentives and accountability', paper presented at Conference on Rules, Incentives and Sanctions: Enforcement in Financial Regulation, Financial Markets Group, London School of Economics, 26 May.

9 Grabosky, n. 7 above, at p. 259.

10 Ayres and Braithwaite, n. 5 above, at p. 30.

enforcement strategy is used. According to Kagan and Scholz,[11] the regulated can be categorised into three rather crude types to allow the regulator to devise the most appropriate strategy to ensure optimum compliance. The first is labelled the 'amoral calculator', motivated purely by profit and the probability of being caught. The second, the 'political citizen', is mindful of what is required and will for a number of reasons comply with the law provided it is considered reasonable in the public interest. The third is the institution which is 'organisationally incompetent': a high proportion of its non-compliance emanates from ineffective internal governance to oversee its business activities.

These images highlight the mixture of institutions which make up the regulated industry. According to Kagan and Scholz, these categories require distinct enforcement strategies.[12] In the case of the 'amoral calculator' the regulator should adopt a strong deterrence-based strategy, because the high degree of management culpability in not complying necessitates more rigorous visits and a retributive penalty to deter others from such action, otherwise the perception of regulatory capture could be suggested. The 'political citizen' requires an altogether different response; a compliance-based approach where regulatory requirements are negotiated and interpreted to avoid a technical breach of the rules. The regulator in this case needs to avoid accusations of simply enforcing rules to the letter and not exercising its judgement as to the cost and benefits of any non-compliance. The third type of institution, the 'organisationally incompetent', also requires the regulator to adopt a compliance-based approach, but to take on a role of a 'consultant' to assist the regulated with remedying the problems experienced by the firm. This is likely to be part of a wider enforcement strategy where some evidence may suggest that the firm has not acted with the appropriate level of care expected of such a business.

The categorisation of businesses and the subsequent enforcement strategy outlined by Kagan and Scholz provide a useful method of assessing whether firms regulated by the FSA have been treated in a manner similar to that suggested.[13] While in some instances this could seem a simple task, as Kagan and Scholz suggest the categorisation is 'crude', so in many instances it may not be a simple choice between deterrence and compliance but rather a combination of both consultation and sanctions. Indeed, the choice of sanctions within the range at the disposal of the FSA is also a gauge as to the seriousness associated with the non-compliance.

Deterrence and Sanctions

The deterrence-based approach is centred on the imposition of sanctions and retribution. In this light deterrence could be construed as a mechanism for ensuring compliance by negative means. This is in contrast to a compliance-based approach which may discourage non-compliance by placing attention on the threat of adverse consequences that can arise from a criminal prosecution or imposition of a punitive

11 Kagan, R. A. and Scholz, J. T. in Hawkins, K. and Thomas, J. (eds) (1984) n 6 above at pp. 67–68.

12 Ibid.

13 Ibid.

civil sanction. The deterrence-based approach is in this respect more reactive, as it places regulatory resources in the area of detecting infringements of the law so that penalties can be successfully applied. According to Reiss, a regulatory strategy based on deterrence would consider the imposition of a penalty as a positive sign of success.[14] The choice of sanction is also dependent upon the seriousness of the breach or offence.

This suggests that a broad range of both non-punitive and punitive sanctions is needed to address the varying degrees of culpability that can underpin non-compliance. Ayres and Braithwaite have set out the choice of sanctions in a pyramid with the most serious sanctions at the top.[15] The base of the pyramid advocates negotiation, but further up the ladder the degree of severity of the sanction increases, recognising the need for a variety of enforcement methods to coerce compliance. This is initiated by negotiation, followed by a 'warning letter' and finally, at the apex of the pyramid, 'licence revocation', which would be literally terminating the right to undertake licensed activities.

The Decriminalisation of Regulatory Offences

Criminal sanctions provide the traditional deterrent against acts which are considered morally wrong by society. The punishment prescribed by the criminal justice system tries to achieve a broad range of goals which are not necessarily attainable with one sanction, such as restraint, retribution, rehabilitation, education, denunciation, compensation or just deserts.[16] The length of the sentence or the size of the fine is a reflection of the severity of the harm caused. A degree of stigma is also attached to incarceration or a criminal fine, which is also a form of chastisement. Consequently, criminal law in any regulatory regime is reserved for some of the most severe offences where there is moral disapproval and a high degree of culpability based on criminal intent or recklessness. This is not the case in society in general, where criminal prosecution takes place regularly for minor as well as serious offences. This process seems to indicate that society is ready to accept the costs of commercial wrongdoing and mitigate the loss or damage it causes by adopting instead civil regulatory sanctions. Succeeding in proving criminal wrongdoing is no simple task, and particularly difficult in the area of complex fraud. Another major concern is the infrequent use of criminal sanctions to punish severe regulatory wrongs.[17] A crucial factor here is whether the culprit is a company or an individual, giving rise to problems associated with establishing the mental element necessary to satisfy a criminal conviction.[18]

---

14 Reiss, n. 4 above, at p. 25.

15 Ayres and Braithwaite, n. 5 above, at p. 35.

16 For a detailed examination of criminal sanctions see Gobert, J. and Punch, M. (2003) *Rethinking Corporate Crime*, London, Butterworths, at pp. 214–252; Croall, H. (2001) *Understanding White Collar Crime*, Milton Keynes, Open University Press, at pp. 123–142.

17 Croall, ibid., at pp. 112 119.

18 Slapper, G. and Tombs, S. (1999) *Corporate Crime*, London, Longman.

The growth in the use of civil sanctions is based on a systematic process of decriminalising regulatory offences, which has curtailed the use of criminal sanctions for all but the most serious offences.[19] Civil sanctions come in various forms: compensation, injunctions, restitution, asset forfeiture or civil fines. For instance, civil law consists of a number of options to achieve equity and fairness between parties, such as injunctions or orders for restitution, which attempt crudely to place the parties in their original or desired positions. The process of decriminalisation in the regulatory sphere has also brought with it, *inter alia*, a new range of civil sanctions such as revocation and restrictions on business activities licensed by a regulator, disqualification of a company or individual from working in an industry and publicity of non-compliance. In the case of publicity, the shame can act as a deterrent because of the link between the offender and the regulatory community.[20] Finally, corporate regulation can also place another layer of civil and even criminal sanctions on the shoulders of companies and directors.[21]

The arsenal of civil sanctions provides a very broad spectrum of methods to ensure compliance. The prevalence of these civil administrative sanctions in regulatory agencies has arisen for a number of reasons: key amongst these is that civil offences are deemed easier to prove in comparison with criminal offences, which embody a number of safeguards to ensure that a person's liberty is not undermined. The power to execute particular sanctions in regulatory agencies, especially civil sanctions, makes it easy to administer them through the designated tribunal rather than through court proceedings. This avoids higher costs and increases the speed of reaching a decision. Moreover, the implementation of administrative civil sanctions means the revenue from such decisions is reaped by the regulatory agency. This can be legitimised in two ways. Firstly, it reduces the burden in terms of budgetary cost on the wider regulatory community. Secondly, non-monetary sanctions such as imprisonment, which should be left for those not deterred by civil sanctions, are socially more expensive.[22] The funds raised through civil sanctions can be more efficiently distributed to those who have suffered loss and require compensation. The attempt to increase the use of non-punitive civil sanctions could directly increase enforcement activity in the intermediate range of offences without society or the market closing its doors on a participant.[23] The use of such sanctions could not only

19 Kerrigan, L. J. (ed.) (1993) 'Project: The decriminalization of administrative law penalties: Civil remedies, alternatives, policy, and constitutional implications', *Administrative Law Review*, vol. 45, 367.

20 Benson, L. M. (1985) 'Denying the guilty mind: Accounting for involvement in a white-collar crime', *Criminology*, vol. 23, 583.

21 See for example Griffin, S (1999) *Personal Liability and Disqualification of Directors*, Oxford, Hart.

22 Posner, R. A. (1986) *Economic Analysis of Law*, Boston, MA, Little, Brown, at p. 209; Shavell, S. (1985) 'Criminal law and the optimal use of non-monetary sanctions as a deterrent', *Columbia Law Review*, vol. 85, 1232.

23 For an excellent examination of this issue see Mann, K. (1992) 'Punitive civil sanctions: The middle ground between criminal and civil law', *Yale Law Journal*, vol. 101, 1795, at p. 1863; Shapiro, S. (1985) 'The road not taken: The elusive path to criminal prosecution for white-collar offenders', *Law and Society Review*, vol. 19, 179, at p. 193.

enhance the public profile of a regulatory agency but also reduce the possibility of allegations of abuse of public office.[24] But notwithstanding these advantages, caution needs to be taken to avoid simply substituting civil sanctions for onerous criminal sanctions.[25]

In the regulatory context, a greater overlap between criminal and civil sanctions exists under the auspices of administrative powers.[26] A specific concern raised by the growing use of civil sanctions is the misconception that they lack the regulatory edge to coerce compliance. The literature on punitive civil sanctions highlights the significant element of deterrence and retributive effect attached to them. For instance, if a company has its licence to conduct business in a particular field revoked, this would almost invariably mean the demise of the business. An order to disqualify an individual from their employment would equally mean the person would have their career brought to an end.[27] The degree of culpability would mean either a short or a permanent ban from a profession or office. The ramifications of these types of civil punitive sanctions mean they are similar to criminal sanctions, and thus hardly ever used.[28] This leads to the conclusion that regulation needs in place a broad range of punitive as well as non-punitive sanctions to show society that enforcement action is taking place to capture the various degrees of non-compliance.

The use of civil sanctions requires the courts to be mindful of claimants simply substituting criminal offences with punitive civil or administrative sanction to avoid the burden of proof required to be discharged in the former proceedings in order to prosecute an individual successfully. In such matters the courts have been sensitive to this issue by ensuring the burden is commensurate to the seriousness of the claim made in civil proceedings.

The Courts' Position on Punitive Civil Sanctions

The central ideas behind criminal penalties and civil remedies have traditionally remained distinct.[29] However, the distinguishing features of criminal and civil sanctions are, on an abstract level, not as distinct as one might think, especially with the use of punitive civil sanctions.[30] In all civil actions the courts have, on occasion,

24 *Three Rivers DC v. Governor and Company of the Bank of England* HL [2001] 2 All ER 513; *Three Rivers DC v. Bank of England* [2006] EWHC 816.

25 Kerrigan, n. 19 above, at p. 433.

26 For the use of criminal sanctions see Kadish, S. H. (1963) 'Some observations on the use of criminal sanctions in enforcing economic regulations', *University of Chicago Law Review*, 30, 423–449; *Harvard Law Review* (1979) 'Developments in the law. Corporate crime: Regulating corporate behavior through criminal sanctions', *Harvard Law Review*, vol. 92, 1227.

27 See the FSA powers of enforcement against individuals and firms that fail to comply with the statutory and administrative regime governing financial services on pp. 128–135

28 See Mann, n. 23 above, at pp. 1814–1816; Coffee, J. C. Jr (1992) 'Paradigms lost: The blurring of the criminal and civil law models – And what can be done', *Yale Law Journal*, vol. 101, 1875.

29 *Atcheson v. Everitt*, 98 Eng. Rep. 1142, 1147.

30 Mann, n. 23 above, at pp. 1803–1813.

sought to insert another burden of proof between the criminal and civil standards where the existing sanctions are deemed so severe that they put the individual's integrity in jeopardy. In some cases civil liability could include a criminal wrongdoing, such as breach of fiduciary duty. The court thus needs to determine the appropriate standard of proof, but the following decisions make it apparent that it is very difficult to strike the correct balance. According to Denning LJ, there is no absolute standard in civil or criminal cases.[31] Though the civil standard is based on a preponderance of probability, he suggested that there are degrees of probability. For example, a fraud case naturally requires a higher degree of probability than that required if one were establishing negligence. Notwithstanding this point, he qualifies his statement by indicating that the degree of probability would not be as high as that expected in a criminal court. This principle was observed, more cautiously, by Denning in the case of *Hornal*, where he decided that when a civil case consists of an allegation of criminality, the standard should still be based on a balance of probabilities, otherwise it would bring the civil process into contempt.[32] According to Coleman J in *Heinl*, the standard of proof to establish dishonesty, although not as high as the criminal standard, should involve a high level of probability.[33] Notwithstanding the above decisions, *Re A Solicitor*[34] and *ex parte Austin*[35] go further and suggest a criminal standard may apply. For example, in *Re A Solicitor*, a case involving the striking-off of a solicitor from the roll of practitioners, it was held that the proceedings of a tribunal should apply the criminal standard of proof because the allegation of misconduct in the case was tantamount to a criminal offence. The decisions in *Re A Solicitor* and *ex parte Austin* assert that when a court considers a person's future position or professional integrity it is crucial that the standard of proof equates to 'beyond reasonable doubt'. This is because, like criminal sanctions of imprisonment, they banish individuals from the society within which they function.

The Historical Position: The Bank's Enforcement Strategy

The Bank's enforcement policy evolved parallel to its *laissez-faire* supervisory approach. Moral suasion/persuasion, colloquially referred to as the 'raising of the Governor's eyebrow', ensured control and discipline within the small and exclusive banking community. Moral suasion acted as the instrument of regulatory control and provided the context for trust and cooperation between the Bank and the City

31 *Bater v. Bater* 2 All ER [1950] 458, 460.

32 *Hornal v. Neuberger Products Ltd* [1957] 1 QB 247, 254.

33 *Heinl and Others v. Jyske Bank (Gibraltar) Ltd*, *The Times* Law Reports, 28 September 1999, 661, 662.

34 *Re A Solicitor* [1993] 1 QB 69, 82. Emphasis was given to a number of Commonwealth decisions, in particular *Bhandari v. Advocates Committee* [1956] 1 WLR 1442, 1452: 'in every allegation of professional misconduct involving an element of deceit or moral turpitude a high standard of proof is called for, and we cannot envisage any body of professional men sitting in judgement on a colleague who would be content to condemn on a mere balance of probabilities', at p. 81.

35 *R v. Milk Marketing Board, ex parte Austin*, *The Times*, 21 March 1983, 202, 202.

of London.[36] Moral persuasion, within the remit of the Bank of England Act 1946 s. 4(3), required a significant amount of coercion. The banks were not always cooperative, and on some occasions they were reluctant to part with information.[37] It would be naive to think that moral persuasion did not experience some resistance and necessitate a formal request. The concern about the traditional form of enforcement via moral suasion is the lack of clarity and transparency, which raises the concern of arbitrary decision-making. Although banking regulation and supervision were formalised with the introduction of the Banking Act 1987, the Bank would use its powers to provide guidance to the banking industry.[38] This suggests a process of formalisation and codification without necessarily diminishing the level of discretion in administrative decision-making.[39]

The Arthur Andersen Report, initiated after the Barings débâcle, noted that the Bank had at its disposal enforcement sanctions of the 'nuclear option'.[40] It highlighted the concern about having over-punitive sanctions with little 'middle ground', such as changes to the 'target' or 'trigger' ratios governing capital adequacy, or more intensive supervision.[41] These sanctions were only utilised when the capital of the authorised institution was far above the target ratio. A decision to increase the target ratio would thus only have had a nominal retributive effect. Moreover, cost concerns also seem to override what may be deemed effective vigilance by the authorised institution.

The Bank's enforcement strategy of suasion was based on the idea of 'remedy'. The literal definition of a 'remedy' connotes the idea of compliance; the underlying ideas are 'treatment' or 'a means of counteracting or removing anything undesirable' or 'rectify and make good'.[42] Moreover, the very word 'enforcement' was rarely used in the guidance notes or the revised Statement of Principles by the FSA. The Principles distinguished between situations of mandatory revocation and those cases which consisted of problematic issues in authorised institutions. They indicated that persuasion and encouragement were used to ensure compliance and make sure that the authorised institution undertook action to 'rectify' or 'remove anything undesirable'.[43]

---

36 Select Committee on the Bank of England Bill (1945), at p. 16, paras 59–61.

37 Ibid., at pp. xxvii xxx, paras 82–90.

38 For an excellent analysis of the Banking Act 1987 see Hadjiemmanuil, C. (1996) *Banking Regulation and the Bank of England*, London, Lloyds of London Press.

39 Shapiro, M. (1983) 'Administrative discretion: The next stage', *Yale Law Journal*, vol. 92, 1487, at p. 1510.

40 Arthur Andersen & Co SC (1996) *Findings and Recommendations of the Review of Supervision and Surveillance* (Arthur Andersen Report), London, Arthur Andersen Consulting, July, at para. 28.

41 Ibid., at para. 107.

42 Thompson, D. (ed.) (1996) *The Oxford Compact English Dictionary*, Oxford, Oxford University Press, at p. 857.

43 For an overview on when to intervene see Baldwin, R. and Cave, M. (1999) *Understanding Regulation: Theory, Strategy and Practice*, Oxford, Oxford University Press, at p. 107.

This is highlighted by the Bank's enforcement decisions in *Hall v. Bank of England*[44] where allegations of misfeasance in public office failed. The Halls undertook deposit-taking as part and parcel of their property management company. Through continuous supervision the Bank was of the opinion that the company's assets, records and systems were not sufficient to safeguard the interests of its depositors and potential depositors. The proposals to rectify the concerns included changes to the management of the company; restrictions on advertising and accepting deposits; and later sale of unoccupied properties to safeguard the company's assets. The case points out that the idea of 'remedy' is not a cosy arrangement between the regulator and regulated, and the proposals that led to the surrender of authorisation were to avoid the public humiliation of the company having its authorisation revoked. In this instance, reconstruction can clearly be a deterrence mechanism.

Discretion and Transparency in Banking Supervision

Transparency in enforcement is normally considered paramount to indicate to the regulatory community that regulation is implemented consistently and proportionally. Opacity and lack of enforcement activity have traditionally been justified on the grounds of safeguarding the interests of depositors and the concerns surrounding systemic risk where the failure of one bank could place in danger the solvency of other related institutions.[45] While concerns about financial stability exist, the argument for opacity does have limits and it is questionable whether it is feasible to use it in the majority of enforcement decisions. For instance, the other regulatory bodies to which the various components of a bank financial conglomerate are exposed do publicise enforcement actions. Moreover, the fact that US regulatory enforcement involves a wide range of publicised sanctions indicates that the traditional perception of the vulnerability of banks can be challenged.

The discretion-based approach adopted by the Bank was generally supported, although concerns about transparency were prevalent.[46] The transparency in the work of other agencies undertaking investigations into authorised institutions did cause concern for the Bank, and in many respects made it very nervous about such actions. This arose particularly with the DTI's investigation into the fraud surrounding the Blue Arrow affair, which involved the take-over of Manpower. The case involved a subsidiary of National Westminster Bank called County Natwest Ltd (CNW). The investigation raised concerns about the role of CNW in fraudulent activities.[47] The public nature of the inspectorate was of particular concern to the Bank, which felt that the matter was better dealt with between the Bank and the DTI because of

---

44 Unreported Court of Appeal decision, *Hall v. Bank of England*, 19 April 2000, CHANI1999/0854/A3 CH1997 H 544.

45 Goodhart, C. A. E. (1995) 'Some regulatory concerns', Special Paper No. 79, Financial Markets Group, London School of Economics, December, at p. 16.

46 Quinn, B. (1996) 'Rules v. discretion: The case of banking supervision in the light of the debate on monetary policy', Special Paper No. 85, Financial Markets Group, London School of Economics, July, at p. 4.

47 Crystal, M., Spence, D. L. and Temple, V. (1989) *National Westminster Bank PLC. Investigation under Section 432(2) of the Companies Act 1985*, London, DTI/HMSO.

CNW's position at the 'pinnacle of the financial establishment'.[48] According to the Governor of the Bank:

> Banking Supervision was still hoping that we might be able to deal with this ourselves but… they were also beginning to wonder whether it was not rather more wide-ranging than we had appreciated. As it… came into the public domain it was going to be more and more difficult to deal with this, as one might say, between ourselves, the Bank of England and National Westminster, simply because of the public interest and I suppose [they] thought there might be a cover-up.[49]

The public was quick to perceive regulatory capture, which was later held to be unsubstantiated when the allegations from the investigation centred around the Bank hindered its completion. Furthermore, the episode brings into question the opacity of the Bank's enforcement activities and investigation process, thus undermining in many ways the public interest in such affairs. Due to its policy of safeguarding the interests of depositors, it placed the threshold of public interest at an unreachable level before disclosure was made. The justification for adopting such an approach is further cemented by Mr Quinn's statement to the investigation. According to Quinn,[50] the Bank's style of supervision was to avoid official investigations into banks in order to safeguard confidence in the institutions, which could be undermined if knowledge of an investigation became public. The Bank's approach would have been to allow Natwest to undertake a thorough internal investigation.

The evidence given by the Governor and Quinn clearly highlights the distinct approach adopted by the Bank in terms of preventing disclosure of potential problems that could undermine confidence in an institution, rather than ensuring that the allegations are thoroughly resolved and the action taken publicised. Moreover, the evidence given to the investigation sheds some light on the force of moral suasion through Natwest's discussions with the Bank and the method used to ensure compliance.

> Although there was no overt criticism clearly the time devoted to the topic and the nature of the questioning left us feeling we had suffered the 'eyebrow raising treatment'… [T]here was no 'overt criticism' at that meeting but the discussion and questioning had been of a serious nature… There was no doubt about it that one felt it was like being in a headmaster's study on this occasion… We got the impression that they were unhappy with the way things developed. The investigation and the failure in submitting an appropriate report into the affair eventually culminated into an investigation and appointment of inspectors at CNW.[51]

The Blue Arrow episode highlights the reluctance to publicise problems at authorised institutions and the desire to avoid undermining confidence in the industry, the very linchpin that holds the markets together. The Bank would rather exercise appropriate remedies within the confines of its supervisory remit than expose problems. However,

48 Ibid., at p. 119.

49 Ibid., at p. 120.

50 Ibid., at p. 122.

51 Ibid., at pp. 145–146, paras 16.3 and 16.4 respectively.

the lack of transparency does pose problems, as it can give rise to a perception that enforcement is simply not happening.

The next section analyses the FSA approach to enforcement, which has moved somewhat away from the opaque approach highlighted above to a more transparent one. The result is that enforcement actions seem to have set the regulatory regime at a level where the industry sees it as counterproductive to the overall interests of the UK financial services industry.

The Financial Services and Markets Act 2000

The FSA's enforcement system combines the traditional powers and sanctions with the formal inclusion of fines and public censure, so it now has an enormous enforcement arsenal at its disposal. Sanctions such as publicity and fines mean that the FSA could improve the legitimacy of the compliance-based approach.[52] Thus the FSA can respond to commercial realities by enhancing market discipline without necessarily restricting or revoking authorisation.

The role of enforcement, as highlighted earlier, is ultimately to ensure market integrity and maintain investor confidence. The FSA exercises its enforcement powers in order to comply with its regulatory objectives that underpin financial regulation.[53] The objectives provide the legitimacy for its decisions and also give a benchmark to measure whether the action taken is 'proportionate' to the objective it attempts to satisfy.[54] A decision to impose some sort of sanction on a firm or approved person does not have to satisfy all four regulatory objectives simultaneously: it could simply fulfil one of them. This is notwithstanding the fact that the regulatory objectives are interdependent rather than mutually exclusive in terms of reinforcing the appropriate values that promote market confidence. The FSA's enforcement decisions are justified on the basis of its objectives and rules, indicating a more adjudicatory 'top-down' approach rather than the remedial-based approach seen in the USA, which is more akin to a 'bottom-up' approach. This is evident from analysing the enforcement decisions published by the FSA and the US regulators.

The FSA in its mandate to regulate the capital markets has a number of principles that govern its approach to making enforcement decisions, in addition to the objectives. First, its work is based on an 'open and co-operative relationship between the FSA and those whom it regulates'; this principle is not new, but it highlights the relationship desired by the FSA to ensure compliance within the industry.[55] This means enforcement powers will only be exercised when the compliance-based approach of openness and cooperation is not forthcoming and taking enforcement action is the only way of effectively addressing regulatory failure. Secondly, work is based on 'the exercise of the FSA's powers in a manner that is transparent, proportionate and consistent'.[56] Finally, the principle that underpins the FSA's enforcement policy is

52 Cf. Arthur Andersen Report, n. 40 above, at p. 20, para. 106.

53 See pp.18 31.

54 ENF 1.2.1G.

55 ENF 1.3.1G(1); see also FSA (1998) *Meeting Our Responsibilities*, August, at p. 56.

56 ENF 1.3.1G(2).

'fair treatment when exercising its enforcement powers'.[57] These principles provide the framework to promote due process in enforcement decisions. This is necessary considering the FSA has at its disposal a broad range of powers of investigation and sanctions in its 'regulatory toolkit'. The FSA approach is said to be one where it does not utilise enforcement sanctions in the first instance but rather proposes to assist in the remedial action agreed with the firm.[58] However, the reality seems far removed from the rhetoric espoused by the FSA and the industry is rather aggrieved with an FSA policy which is considered more akin to an 'authoritarian approach' based on deterrence; utilising sanctions to ensure orderly markets rather than compliance, consultation and education.[59] This is particularly the case where firms have come clean with compliance failures, but the FSA still considers it necessary to impose a penalty rather than educate the industry through disclosure and consultation.

The Regulatory Decisions Committee

The Regulatory Decisions Committee (RDC) is probably the most prominent and influential body within the enforcement decision-making system, and certainly influences the enforcement climate within the industry.[60] The enforcement decisions taken by the RDC are based on FSA staff findings gathered through their reports or investigations, which are then transferred to the enforcement division for a decision as to whether the matter should go any further. The RDC is responsible for 'statutory notice decisions' and 'statutory notice associated decisions'. These notices are the avenues for the actions the FSA proposes to take against a firm or approved person.

The RDC is responsible for a broad range of enforcement decisions that regulate the permission to undertake authorised activities. For example, it can *inter alia* impose limits and requirements, and restrict or withdraw a firm's or an approved person's permission to undertake regulated activities.[61] These responsibilities entail the issuing of warning notices,[62] decision notices[63] and in some cases supervisory decisions.[64] The FSA is required to issue a warning notice indicating the reasons for initiating an action, identifying the misconduct deemed to have taken place and the proposed sanction to be imposed. It then proceeds with a decision notice that will outline the decision and state when it will take effect. The approved firm or person will have the right to refer the decision to the Appeals Tribunal.[65]

The RDC exists outside the FSA's management structure but is accountable to the FSA board for its decisions; this provides a distance and a perception of

57 ENF 1.3.1G(3).

58 ENF 1.3.4; see also ENF 11, ENF 11.3. For background see FSA (2000), *Enforcement Manual*, CP 65.

59 *The Financial Services Practitioner Panel, Annual Report* (2005/6), at p. 5.

60 DEC 4.

61 DEC 4.1.4G–5G.

62 FSMA 2000, s. 387.

63 FSMA 2000, s. 388.

64 FSMA 2000, s. 394.

65 DEC 5, 'References to the Tribunal, publication and service of notices', see DEC 5.1.3G.

independence through the separation of the body administering enforcement decisions and the regulator/supervisor of firms and individuals.[66] The RDC is not a statutory body like the Practitioner Panel or the Consumer Panel, even though it exercises enforcement powers under s. 395 of the FSMA 2000, so it does not have the same kind of resources to function independently. The individuals appointed to the RDC are not directly employed by the FSA, other than its chair; the members are people with experience of the financial services industry and consumer interests. To create a spirit of independence, the chair of the RDC is appointed by the FSA on the recommendation of an independent group set up for that specific reason. Subsequently the chair nominates members of the committee, whom the FSA then appoints. The separation of the RDC and the FSA seems to suggest that an appropriate degree of independent decision-making exists, but the underlying basis of RDC decisions is heavily dependent on the FSA's findings and conclusions, thus reducing the likelihood of the RDC actually hearing the other side of the story and coming to an 'independent decision'. The dialogue between the two undermines in some respects the Chinese wall that should exist between them to enhance the independence of the RDC. The review of enforcement post-Legal & General has fleshed out a number of findings and recommendations which have attempted to strengthen the independence of the RDC, as reviewed later in this chapter.

FSA Powers of Investigation

The FSA has a number of gateways to seek information and documents from a firm.[67] The powers of investigation also include the appointment of third parties – skilled persons to investigate and report on nominated areas.[68] Section 165 of the FSMA 2000 outlines the FSA's power to seek information and documents from firms which are needed to assess compliance. These powers extend to a broad range of operations and associated parties – for instance, members of the firm to monitor ownership or to assist an overseas regulator.[69] An investigation may be initiated if the FSA is concerned that a firm or individual has contravened its permission, breached an FSA rule or is no longer fit or proper to perform functions in relation to a regulated firm.[70] The investigation may require the firm or individual to assist the investigator by answering questions on the matter.[71]

Publicising investigations into the affairs of a firm or approved person is a rather more sensitive issue than simply advocating the use of publicity to deter future non-compliance by a name-and-shame strategy. The investigation process is a formal attempt to gather information and documents to assess whether a concern needs further examination by the enforcement division. While this role is clearly legitimate, publicity of investigations could lead to a stand-off between the firm

66 DEC 4.2.3G.

67 See pp. pp.57–58.

68 For an analysis of skilled persons see pp.153–173.

69 ENF 2.3G.

70 FSMA 2000, s. 168(4)–(5).

71 ENF 2.4G.

and the regulator, giving the latter the arduous task of seeking information and documents with little cooperation from the investigated institution or person. This would inevitably lead to a cat-and-mouse scenario with the possibility of firms or persons not 'coming clean' because the disclosure of the investigation will have already caused damage to its reputation, and more will come with the publication of the final enforcement notice.

However, a balance must be struck because market rumours are not always based on idle gossip and can indicate a credible concern, in which case the FSA may have to exercise its right to disclose that it is investigating the issue. It can disclose the fact that it has initiated an investigation if *inter alia* it considers it necessary to maintain market confidence or consumer protection.[72] If the FSA simply ignored such rumours then it would seem as though it was not taking seriously its role of surveillance in the capital markets through which such information would be gathered. BCCI and Barings demonstrate that the financial markets were 'ringing alarm bells' long before formal action was taken. Consequently, disclosure of sensitive information about an investigation would undermine confidence in a firm or approved person (more so than publicising enforcement decisions) in a market where confidence is inextricably linked to integrity and honesty. This is based on the point that an enforcement notice acts as a 'final decision', thus closing the case, whereas disclosure of an investigation effectively initiates prolonged exposure of a possible wrongdoing without necessarily leading to any sanction.

FSA Enforcement Powers

The FSA has a variety of administrative, civil and criminal sanctions within its power to deal with a range of compliance failures, from the most routine to the most serious that evince criminal wrongdoing; offences range from a failure to file regulatory returns to undertaking regulated business without permission. This section will review some of the sanctions the FSA has and the types of failure that have led to their application. It will particularly focus on the FSA's use of publicity and administrative fines to deal with compliance failures, as an example of decriminalising criminal monetary penalties. In addition it will consider whether the enforcement approach is commensurate to the failures that are evident and result in their application. Indeed, the FSA seems to have taken to task those Kagan and Scholz[73] consider to be 'amoral calculators', 'organisationally incompetent' and even the 'political citizens' to express to the industry that it is willing to initiate enforcement proceedings for the purposes of ensuring compliance by either refusing permission for firms to undertake regulated activities, imposing a fine or publicising the wrongdoing.

The FSMA 2000 provides the FSA with powers to control entry to and exit from the financial markets.[74] First, it prohibits those unauthorised from carrying on regulated activities; secondly, permission is granted to carry on regulated activities

72 ENF 2.13.4G.

73 Kagan and Scholz, n. 11 above.

74 FSMA 2000, Part IV, 'Permission to Carry on Regulated Activities', ss. 40 55.

provided the firm or individual conforms continuously to prudential rules, standards and principles that govern their business.[75]

An application for Part IV permission requires satisfaction of the 'threshold conditions' in Schedule 6 on a continuing basis.[76] The power of the FSA here is broad, and includes the authority to change permission if it thinks the regulatory objectives would not be achieved or would be in some way damaged.[77] The FSA has the authority to vary the Part IV permission on its own initiative if, for example, the authorised person fails or is likely to fail to meet the threshold conditions, or it is desirable to vary the permission to protect the interests of consumers and potential consumers.[78] This sanction would be used for the most serious failures to comply with the threshold conditions, giving rise to connotations of 'amoral calculator' or 'organisationally incompetent'.

The two most prominent reasons for refusing an application for permission are a lack of adequate resources and the suitability of those applying to undertake regulated activities. The evidence suggests that the firm or individual must be either an 'amoral calculator' or 'organisationally incompetent' for the permission to be refused or revoked. For example, the FSA varied the permission granted to Oaktree Financial Services as it found evidence of mishandling clients' money.[79] In the interests of consumers the permission was varied as the FSA did not consider the firm to be fit and proper on the basis that it did not conduct its business with integrity and in accordance with proper standards. The variation culminated in the firm effectively being refused permission to conduct any regulated activities. The FSA could also exercise these powers to satisfy a request from an overseas regulator where *inter alia* the assistance would be reciprocal. Alternatively it could act on the evidence of legal actions in other jurisdictions. This provides the FSA with extensive scope to exercise its judgement about authorisation. In the case of Target Asset Management the application for Part IV permission was refused on the grounds that the company was associated with a Mr Shefket (sole owner), who was subject to a US criminal fugitive arrest warrant issued in North Carolina for investment fraud; evidence such as this called into question in the FSA's mind his honesty, integrity and reputation.[80]

The FSA can also impose, vary or remove requirements relating to acquiring control or assisting an overseas regulator, and it can change the asset requirements of regulated firms.[81] For example, the FSA could impose limitations to control the number of customers a firm could deal with, stipulate the types of investment it could undertake or impose requirements on not undertaking new business. A distinction between limitations and requirements does exist: the latter are more burdensome in that they instruct the firm to take or refrain from certain activities, whereas the former restrict the degree to which the firm can undertake an activity. The imposition of a

---

75 FSMA 2000, ss. 19–23, and in particular s. 29.

76 FSMA 2000, s. 41.

77 ENF 3.2.1G.

78 ENF 3.3.1G–3G.

79 First Supervisory Notice, Oaktree Financial Services Ltd, 20 February 2004.

80 FSA (2004) 'Final Notice: Target Asset Management Ltd', 8 April.

81 FSMA 2000, ss. 45–48.

requirement means that it needs to be fulfilled for the firm to retain its permission to undertake a regulated activity. At the other end of the spectrum of enforcement is the power to cancel and withdraw authorisation. This power is exercised by the FSA when it has serious reservations about the way in which the business of a regulated firm is conducted. The gap between varying and cancelling an authorisation is very fine: the distinction lies in the fact that latter requires the completion of a hearing on the decision before it can be made.[82]

The FSA must exercise its powers to vary a Part IV permission in a way that is proportionate to the concern raised by the conduct of the firm.[83] The responsibility to ensure that a firm is compliant rests on its directors and senior management. The FSA would thus focus on *inter alia* whether the firm has internal controls to capture the risks that emanate from its activities, and where internal controls do exist whether they capture the risk portfolio of new ventures. In order to assess whether a firm exercises its own initiative powers, the FSA would assess the level of cooperation it experiences during the supervisory process. If it appears that the firm is not able to implement the changes necessary to ensure compliance, the FSA may consider varying the permission because the manner in which the firm is conducting its affairs raises serious concerns – for example if the firm's conduct calls into question its compliance with the threshold conditions or it does not achieve the appropriate standard of fit and proper behaviour, which could even expose it to the risk of criminal prosecution.[84]

The authority to withdraw approval or prohibit an individual from undertaking controlled functions is set out in ss. 63(1) and 56(2) of the FSMA 2000. These powers are available if the FSA considers the individual approved person or firm is not fit and proper to perform controlled functions. In respect to both powers the FSA's decision needs to comply with the regulatory objectives that underpin financial regulation and supervision. It is the severity of the case that distinguishes an order for a withdrawal or prohibition. The FSA in its power to withdraw approval could take into account a variety of factors, and even events outside the remit of controlled functions.[85] It assesses whether an approved person undertakes controlled functions with the appropriate level of probity, integrity and competency. In the case of Geoffrey Darin Brownlee-Jones, the FSA refused an application for approval on the grounds that he did not disclose all his criminal convictions, including a caution for indecent assault on a female and criminal damage.[86] In respect to the exercise of a prohibition, which is more severe, the order could be either a complete ban on performing any function connected with regulated activities or restricted to a specific controlled function.[87]

The FSA has the power to discipline firms and approved persons without imposing limitations or requirements or cancelling their permission to undertake regulated

82 DEC 5.5.1G and 5.5.3G.

83 ENF 3.3.3G.

84 ENF 3.5.8G.

85 ENF 7.5.1G 7.5.5G.

86 FSA (2003) 'Final Notice: Geoffrey Darin Brownlee-Jones', 28 November.

87 ENF 8.2.1G.

activities.[88] These tools provide the FSA with the power to ensure compliance with the FSMA 2000 and, more importantly, demonstrate to the public that its rules, standards and principles are being upheld. The enforcement sanctions at its disposal under Parts V and XI are public statements, public censures and financial penalties. It also has protective and remedial actions to ensure a firm continuously meets the threshold conditions and the appropriate standard of care when undertaking controlled functions. While the FSA has a range of enforcement sanctions at its disposal, it is clear from its guidance that it will also indicate concerns informally within the supervisory process. In these circumstances the FSA would not publicly sanction a firm or approved person for minor instances of non-compliance, but may uphold the FSMA 2000 by issuing either an informal warning or a more formal private warning to deter imprudent behaviour. The private warning would formalise the FSA's objection by 'cautioning' the firm or approved person about their inappropriate behaviour. This warning would form part of its compliance history and would be taken into account in future incidents of non-compliance. The FSA is, in these circumstances, given the discretion to consider a private warning despite the length of time that has lapsed between any previous private warning and the new breach of rules. Moreover, a pattern could emerge in the issue of informal and private warnings which, taken cumulatively, suggests an inappropriate culture towards compliance in the organisation.

The FSA uses a broad criterion to determine whether to take disciplinary action, applied on a case-by-case basis. The factors listed by the FSA are mutually exclusive, so they do not all have to be evident in a single case. A breach of the regulatory objectives is a significant indication of whether disciplinary action should be taken, as is evident in the criterion. Moreover, the FSA would consider whether the firm or approved person sought to comply with any guidance it issued on the subject, and the degree to which they tried to comply. The first factor the FSA could take into account is the seriousness of the suspected breach of the rules and whether it evidences a deliberate or reckless attitude. This factor would gauge the degree of culpability of the firm or approved person in the non-compliance. The FSA would also consider the length of time over which the breach continued and the point in time the breach was identified by those with responsibility; whether the firm or approved person has gained any benefit from the breach by either making a profit or avoiding a loss; and the extent to which a firm or approved person cooperated in the investigation or the measures it put in place to rectify the breach.[89] In the decision to exercise disciplinary action the FSA could also take into account the previous conduct of the firm or approved person, such as previous disciplinary action by itself or a former regulator.[90]

The FSA clearly places the responsibility for compliance on the firm rather than on the approved persons within that firm. Its guidance for both firms and approved persons is very elaborate, based on statute, rules, statements of principles and a

88 ENF 11.2.2G.

89 ENF 11.4.1G(1)–(2).

90 ENF 11.4.1G(3) and (5) respectively; see also FSA, CP 65, n. 58 above.

code of conduct.[91] The firm would, in a suspicion of a breach, need to establish that it took reasonable steps to prevent non-compliance by its approved persons. In circumstances where the firm can satisfy this standard of care the FSA would seek to assess the personal culpability of the approved person involved and the due diligence which is expected of an individual exercising the relevant controlled functions. For instance, to exercise disciplinary action against an approved person the FSA would want to assess whether the individual had complied with the relevant principles.

The FSA has the power to initiate criminal sanctions for a broad range of offences which undermine the financial system and threaten depositors' and investors' interests. A significant number of the offences protect the perimeter of the regulated activities – for example, undertaking a regulated activity without permission or deceiving the public by claiming to be regulated.[92] The FSA, the Secretary of State or the Director of Public Prosecutions can institute criminal prosecution.[93] This power does not prevent the FSA from initiating civil actions or remedies to protect individuals and compensate them for any losses they have incurred by imposing an injunction or seeking restitution. It may also seek to exercise its regulatory powers to withdraw permission or prohibit the carrying on of regulated activities or functions by a firm or approved person. The decision to institute criminal proceedings is based on the criteria used by the Crown Prosecution Service (the Code for Crown Prosecutors), which involve the key factors of whether there is sufficient evidence to prosecute each charge and whether it is in the public interest to do so.[94] The Code for Crown Prosecutors also provides a broad list of factors that need to be taken into account when deciding on a criminal prosecution, such as the seriousness of the offence, whether the defendant was in a position of authority or trust and whether the offence evidences premeditation.

Publicity

The formal introduction of publicising misconduct in the marketplace through 'public censure' or 'public statement' highlights the importance the industry places on its business reputation.[95] This regulatory tool is not the same as that conferred on the FSA, pursuant to *inter alia* s. 391(5) of the FSMA 2000, to publicise variations of Part IV permission. Public censure can be used when disciplinary action is required but the misconduct does not warrant a financial penalty. This penalty could be imposed on those deemed to be 'political citizens' or 'organisationally incompetent'. The guidance does not indicate how the FSA will determine its decision on either issuing a public censure or a public statement in a given case. The former obviously gives rise to a policy of shaming rather than simply naming individual firms or approved persons, which is concurrent with the latter type of regulatory tool. Public censure as a means of punishment is also considered a less punitive sanction than a financial

91 See pp. 79–105.

92 ENF 15.

93 ENF 15.3.2G; FSMA 2000, ss. 401–402.

94 ENF 15.5, Annex 1G.

95 FSMA 2000, ss. 66 and 205; for guidance see ENF 12.

penalty, so it is ordered provided the firm or approved person has not benefited from the non-compliance and compensation does not ensue from the breach. This policy highlights that 'naming and shaming' has a distinct deterrent effect above and beyond simply publicising final notices.[96] The introduction of publicity of non-compliance is said to achieve confidence in the financial system and increases public awareness of the standard expected of firms and approved persons. The justification for such a power is to promote the FSA's accountability for the performance of its functions in enforcing the regulatory regime. Publicity of such actions provides a further mechanism to secure compliance and, in many respects, fills the intermediate range of sanctions that has been encouraged.

Publicity of non-compliance can act as a deterrent because of the damage it can cause to the reputation of institutions – damage they would wish to avoid. More importantly, it shows that regulation is enforced, thus satisfying the objective of protecting the consumer.[97] The necessity for publicity needs to be monitored due to concern regarding the perception of 'swelling' prosecution that can create an environment which is considered harassing and inefficient.[98] This is because enforcement decisions need to consider a number of factors in order to ensure observance of the regulatory order, which usually requires the cooperation of the regulated. A hostile environment could be detrimental to the overall regulatory strategy.[99] According to Hawkins, the imposition of sanctions demonstrates that the regulator has the appropriate level of authority over the regulated and avoids suggestions of regulatory capture in the public's mind.[100] The imposition of sanctions also acts as a warning to the public of what to avoid in the marketplace as a consumer. According to Hawkins, publicity exonerates the regulator by showing that it is a credible enforcement authority, as it highlights rule-breaking and evidences the effectiveness of the agency to deal with such matters in an efficient manner.[101]

Publicity has generally been used as a mechanism to censure the regulated by disclosing to the industry the wrongdoing that has taken place, whether on a firm or an industry-wide level, and warning of possible enforcement and supervisory action if failures are not addressed. For example, industry-wide publicity of possible problems is brought to firms' attention through the FSA's 'Dear Chief Executive' letters. However, publicity could also be used in a positive way to show the industry good practice that has been found through the supervisory process or brought to the FSA's attention through other means, such as from a firm itself. This would avoid the perception that the FSA is simply focused on exposing wrongdoing in the industry and is not using its machinery to disclose best practice as well. Such publicity could

96 ENF 12.2.1G and 12.3.3G.

97 ENF 1.2.1G(2).

98 Hawkins, K. (1998) 'Law as last resort', in Baldwin, R., Scott, C. and Hood, C. (eds) *A Reader on Regulation*, Oxford, Oxford University Press, at p. 289.

99 Braithwaite, J. (1989) *Crime, Shame and Re-integration*, Cambridge, Cambridge University Press, at p. 75; Box, S. (1983) *Power, Corruption and Mystification*, London, Tavistock, at p. 9; Chambliss, W. J. (1988) *Exploring Criminology*, New York, Macmillan, at p. 54.

100 Hawkins, n. 98 above, at p. 291.

101 Ibid., at p. 292.

be undertaken on an industry-wide basis or individually at a firm level. The use of best practice would act as an incentive for the industry to 'clean up' its act so that firms do not lose competitive advantage, rather than trying to achieve this through censure. The FSA does, through its consumer education role, try to inform consumers about what to look for when deciding on buying financial products. Publicity of best practice for the purposes of regulatory compliance is somewhat different, as it draws attention to what the FSA views as good compliance practice in a certain area, such as compliance with laundering guidelines. This also fulfils the FSA's role as educator and consultant, not by it being drawn into acting in a capacity of 'shadow director' but by harnessing the industry and its participants to improve compliance.

Fines

Financial penalties are another new sanction to add to the FSA's arsenal of enforcement tools. This sanction can be imposed on a firm and approved persons under ss. 206, 64 and 66 of the FSMA 2000, respectively. The use of financial penalties is another way for the FSA to achieve compliance with the regulatory objectives and deter those regulated from acts or omissions of non-compliance. It is suggested that such penalties would only be utilised in the most extreme forms of regulatory misconduct. The decision to impose fines depends upon the nature of the derogation, in a similar manner to other enforcement sanctions.[102] The FSA assesses factors such as the seriousness of the misconduct and the degree of culpability of the firm or approved person. The impact of the fine on the firm or approved person is also important, and must take account of the hardship that may ensue from imposing the penalty.[103] The FSA is mindful of the need to pitch civil fines at the right level to ensure that they are neither too low nor too high. In the former case the sanction would have little impact to deter or have a retributive effect, whereas in the latter the sanction would be too punitive and may not be proportionate to the offence committed. In this regard the level of cooperation exercised by the firm is also taken into account and can lead to a reduction in the size of the fine.

It is often noted in enforcement decisions whether or not firms have been cooperative. Indeed, it is crucial for a firm to cooperate in such matters, first to ensure it does not get tarnished with a reputation of being difficult, which could imply that it has something to hide, and secondly to avoid a needlessly larger sanction than may otherwise be imposed. This cooperation may be in the form of setting up an internal investigative team, giving information to the investigators or initiating investigations by independent accounting firms. For example, AXA Sun Life was fined £500,000 by the FSA for its failure to have in place effective systems and controls over its group entities for the purpose of selling its life and pensions products. Another failure was not to have notified the FSA about the breach in a timely manner. As a result of these failures a fine was considered an appropriate sanction.[104] The size of the fine was reduced as a result of AXA's cooperation in remedying the matter, including

102 FSMA 2000, ss. 66 and 206; ENF 13.3.2G–3G.

103 ENF 13.3.3G(3).

104 FSA (2004) 'Final Notice: AXA Sun Life Plc', 21 December.

withdrawal of its advertisements, voluntarily appointing Ernst & Young to report on its systems and controls, sending remedial letters to its customers and assisting the FSA during its investigation.[105]

A concern about civil fines is the unspecified limit to the level of the fine, but this is not across the board. The FSA has adopted a tariff of fines for many routine violations of administrative regulations, such as failure to provide timely prudential returns or other critical reports.[106] The guidance in this area provides in its annex an indicative scale of penalties for late submission of reports: a delay from one to seven days late to 22–28 days late in submitting reports is given, with a range of financial penalties depending on the size of fees the firm pays. A tariff system moves towards a rules-based approach and culminates in a checklist to assess whether the institution or person is in compliance. But for routine enforcement such an approach ensures consistency and, more importantly, highlights to the industry that the regulator will act in this area.

Financial penalties can also be used for breaches of prudential regulations. In this case, however, further examination suggests the measure may not be as retributive as first thought, unless the FSA proposes to follow up the fine and change the target and trigger ratios to a considerable extent. According to the Arthur Andersen Report, changes to these ratios generally occurred when the institution's current ratios were considerably over target.[107] Furthermore, according to a study by Lucas on the Basel measures, the compliance strategy of backtesting internal models leads to an underreporting of market risk to supervisors and thus does not entirely achieve supervisory objectives. Lucas advocates stricter enforcement sanctions to ensure that banks implement appropriate internal models.[108] The use of fines in this area could thus be simply 'creative enforcement'. This problem is exacerbated because the underlying standards governing prudential requirements are broad and so introducing financial penalties could raise other problems, such as how to identify the point at which a breach has occurred.

The FSA and Cooperation with Overseas Authorities

The global nature of the financial system necessitates cooperation between regulatory authorities, as it is an inevitable fact that corporate failures and financial crime will affect other jurisdictions and require their assistance to manage the fallout. The FSMA 2000 provides a general obligation on the FSA to cooperate where appropriate to reduce financial crime and share information with overseas authorities. This provision constitutes the platform, together with a range of formal gateways and memoranda of understanding between the FSA and overseas regulators, by which it can cooperate with extra-national authorities. This responsibility will be assessed, like the exercise of its other responsibilities, on the basis of the FSA's regulatory

105 Ibid., paras 3.3 3.4.

106 ENF 13.5.1G.

107 Arthur Andersen Report, n. 40 above.

108 Lucas, A. (2001) 'Evaluating the Basel Guidelines for backtesting banks' internal risk management models', *Journal of Money, Credit and Banking*, vol. 33, 826.

objectives; these are territorial in nature, whereas the provision for cooperation with extra-national regulators may see a wider notion of 'public interest' applied in the execution of the statutory framework and legitimated under the FSMA 2000 s. 2(2)(a) provisions about market confidence and s. 2(2)(c) provisions about consumer protection, both of which have the capacity to transcend national boundaries.

Cooperation with overseas regulators also includes taking enforcement actions when there is evidence that UK-regulated firms are not cooperating with the FSA's overseas counterparts. The FSA fined Credit Suisse First Boston International (CSFBi), authorised in the UK, £4 million for its failure to cooperate and misleading the Japanese authorities regarding its derivatives business in Japan.[109] The fine was deemed a signal to the financial industry that misleading regulators is a very grave offence which undermines the credibility of financial markets. The case also epitomises the characteristics of Kagan and Scholz's 'amoral calculator':[110] the facts disclosed examples of concealing the true nature of activities from regulators to ensure the firm continued undertaking the business it was pursuing in Japan. CSFBi, formally known as Credit Suisse Financial Products, between April 1995 and December 1998 sold sophisticated derivatives which concealed bad company assets that had depreciated by not disclosing them in financial statements. Credit Suisse Financial Products also systematically disguised its operations in Japan to suggest it was undertaking securities business, fearing that the operations would be construed, legitimately, as banking business for which it was not licensed: the Japanese authorities prevented banks from undertaking securities business and required firewalls between specific business entities, and this particularly exposed foreign banks accustomed to different organisational structures. The extent of CSFBi's actions to avoid detection included concealment and in some instances destruction of documents to avoid the Japanese authorities detecting the true nature of the business.

The evidence pointed to a number of systematic incidents across Japan and London of non-compliance by a large number of employees. For instance, Antony Blunden, the CSFBi global head of compliance, was prohibited from acting in any compliance function connected with regulated activities due to his conduct falling short of what is construed as fit and proper: the evidence pointed to a complete disregard of the local regulations and support of a policy to prevent full disclosure of the business to the Japanese authorities.[111] The facts associated with the company and its employees pointed to a high degree of culpability, with a deliberate attempt to avoid disruption to its business in Japan and avoid tax liability by concealing the truth about its operations.

109 FSA (2002) 'Final Notice: Credit Suisse First Boston International', 11 December; FSA (2002) 'FSA fines Credit Suisse First Boston International £4 million', press release, FSA/PN/124/2002, 19 December, available at www.fsa.gov.uk/pubs/press/2002.

110 Kagan and Scholz, n. 11 above.

111 FSA (2003) 'Final Notice: Antony Blunden', 10 November; FSA (2003) 'Final Notice: Robert Stevens', 10 November. Stevens was prohibited from performing any function in relation to any regulated activity because of his conduct, which included the dissemination of information to the Japanese authorities to mislead them deliberately during the audit of CSFBi's business operations.

FSA Sanctions and the Human Rights Act 1998

The decriminalisation of sanctions has required a number of checks and balances to be put in place, as seen earlier in the discussion of the changing burden of proof, so that regulators do not abuse their power by simply reclassifying offences into less serious ones where the ability to impose punitive administrative and civil sanctions has a simpler basis and avoids the due process attached to successfully prosecuting an individual. This is especially the case with the introduction of the Human Rights Act 1998, as it provides additional safeguards to avoid the abuse of decriminalising sanctions. This is a particularly important issue for the FSA, given its arsenal of sanctions and the application of the Human Rights Act to the responsibility exercised by the FSA over the UK financial markets.[112] The principles emanating from the 1998 Act are far-reaching: they apply to both firms, as legal persons, and individuals undertaking regulated activities or significant functions on behalf of a firm. The 1998 Act requires the FSA and the Appeals Tribunal to interpret the enforcement powers of the FSMA 2000 in the light of, *inter alia*, decisions and opinions of the European Court of Human Rights governing the European Convention on Human Rights (ECHR).[113]

The FSA policy of having a broad range of enforcement sanctions of both a non-punitive and a punitive nature is crucial to curb the various degrees of non-compliance, from the least to the most culpable of offences. The distinction between civil and criminal sanctions is not clear-cut, with the introduction of severe civil sanctions which could prima facie be construed as criminal sanctions disguised to avoid the strict procedures governing criminal prosecution. The severity of the sanctions and the safeguards governing them to protect an individual's integrity and liberty are thus inextricably linked.[114] The controversy over this issue was heightened by a concern that the architects of the FSA were simply decriminalising enforcement sanctions.

The point with civil regulatory sanctions is whether the principles governing the Human Rights Act 1998, which emanate from the jurisprudence of the ECHR, could construe them as criminal sanctions. Article 6(1) upholds the principle of the 'rule of law', with the right to a fair trial for both a civil and a criminal action, by asserting an individual's right to a timely, independent public hearing.[115] Article 6(2)–(3) also provides further procedural safeguards, such as the need for a presumption of innocence in law, legal clarity and assistance to ensure a fair hearing.[116] These

112 Singh, D. (2000) 'Civil and criminal enforcement methods and sanctions in banking regulation and supervision', paper delivered at Conference on Rules, Incentives and Sanctions: Enforcement in Financial Regulation, Financial Markets Group, London School of Economics, 26 May.

113 Human Rights Act 1998, s. 2(1).

114 See section on burden of proof on pp. 120–121.

115 *H v. Belgium* (1988) 10 EHRR 339; see also *Ringeissen v. Austria* (1979) 1 EHRR 455, para. 95; *Pretto v. Italy* (1984) 6 EHRR 182.

116 *Austria v. Italy* (1963) 6 Yearbook 740, 782; *Ekbetani v. Sweden* (1991) 13 EHRR 457; *Stanford v. UK* (1986) 8 EHRR 272.

safeguards form the basic measures; other assurances are, for instance, a right of access to the courts[117] and equality of arms.[118]

The crucial issue governing sanctions, for this purpose, is their classification into criminal and civil divisions. The jurisprudence of the ECHR points out that the issue of classification is to be determined by its own decisions rather than domestic opinion:[119] the nature of the offence and the severity of the sanction are more authoritative, objective principles than simply following the domestic approach. A domestic policy of decriminalising sanctions is thus not prohibited, but the ECHR provides a check to make sure the appropriate procedures are followed to ensure a fair trial where criminal sanctions have been substituted by civil or administrative penalties. In these circumstances the court will accept the domestic position if the offence is classed as criminal, whereas it will not be so clear-cut in the case of a civil or regulatory offence. First, the court would need to consider whether the offence is classified as criminal in other European jurisdictions; if it is the court may lean towards taking the same approach.[120] Secondly, does the offence apply to a specific group of individuals or to the population at large? In the former case the courts have ruled the offence is civil by nature for Article 6 purposes.[121] In *Wickramsinghe* the Privy Council ruled that a disciplinary hearing to determine whether an individual was fit to practise medicine was a civil rather than a criminal case.[122] In instances where the civil offence is deemed to be severe (by the underlying deterrent and punitive nature of its sanctions) it is important to assess whether it is more appropriate to classify it as a criminal offence. For example, a disqualification order or a heavy fine could suggest the offence requires the safeguards more akin to a criminal trial to ensure an individual's livelihood or integrity is not permanently damaged without the proportionate due process.[123] The use of disqualification or prohibition is the last resort in financial services, and would be like issuing a death penalty for a firm or individual. In the extreme case a firm or individual may seek to surrender their permission rather than face the embarrassment of losing the right to undertake regulated activities. Thus simply suggesting that the offence is civil and governs a small subset of individuals is too simplistic a position. The severity of the civil or regulatory sanction needs to be given more prominence when the effect is so detrimental. Moreover, as seen above, the tribunals do in many instances make concessions in such circumstances so that the appropriate safeguards are in place to ensure a fair trial.

The Court of Appeal decision in the case of Bertrand Fleurose,[124] a senior cash arbitrage trader employed by JP Morgan Securities, clarifies the application of the

117 *Golder v. UK* (1979) 1 EHRR 524.

118 *Dombo Beheer BV v. Nertherlands* (1994) 18 EHRR 213, para. 33.

119 *Engel v. Netherlands* (1976) 1 EHRR 647.

120 *Ozturk v. Germany* (1984) 6 EHRR 409.

121 Cf. *Campbell and Fell v. UK* (1985) 7 EHRR 165.

122 *Wickramsinghe v. UK*, App. No. 31503/96, 9 December 1997; *Brown v. UK*, App. No. 38644/97, 24 November 1998.

123 *Ozturk*, n. 120 above; *Lutz v. Germany* (1988) 10 EHRR 182.

124 *R v. Securities and Futures Authority Ltd and another ex parte Fleurose* [2001] EWCA Civ 2015 [2002] IRLR 297.

HRA 1998 to civil or regulatory disciplinary action in the financial services sector. The SFA investigated allegations that Fleurose and his manager manipulated the FTSE 100 Index to avoid an obligation to pay £475,500 on an option contract they had entered into with a counterparty based on the price differential between the FTSE 100 Index and the S&P 500 Index. The SFA suspended Fleurose from acting as a registered person for two years and ordered him to pay £175,000 towards the costs it incurred. Fleurose sought a judicial review of the SFA proceedings on the grounds that they breached Article 6(1) of the HRA 1998: the proceedings were analogous to a criminal hearing, so appropriate measures in accordance with Articles 6(2)–(3) and 7 needed to be in place to ensure a presumption of innocence, a right to legal assistance and a right to be informed about the nature of the accusation. Fleurose also claimed his right to avoid self-incrimination was breached because he was compelled to give evidence during the investigation.

The appeal against the High Court decision (not to classify the allegations against Fleurose as criminal charges) failed and the decision by Morrison J was upheld. The Court of Appeal decided the SFA proceedings were proportionate to the allegations and did not give rise to criminal charges that would have required further safeguards to ensure a fair trial. The court placed particular reliance on the decision in *Han and Yau*,[125] where it was held the criteria provided in *Engel*[126] needed to be interpreted cumulatively if the single criterion of the nature of the offence and its severity does not give rise to a clear outcome. The courts' case-by-case approach to such a claim is significant: the inference can be drawn that the proceedings and the decision by the SFA were, in this case, proportionate in the light of the penalty imposed. However, scope still remains to challenge such regulatory proceedings if the punishment is, for instance, an order to disqualify an individual from permanently pursuing their livelihood.[127]

Reflections on the FSA Approach to Enforcement

The FSA's approach to enforcement has come under considerable scrutiny in many respects due to the move towards modernising financial regulation and placing confidence in the industry and the interests of consumers above those of individual firms. This approach can therefore be examined by placing the interests of practitioners and consumers at opposite ends of the compliance continuum. The other end of the enforcement continuum is the deterrence-based sanctions. The Consumer Panel has attempted to place more emphasis on this end of the spectrum in light of its view that the industry gives little due regard to the safety of consumers. Its findings indicate that the FSA's approach of strong sanctions and publicity of non-compliance evidences its commitment to protect consumer interests, and the panel advocates a similar approach to ensure the industry is mindful of these interests when financial products are sold. However, whether publicity and fines are the appropriate way is obviously challenged by practitioners: the practitioner voice is calling for more

125 *Han and Yau v. Commissioners of Customs and Excise* [2001] EWCA Civ 1048.

126 *Engel*, n. 119 above.

127 *Ex parte Fleurose*, n. 124 above, at p. 301, para. 66.

dialogue and pragmatism in the enforcement approach and the consumer voice is calling for more punitive sanctions to heighten the right of consumers to be treated fairly. These are interests the FSA needs to balance; the view so far is that it is rather heavy-handed in its enforcement approach and lacks the appropriate level of dialogue with the industry.

The complex nature of the financial services industry also means that the FSA needs to have a more sophisticated method of enforcement than simply a 'command-and-control' approach. Indeed, a significant amount of dialogue is required for the rules to be applied properly in light of the fact that the industry is complex and financial products are exposed to a variety of risks. Thus the first mechanism to ensure compliance needs to be cooperation and consultation. A difficult issue to balance is the extent to which a regulator should be over- or under-accommodating in cases of non-compliance. It is inevitable that the regulated will on occasion get things wrong. But it is important that a regulator takes a pragmatic view and avoids being too draconian, which would create a climate of hostility between itself and the regulated; such a climate could result in compliance failures being brushed under the carpet to avoid the regulator detecting them, leading to obviously more serious concerns. The practitioners' views of the FSA's approach to enforcement were highlighted in the qualitative aspects of the 2004 Practitioner Panel survey. It indicated that practitioners did not consider the process to be fair, but rather to be 'hostile' and 'costly'.[128] This survey also highlighted that the FSA did not accommodate minor errors and practitioners considered the enforcement process as too mechanical, leading to a culture of having constantly to refer to lawyers for advice. In practitioners' minds this deflected attention away from important issues of greater regulatory significance.

The regulatory climate can be undermined by a lack of positive feedback published by the regulator about the industry. To ensure a climate of cooperation a regulator needs to do more than simply disclose and punish non-compliance; it also needs to publish evidence of good practice to bring the two-way traffic in line. Publication of good practice can encourage the industry to stop and look at what competitors are doing and how they are doing it. A dialogue of this sort, with positive and negative highlights, is an incentive to change their practices. The Practitioner Panel survey called into question the FSA's approach because it does not adopt a style of enforcement with negotiation and dialogue at its centre: the FSA failed to publicise good practice in the industry.[129] Its approach to enforcement is considered to have caused an imbalance in the application of regulation: the survey suggests the FSA is trying to appease consumer concerns by digging for non-compliance at large institutions to show that it is being proactive.[130]

---

128 Financial Services Practitioner Panel (2004) *Third Survey of the FSA's Regulatory Performance*, December, at p. 80.

129 Ibid.

130 Ibid., at p. 82.

The Legal & General Tribunal Decision

L&G's referral of an FSA decision to the Financial Services and Markets Tribunal exposed a number of gaps in the enforcement process, and indeed led to the subsequent review of enforcement.[131] The action challenged the FSA's decision to impose a fine on L&G for failing to comply with procedures governing the sale of endowment mortgages, and instances of mis-selling these products to people considered to be low-risk customers between 1 January 1997 and 31 December 1999. This was an industry-wide problem that needed a concerted approach to rectify the mis-selling and compensate those who incurred shortfalls in their investment to cover their mortgage.[132] The major public concern warranted the FSA taking appropriate action to deal with it.

The first limb of the case, and indeed the central failure suggested by the FSA, was that L&G did not have procedures in place to identify whether customers were reluctant to take on the risks that could emanate from such policies, namely a possible capital shortfall resulting in the original mortgage not being paid off in full.[133] The L&G action challenged the FSA's justifications for the decision and the role of the RDC in the enforcement decision-making process. The applicable principles and rules at the time were those provided by the SIB and the PIA (and its predecessor LAUTRO). The tribunal indicated its surprise that these guidance and rules were somewhat limited given the fact that they related to quite onerous financial products. In the light of the facts the tribunal decided that L&G failed to ensure its advisers had sought clients' attitude to risk about the possibility of a capital shortfall. However, notwithstanding this the problems needed to be set in context, as the PIA had failed to identify the shortcomings of the documentation and nor did it take any disciplinary action when defects were identified in 1999, other than to ensure that problems with ambiguous wording were resolved.[134]

The second limb of the case concerned allegations of L&G mis-selling its mortgage plans to customers.[135] The key issue in dealing with this was whether the review of endowment mortgages undertaken by PricewaterhouseCoopers (PwC), on behalf of the FSA, was a reliable basis to decide whether mis-selling had occurred. The review of a sample of cases was used to gauge the size of the problem, and resulted in the FSA taking action against L&G. L&G instructed KPMG to review the work done by PwC, and the general conclusion was the methodology of the work was flawed.[136] The conclusions reached by PwC were doubtful, as they 'did not believe that this approach should be relied on solely to determine the true circumstances at the time of the endowment sale'.[137] The tribunal decided that the

131 *Legal & General Assurance Society Ltd v. The Financial Services Authority*, Financial Services and Markets Tribunal, 18 January 2005.

132 Ibid., at p. 2.

133 Ibid., at p. 13.

134 Ibid., at pp. 44–48 and 50 51.

135 Ibid., at p. 51.

136 Ibid., at p. 52.

137 Ibid., at p. 56, and for an analysis of the sample see paras 182–204.

action for mis-selling alleged by the FSA failed because of the way the sample of cases was assessed to measure the size of the problem at L&G, which resulted in a misrepresentation of the position.[138] The tribunal held that the review of the sample cases was flawed and the second limb of the case failed.

The criticism of the FSA's decision extended to the very body given responsibility for making it, namely the RDC.[139] L&G's criticism challenged the FSA's submission of evidence to the RDC. The FSA emphasised in more definite words than the PwC report (which simply highlighted a possibility that there may have been mis-selling) that 'these customers were sold policies that were unsuitable for them and [the FSA] considers this to be a significant proportion of the customers' review'.[140] The tribunal highlighted that assuming this was an oversight is 'unfortunate', as the RDC is likely to have relied on it.[141] Indeed, the certainty expressed by the FSA about the findings could have deflected attention away from the concerns raised by L&G over how the findings were put together and reduced the need to review the evidence presented by L&G. L&G contended that the RDC was wrong simply to rely on the PwC findings given that it did not itself conclude L&G was actually guilty of mis-selling. The tribunal concluded that this was a 'significant error',[142] and supported L&G's grievances about the RDC's over-reliance on the accuracy of the PwC report and the FSA rejection of L&G's recommendation of doing an extended sample review. The tribunal also highlighted the usefulness of placing on record the case put forward by L&G, as done in other judicial and disciplinary proceedings, so that counterclaims are given a sufficient amount of attention by all parties. The tribunal decided that the RDC was 'in error' in its approach to the mis-selling case and reached conclusions not justified by the material before it.[143]

A problem facing the FSA is that it is dealing with a number of issues dating back to the previous regime, when the regulatory standards were quite different in comparison to standards and expectations that exist today. Indeed, the approach to enforcement decisions needs to be put in that context, because the approach of previous regulators was distinctively less punitive and standards less rigorously scrutinised. Therefore the FSA needs to be mindful of the standard of behaviour expected at the time, so that the expectations of today do not distort any decision about what happened under a previous regulatory regime with differing expectations of those it regulated. Consequently, enforcement decisions need to be proportionate and fair in the light of the standards that existed at the time.

These issues, however, do not deflect attention away from the way the FSA decided to embark on its decision to impose a fine on L&G for its alleged procedural failures and mis-selling of endowment mortgages. The case highlights the significant power that the FSA wields, and how the RDC could overly rely on the FSA's investigation and findings to come to its own conclusions in favour of the FSA's case against the

138 Ibid., at p. 66, para. 205.
139 Ibid.
140 Ibid., at pp. 66–67.
141 Ibid., at p. 67.
142 Ibid.
143 Ibid., at p. 69.

regulated firm or individual. In the Practitioner Panel survey in 2004 the underlying tone of the relationship between regulator and regulated was described as one where the regulator is simply erring on the side of consumers and somewhat distancing itself from the industry.[144] The FSA was described as 'Stalinesque' in its approach.[145] In addition the survey highlighted dissatisfaction with the decision-making process, especially the independence of the RDC where the case is 'heard from one side only'.[146]

These concerns in 2004 about the enforcement process and the role of the RDC are in many respects echoed by the tribunal. It highlighted that the RDC does not have the same time to assess the evidence as it does. But this does not negate the fact that the RDC is making decisions about firms and individuals that can have very serious consequences. Therefore, one issue is whether the RDC has the appropriate mix of independent members to ensure the proper level of independence is maintained. Another concern is whether it is able to deal with the issues in an impartial way given the access the FSA has to the RDC – access which regulated firms and individuals do not seem to have. These issues are of major concern because not every firm or individual will be inclined to take their case to the Financial Services and Markets Tribunal for it to scrutinise the matter afresh.

Enforcement Process Review

The enforcement style of the FSA has come under considerable criticism from the Practitioner and Consumer Panels and those who have had the misfortune of experiencing the enforcement process. In addition the anomalies exposed by the L&G action highlighted the further need for a thorough review of the process, in particular the role of the RDC. The issues raised have challenged the underlying principles that govern the enforcement process, namely the fairness and efficiency with which the FSA makes its decisions. In the light of this pressure the FSA sought to review its management of the process.[147]

The committee set up by the FSA in its review made a number of recommendations to improve the process and reduce the perception of its unfairness. In all there are 44 recommendations, which *inter alia* place particular emphasis on the role of the RDC and changes to this to re-establish confidence in the system. These recommendations attempt to appease the concerns expressed by both practitioners and consumers. The review committee focused on a number of issues: a clearer rationale for enforcement, more monitoring of the process, a separation of the investigative and enforcement decisions and practical steps to enhance the objectivity and independence of the process. This latter issue was of most contention, as a result of the findings of the L&G tribunal decision. The review committee recommended that the RDC be strengthened by the introduction of a separate legal team dedicated to assisting it in its decisions, rather than relying on the actual enforcement division that is deciding

144 Practitioner Panel, n. 128 above, at p. 79.

145 Ibid., at p. 80.

146 Ibid.

147 FSA (2005) *Enforcement Process Review: Report and Recommendations*, July.

on whether the breach warrants a sanction. The main recommendation on the RDC is to separate its role clearly from the enforcement division to reduce the perception that their dialogue could prejudice its decision. The committee recommends disclosure of all communication between the enforcement division and the RDC to the other parties, to ensure those accused are able to get an idea of what to expect. In addition the recommendations include measures to end the dialogue between the enforcement division and the RDC after the 'representations meeting' has taken place.

These measures make incremental changes to enhance confidence in the role of the RDC by improving its independence. But the review begs the question whether independent panel members acting in the interests of a regulatory system can actually deal with matters in an impartial way, and indeed decide contrary to the regulator who has brought the action in the first place. It is difficult to find but it would be interesting to investigate the number of times the RDC has actually gone against the opinion of the enforcement division in the same way as the Financial Services and Markets Tribunal.[148]

The US Experience of Enforcement

The US structure of banking regulation is unique in that there are a number of regulatory agencies with responsibilities for safeguarding the safety and soundness of the whole banking system. However, in terms of enforcement policy and rules the legal structure is more centralised,[149] and indeed the federal regulators have acted jointly in enforcement proceedings.[150] The problems associated with establishing liability in common law have already been explored. It is no wonder the federal agencies had their administrative arsenal of sanctions bolstered by the FIRREA 1989 to deal with failures where simple negligence rather than gross negligence or recklessness needs to be established in a common law action pursued by the FDIC

148 Such statistical information is not readily accessible from the FSA publications.

149 OCC (2001) *Policies and Procedures Manual, Enforcement Act Policy*, PPM 5310-3 (Rev), 30 July; Peek, J. and Rosenberg, E. (1995) 'Bank regulatory agreements in New England', *Federal Reserve Bank of Boston New England Economic Review*, May/June, 15; Peek, J., Rosenberg, E. and Jordan, J. J. (1999) 'The impact of greater bank disclosure amidst a banking crisis', Working Paper Series No. 99-1, Federal Reserve Bank of Boston; Huber, S. K. (1998) 'Enforcement powers of federal banking agencies', *Annual Review of Banking Law*, vol. 7, 123; Curry, T. J., O'Keefe, P. O., Coburn, J. and Montgomery L. (1999) 'Financially distressed banks: How effective are enforcement actions in the supervision process', *FDIC Banking Review*, 1; Federal Deposit Insurance Corporation (1997), 'Bank examination and enforcement', in FDIC *History of the Eighties – Lessons for the Future. Vol. I: An Examination of the Banking Crises of the 1980s and Early 1990s*, available at www.fdic.gov/bank/historical/vol1.html, at p. 421.

150 See, for example, Board of Governors of the Federal Reverse System & Office of the Comptroller of the Currency, Washington, DC: In the matter of Bob L Sellers of First National Summit Bankshares Crested Butte, Colorado & First National Summit Bank Gunnison, Colorado (FRB Docket No. 98-029-E-I) (OCC Docket No. AA-EC-98-28).

as a receiver or conservator.[151] A federal agency such as the OCC can initiate this and then give responsibility for dealing with the bank to the FDIC.[152] Thus the federal regulators have a broad range of sanctions to deal with everything from minor failures such as inaccurate records[153] up to offences that fundamentally threaten the safety and soundness of the institution and its depositors – which can lead for example to a bank losing its access to the FDIC deposit insurance scheme.[154]

The US enforcement powers that exist today are the consequence of various financial failures. These failures brought the discretionary/persuasion-based approach in banking regulation into question, raising the criticism that it was 'outmoded'.[155] This is notwithstanding the fact that K. C. Davis advocates the approach as 'probably the outstanding example in the federal government of regulation of an entire industry through methods of supervision'.

The criticism resulted in greater use of formal enforcement actions and the imposition of sanctions by the various regulatory bodies, and a move away from the 'come-let's-reason-together' approach.[156] However, the evidence from the USA does suggest that a discretionary enforcement policy could lead to very extreme measures, such as the displacement of the entire management of an institution without direct statutory authority.[157] The US bank regulators have nevertheless retained a remedial-based approach where the published enforcement outcome sets out how the regulator expects a bank to resolve problems that could undermine its 'safety and soundness'[158] rather than a purely retributive approach, despite the earlier suggestions of a move away from the informal system. For example, the OCC has highlighted that it retains a remedy-based approach including 'advice' and 'moral suasion' to ensure that a bank undertakes its business in a safe and sound manner.[159] The maintenance of this approach rather than a more punitive and retributive stance is possibly to avoid overburdening the FDIC's deposit protection scheme by simply closing banks by revoking their charter.

A central policy aim for all bank supervisors is to ensure banks are compliant with the appropriate rules and regulations, and to have at their disposal an appropriate

151 This issue is extensively examined by Schooner, H. M. (1995) 'Fiduciary duties' demanding cousin: Bank director liability for unsafe or unsound banking practices', *George Washington Law Review*, vol. 63, 175, at pp. 215–219.

152 OCC (1997) *The Role of a National Bank Director: The Director's Book*, at p. 102.

153 12 USC § 1818 (3) (A).

154 12 USC § 1818(a).

155 Davis, K. C. (1982) *Legal Times*, 25 October, cited in Hawke, J. D. Jr (1985) *Commentaries on Banking Regulation*, Washington, DC, Harcourt Brace Jovanovich, at p. 51.

156 Hawke, ibid.; see also Baxter, L. G. (1991) 'Judicial responses to the recent enforcement activities of the federal banking regulators', *Fordham Law Review*, vol. 59, 193; Baxter, L. G. (1993) 'Fiduciary issues in federal banking regulation', *Law and Contemporary Problems*, vol. 56, 7.

157 *Miami Beach Fed. Sav. & Loan Ass'n v. Callander*, 256 F.2d 410 (5d Cir. 1958), pp. 414–415.

158 The principle of 'safety and soundness' is analysed on pp. 70–72.

159 OCC, n. 149 above, at pp. 3–4.

mix of enforcement sanctions if this is not the case. There is clear recognition that the draconian power of 'termination is analogous to wielding a blunt instrument in a surgical procedure that really requires a more refined tool'.[160] The US experience shows that the Bank of England's approach of treating banks within an informal opaque environment should be applied only in a narrow set of circumstances, and in many respects undermines the importance of utilising market response as a mechanism for ensuring compliance. Studies undertaken in the USA into the effect of formal enforcement actions highlight that institutions implement the steps required, ensuring compliance. More importantly, the effect of market discipline through publicising formal enforcement actions can, without necessarily leading to their demise, negatively affect share prices of publicly listed institutions. The conclusions from these studies suggest that this type of information provides the market with material to make realistic assessments of bank risks, and leads to a diminution in the likelihood of contagion.[161] In addition to this market response, depositors' response to enforcement decisions also seems to be somewhat limited, thus challenging the traditional idea that such publicity could result in a bank run. An empirical study by Gilbert and Vaughan refers to the debates in the House of Representatives on publicity of enforcement decisions.[162] The debates suggest that the lack of publicity of wrongdoing hides the sins of bankers away from the public and thus prevents them from taking appropriate actions. The work also highlights that the House of Representatives did not accept the argument put forward by the supervisors that publicising enforcement decisions would result in bank runs, considering the fact that this had not happened when such action had been taken against a bank or one of its officials.[163]

The Financial Institutions Reform, Recovery, and Enforcement Act 1989 (FIRREA)[164] was enacted to deal with a number of failures exposed by the US 'savings & loans' disaster, and consequently provided much wider enforcement powers to banking regulators.[165] The FIRREA gives a broad right to initiate enforcement sanctions

160 Curry et al., n. 149 above, at p. 2.

161 FDIC, n. 149 above, at p. 47.

162 Gilbert, R. A. and Vaughan, M. D. (2000) 'Do depositors care about enforcement actions?', *Journal of Economics and Business*, vol. 53, 2175.

163 Ibid.

164 Public Law 101-73: Financial Institutions Reform, Recovery, and Enforcement Act 1989 ('To reform, recapitalize, and consolidate the federal deposit insurance system, to enhance the regulatory and enforcement powers of Federal financial institutions regulatory agencies, and for other purposes'). See examination of US bank directors' duty of care on pp. 105–110. The provisions of the FIRREA are incorporated in various parts of 12 USC.

165 Ibid., § 101 sets out the purposes of the legislation. The first purpose is 'to improve supervision by strengthening capital, accounting, and other supervisory standards'. The eighth purpose is 'to provide for improved supervision and enhanced enforcement powers and increase criminal and civil monetary penalties for fraud against financial institutions and depositors'. Providenti, A. C. Jr (1991) 'Playing with FIRREA, not getting burned: Statutory overview of the Financial Institutions Reform, Recovery, and Enforcement Act of 1989', *Fordham Law Review*, vol. 59, 323, at p. 333.

against affiliated parties, which not only include the institution's directors, officers and employees, but also other persons who are affiliated with the bank such as accountants and lawyers.[166] It builds upon the existing regime by providing various formal sanctions to ensure compliance and act as deterrents.

The Federal Deposit Insurance Corporation Improvement Act 1991 (FDICIA), in addition to the FIRREA, provides the regulators with the power to insist on 'prompt corrective action' to make banks remedy insufficient levels of capital.[167] The 'prompt corrective action directive' is an attempt to intervene before a bank faces the possibility of failing. It is no surprise the directions of the regulator are far-reaching to avoid a bank failure, although the directive gives the option to the bank to remedy its position rather than simply close for fear of failing. For example, such a directive was made to the First National Bank of Northern Kentucky, which was deemed by the OCC to be 'critically undercapitalised'.[168] To rectify this position the bank was required to initiate plans to increase its minimum level of capital, and to put forward plans to either sell, merge or liquidate its business if it could not improve its capital base.[169]

The federal banking regulators have a number of enforcement options, embracing informal[170] and formal powers.[171] These can be subdivided into enforcement actions that are publicised[172] and those that are not.[173]

Informal actions are used in instances where the act or omission of the bank warrants a less severe sanction: commitments, board resolutions and memoranda of understanding. Nevertheless they can vary in their severity depending on, for example, the 'nature, extent, of the bank's problems and weaknesses' and the extent to which the regulator is confident that the bank can rectify the issues.[174] While the respective regulators can initiate these informal sanctions, they are deemed voluntary arrangements with no formal compulsion. However, Jackson and Symons point out that not complying with an informal action would lead to formal supervisory action, as it suggests a lack of commitment on the part of the bank to deal with issues as they arise.[175] A bank board resolution (BBR) is a resolution adopted by the

166 For a definition see 12 USC § 1813(u) Institution – Affiliated Party.

167 Jackson, H. E. and Symons E. (1999) *Regulation of Financial Institutions*, St Paul, West Group.

168 Pursuant to 12 USC § 1831(o); US Department of the Treasury Office of the Comptroller of the Currency: In the matter of First National Bank of Kentucky, Fort Mitchell, Kentucky, #2002-90, Prompt Corrective Action Directive.

169 Ibid., Article I.

170 OCC, n. 149 above, at p. 18.

171 Ibid., at pp. 18–21.

172 For power to publicise enforcement actions see 12 USC § 1818(b) and (u); in relation to a prompt corrective action directive the authority to publicise is pursuant to 12 USC § 1831(o); for safety and soundness orders see 12 USC § 1831p-1(e); for a description of publicising enforcement decisions see OCC, n. 149 above, at p. 15; Federal Reserve Bank, *Commercial Bank Examination Manual*, s. 5040.1.

173 See for example OCC, n. 149 above, at p. 15.

174 Ibid., at p. 7.

175 Jackson and Symons, n. 167 above, at p. 335.

board of directors to implement reforms initiated by the respective regulator.[176] A 'commitment' is a request by the regulators to resolve small issues at the bank.[177] A memorandum of understanding (MoU) builds on the former resolution of an action plan to rectify a number of minor problems at the institution.[178]

The approach changes with formal enforcement actions, which are publicised.[179] These are used where serious problems exist which affect, for example, the safety and soundness of an institution or evidence non-compliance with regulatory rules.[180] The action taken by the regulators centres on whether the bank has acted in an 'unsafe and unsound' way which undermines, for instance, the interests of depositors.[181] The standard of 'unsafe and unsound' is wide, and amenable to various sorts of non-compliance. It refers to a broad range of incidents which are serious acts of imprudence that give rise to abnormal risks to the safety of a bank. The US courts have shed further light on the standard and have not simply accommodated the decision of the regulator.[182] For instance, in a case of simple breach of contract, the court held that it is important to assess how remote the breach is from threatening the existence of the bank, and if it were to continue whether it would result in only a minor financial loss.[183] Written agreements are issued to ensure compliance in a broad range of areas which point to less severe forms of non-compliance.[184]

The key sanction is the cease and desist order (C&DO).[185] This can require the institution or its affiliated party to refrain from unsafe or unsound practices, or violating applicable rules and regulations.[186] The order is accepted by the institution or individual before it is formally issued by the regulator; this avoids having to go through a lengthy administrative hearing simply to issue the order, which is already accepted by both sides. The order requires the deficient party to take appropriate action to rectify the problem that resulted in the order being given.[187] Under the FIRREA 1989 a fine in the region of S1 million per day can be levied on an institution or individual.[188] The level of the fine relates to the gravity of the failure, the question of recklessness and/or breach of fiduciary duty and the benefit accrued by the individuals or institutions.[189] A fine could be levied for violation of a broad range of regulations, or for non-compliance with an existing enforcement order. For example,

---

176 OCC, n. 152 above, at p. 97.

177 Ibid.; see also OCC, n. 149 above, at p. 18.

178 OCC, n.152 above, at p. 98.

179 OCC, n. 149 above, at p. 4.

180 Ibid., at pp. 7 8.

181 12 USC § 1831p-1.

182 The principle of safe and sound is described and analysed on pp. 70–72.

183 *Gulf Federal Saving & Loan Association v. Federal Home Loan Bank Board*, 651 F.2d 259, 264 (5d Cir. 1981).

184 For written agreements see, for example, 12 USC § 1818(b)(1) and formal written agreements see 12 USC § 1831(i).

185 12 USC § 1818(b).

186 12 USC § 1818(u).

187 12 USC § 1818(b)(6).

188 12 USC § 1818(i).

189 12 USC § 1818(i)(2)(C)–(D).

Credit L Credit Agricole, SA, France and its New York affiliates[190] were fined in total $13 million for not complying with a written agreement and additional 'unsafe and unsound' practices which pointed to poor management supervision of internal controls and risk management techniques in its business operation. The ultimate sanction the regulators can initiate is an order to prohibit or remove authority to conduct 'banking business'.[191] This power can be initiated in circumstances similar to a C&DO where there is evidence that an enforcement order has not been complied with, or 'safe and sound' rules and regulations have been violated or depositors' interests are threatened. However, the degree of culpability and knowledge on the part of the institutions or individuals would need to be extensive when exercising the power to prohibit them from operating in the industry.[192] The federal regulator can issue a suspension order with immediate effect if it considers the interests of depositors are under threat. The evidence would need to point to 'continuing disregard' of regulation, which is interpreted to mean 'heedless indifference to the prospective consequences'.[193]

Allfirst INC, a US subsidiary of Allied Irish Bank based in Ireland, accumulated losses in the region of $691.2 million through the activities of its 'star trader' in its US foreign exchange business.[194] This case illustrates the remedial-based approach adopted by US regulators, in this instance the Federal Reserve, and the extent of the enforcement action taken by the US supervisors in stipulating the measures the Irish bank needed to implement to ensure it was managed in a safe and sound manner.

The losses Allfirst INC accrued were the result of ill-judged foreign exchange trading involving the US dollar and Japanese yen over an 11-year period.[195] The centre of the management failure was the treasury operations undertaken by Allfirst INC overlooking the 'star trader', John Rusnak. The trader betted, wrongly, on the movement of the Japanese yen against the US dollar. To camouflage the continuing losses he created fictitious options to suggest the positions were hedged to mitigate any potential loss. These fraudulent activities continued due to the weak internal controls in place.[196] For instance, the back office, responsible for processing and settling trades, failed to get trade confirmations from Rusnak for the options part of the business. This was exacerbated by the fact that foreign exchange transactions were not systematically verified by an independent source to check the accuracy of the trades. The large deficiencies in the culture of compliance led to an overall attitude that the 'confirmation process was a pointless formality'.[197] This lack of

190 Enforcement Action is available at www.federalreserve.gov/boarddocs/press/enforcement/2004/20040310/.

191 12 USC § 1818(e)(1) and (7).

192 12 USC § 1818(e)(3).

193 *Kim v. Office of Thrift Supervision*, 40 F.3d 1050 (9d Cir. 1994).

194 Promontory Financial Group and Wachtell, Lipton, Rosen & Katz (2002) *Report to the Boards of Directors of Allied Irish Bank PLC, Allfirst Financial INC and Allfirst Bank Concerning Currency Trading Losses* (Promontory Financial Group Report), 12 March.

195 Ibid., at pp. 9–15.

196 Ibid., at pp. 15–18.

197 Ibid., at p. 21.

corporate vigilance led to a culture of complacency, allowing Rusnak to continue with his fictitious trading for years without detection.

John Rusnak pleaded guilty to one count of bank fraud in connection with the losses sustained by Allfirst Bank by his foreign currency trading, which resulted in a sentence of 90 months' imprisonment.[198] Notwithstanding the criminal conviction, the US supervisors entered into the less severe sanction of a written agreement with Allied Irish Bank Plc, Allfirst Financial Inc and Allfirst Bank.[199] This public agreement requires the bank to ensure it implements changes to comply with a review undertaken by consultants appointed by Allied Irish.[200] The agreement identifies the remedial action required: for instance, to 'strength the organisation's management' in compliance with the consultants' findings. This included clear plans on proposed risk management, internal controls and management information systems, and an internal audit programme which set out the review of each operational area. These changes, implemented within the allotted time frames, need to satisfy the US supervisors that the bank's operations are safe and sound.

Conclusion

This chapter has highlighted that a pragmatic enforcement method is required which does not rely on one particular strategy, but rather a mixed approach where one has to accept that, in the process of carrying out supervision, a degree of accommodation of certain minor departures from the regulations might be necessary. These departures are tolerable and may need to be accommodated in order to avoid undue and adverse effects on the market, thus disturbing the rapport between the regulator and the banks. Over-accommodation of derogation, as suggested by Kagan,[201] should be looked at from a pragmatic standpoint. What matters most is the nature of the derogation which is being accommodated. No sensible regulatory body should accommodate a derogation of a significant nature which can have adverse repercussions on depositors or investor confidence in a marketplace. Nevertheless, the judgement required to balance these issues needs to ensure the interests of both the industry and consumers are addressed proportionately; consultation may be a more efficient approach than simply imposing sanctions to show that wrongdoing is being dealt with by the regulator.

The FSA has adopted a much more robust enforcement approach to ensure its regulatory objectives are seen to be achieved. The rationale of its enforcement decisions is based on its objectives and principles, in addition to the rules set out

198 US Attorney Office, District of Maryland (2002) 'Former Allfirst currency trader pleads guilty', press release, 24 October, available at www.usdoj.gov/usao/md/press_releases/press02/john_m_rusnak_pleads_guilty.htm.

199 Board of Governors of the Federal Reserve System, Washington, DC, by the Federal Reverse Bank of Richmond, Virginia, State of Maryland, Division of Financial Regulation, Baltimore, Maryland, Central Bank of Ireland, Dublin, available at www.federalreserve.gov/boarddocs/press/enforcement/2002/20020516/attachment.pdf.

200 Promontory Financial Group Report, n. 194 above, at pp. 45–56.

201 Cited in Hawkins and Thomas (1984) n 4 above, at p. 7.

in the FSMA 2000 and the FSA handbooks. It has attempted to address regulatory failures on industry, firm and individual levels. The move towards the use of publicity and fines has certainly led to an increased volume of enforcement activity. The consequence of this is the industry now considers itself to be in a regulatory climate where the interests of consumers are paramount. The move by the FSA to address their problems seems to have overridden the interests of the industry *per se*. This may be a result of the regulatory lapses with which the FSA has had to deal during its short life. The robust approach may mean the industry finally recognises that the interests of depositors and investors are central to the success of its business. Nevertheless, the enforcement approach adopted is adjudicatory, giving a justification for the FSA's actions rather than trying to correct a wrong that has taken place. The move to try to ensure compliance through education and consultation has focused on the individual consumer. This should be broadened to disseminate good practice within the industry itself, utilising publicity to disclose both positive and negative news.

The UK position places reliance on the FSA's objectives to support enforcement decisions. This strategy suggests that the FSA is adopting a rather defensive position, taking a 'top-down' approach to demonstrate why a decision is necessary. This is in contrast to the US position, which is more of a 'bottom-up' approach where an enforcement order is an engagement between the regulator and the authorised institution to investigate how a breach can be rectified. The enforcement order, while positioned as a sanction to deter or punish non-compliance, actually takes a remedial approach in that process by identifying how a breach can be remedied. This applies even in the most serious of cases, such as where a bank is considered critically undercapitalised. While it may be the case that not all directives are publicised, there is certainly a commitment on the part of the US regulators to publicise such matters. This challenges the idea again that abrogations can be best dealt with behind closed doors. The FSA notice, on the other hand, seeks to expose the wrongdoing which led to the punishment, thus legitimising its actions, but does not publicly engage with the firm or approved person in the steps necessary to rectify the breach. This gives rise to a distinctive enforcement system in comparison to the US approach. The UK system is more akin to an 'adjudicatory' method where the outcome is a justification for the decision rather than an attempt to resolve the problems that led to the sanction in the first place. This aspect of the dialogue is not included, although it takes place during the enforcement and supervisory process.

Chapter 5

The Role of the External Auditor and Skilled Person

Introduction

The regulators of financial services in the UK have traditionally sought the assistance of external auditors in their work. The Bank of England formally adopted the use of external auditors in the 1980s; the FSA followed suit, but has taken a cautious approach and restricted their use. While regulators and external auditors undertake similar functions, they can be categorised as serving public and private interests respectively. The regulator is conferred statutory responsibility for regulation and supervision of financial services with the ultimate aim of protecting market confidence and depositor and investor interests. For example, the regulator is not necessarily interested in how the firm is ensuring shareholder value but is more concerned about protecting the interests of depositors and investors. The external auditor, on the other hand, serves the primary interests of company shareholders by expressing an opinion as to whether the financial statements provide a 'true and fair' view. To fulfil their respective responsibilities the regulator and external auditor undertake a process of verifying information and representations as to its accuracy and reliability provided by the directors and management of a firm. This process requires an independent and objective mind-set with a suitable level of scepticism and vigilance to assess the reliability of the information.

This chapter will look at the roles of both the external auditor and the skilled person in the UK, which are governed by the FSMA 2000 and the auditing profession's standards and guidelines. The first section focuses on the auditing of bank accounts from its inception. It outlines how external auditors were used by the Bank in the mid-1980s, and highlights some of the concerns surrounding their use during that period. The second section focuses on the external auditor and its client, analysing the salient features of the professional guidelines to ensure external auditor independence and assessing the new initiatives to ensure work is undertaken with independence in mind, in particular the action taken by the professional bodies against individual external audit firms and auditors. It refers to several Joint Disciplinary Tribunal decisions, such as the recent BCCI case, as examples of the type of acts or omissions that have given rise to a failure to show the requisite level of scepticism and vigilance. The third section outlines the duty of care owed by external auditors to their clients in common law. It specifically examines the collapse of Barings Bank, analysing the legal duty of care required by external auditors in forming a 'true and fair view' about a bank's financial statements, and the issue of contributory negligence to apportion liability. The fourth section outlines the use of external auditors by the FSA and the extent to which it has changed the way they are now used. It describes the mechanisms put in place to ensure auditors act in the interests of the regulator rather than the client, and also outlines the duty of care owed by skilled persons to the FSA. In the fifth section the US position on the use of external auditors is introduced. The external audit of financial statements does not extend across all banks in the USA on an annual basis, but certain regulatory responsibilities are placed on external auditors where they are required by banks to assist the regulatory examiners with their work. It is evident that the relationship between the regulator and the external auditor is in certain areas more 'intrusive', with the regulator having the authority to request working papers produced during the audit of financial accounts. Finally, the sixth section will provide some concluding points and comparative observations about the UK and US approach.

The Audit of Bank Accounts

The auditing profession has acquired a unique status in the world of commerce as the arbiter of good stewardship of a company on behalf of shareholders. This has arisen as a result of the growth of financial markets that necessitated supervision of their integrity, and the efforts of the profession itself to create its own monopoly of the audit function.[1]

The compulsory audit of bank financial statements was first introduced with the Companies Act 1879,[2] emanating from a fraud at the City of Glasgow Bank and other bank failures at that time. The essential failure was the fact that none of the banks had arranged a thorough audit of their accounts. Whilst it was recognised at the time that the audit was not a panacea for preventing all bank failures, according to Lord Cross, placing a duty on auditors to state a bank's actual position would be a task which 'no human could perform'.[3] Notwithstanding the limits of the audit, it was clear that it could have pre-empted the problems and prevented the losses that occurred.[4]

---

1 Maltby, J. (1999) 'A sort of guide, philosopher and friend: The rise of the professional auditor in Britain', *Accounting Business & Financial History*, vol. 9, 29, at p. 33; Power, M. (1999) *The Audit Society: Rituals of Verification*, Oxford, Oxford University Press; Dicksee, L. (1892) *Auditing: A Practical Manual for Auditors*, London, Gee Publishing; Brown, R. G. (1975) 'Changing audit objectives and techniques', *Accounting Review*, April, 285; Chandler, R. A. (1995) 'Changing perceptions of the role of the company auditor 1840–1940', *Accounting and Business Research*, vol. 23, 443, at p. 444; Willinham, J. J. (1975) 'Discussant's response to relationship of auditing standards to detection of fraud', *CPA Journal*, April, 18.

2 Cooper, E. (1886) 'Chartered accountants as auditors of companies', *The Accountant*, November, 644.

3 House of Commons, Session 12 August (1879), col. 857.

4 House of Lords, Session 14 August (1879), col. 967.

While the audit remained important as a deterrent of fraud, the post-war period saw a change in direction away from the audit function and towards greater reliance on disclosure policies complementary to the audit.[5] However, the Jenkins Committee considered that the policy of disclosure should not be applied to banking and insurance institutions because there was always the concern of disclosing an adverse opinion that could threaten their existence.[6] At this time shareholder rights were considered secondary to the wider public interests of stability and ensuring confidence within the banking industry. The policy of non-disclosure was criticised in the Jenkins Committee and reversed in the 1970s.[7] This process continued later with the introduction of the Bank Accounts Directive[8] and through the work of Basel.[9] The directive brought the disclosure requirements of banks in line with member states and companies incorporated under the Companies Act 1985.

External Auditors and Banking Supervision

The Banking Act 1987 formally introduced the role of the external auditor in the supervision of authorised institutions after the Johnson Matthey affair,[10] from which point the role of the auditor grew in terms of involvement in banking supervision. The right to disclose issues of concern put aside the duty of confidentiality between auditor and client.

The closure of BCCI highlighted the concern surrounding external auditors' responsibility and the potential conflict between the auditor's duties to shareholders and the company and its obligations to the regulator. This issue can be demonstrated by examining the advice Price Waterhouse had given to BCCI to move its treasury operations to avoid tax liabilities relating to its treasury losses. The minutes of their meeting illustrate what Price Waterhouse advised BCCI to do:

---

5 Jenkins Committee (1962) *Report of the Company Law Committee Appointed by the Board of Trade*, Cmnd 1749, HMSO.

6 From Gladstone: 'Publicity is all that is necessary. Show up the roguery and it is harmless', Hansard LXV [1844] 277: The Cohen Committee (1945) Cmnd 6659; and Jenkins Committee (1962) examined the issue of auditing bank accounts and came to the conclusion that disclosure and expressing a 'true and fair' view were not in the public interest, at p. 158.

7 See the dissenting opinion, Jenkins Committee, n. 5 above, at p. 215. SI No. 327. Companies: The Banking Companies (Accounts) Regulations, 1970, 1205.

8 Council Directive on the Annual Accounts and Consolidated Accounts of Banks and other Financial Institutions, 86/635/EEC, 8 December 1986; SI (Bank Accounts) Regulation 2705 (1991).

9 Basel Committee on Banking Supervision (1998) *Enhancing Bank Transparency, Public Disclosure and Supervisory Information that Promote Safety and Soundness in Banking Systems*, Basel, Committee on Banking Supervision; G22 Working Group (1998) *Summary of Reports on the International Financial Architecture: Working Group on Transparency and Accountability*, G22 Working Group, October.

10 Bank of England (1985) *The Relationship between the Supervisors, Auditors and Management of Banks*, consultation paper, 20 August.

> 3.9. A further feature arising from the review of Treasury operations in 1985 was the potential liability to the Corporation Tax arising from the Division's activities in the period 1982 to 1985. Following advice from ourselves and from the Tax Counsel during 1986 it was determined that this liability could be significantly reduced if the Bank ceased trading in the United Kingdom and claimed a terminal loss. As a consequence of this advice, the Treasury activities were moved from London to Abu Dhabi with effect from 31 October 1986. Price Waterhouse assisted with the Transfer from London to Abu Dhabi and we are pleased to report that the transfer was conducted smoothly.[11]

This episode highlights the conflicts of interests that can arise between the audit, regulatory and commercial interests of external auditors as a result of legitimate tax advice. The establishment of the central treasury in Abu Dhabi was strongly criticised in the Bingham Report, according to which the move was like placing 'a refractory pupil ... in a dark corner at the back'.[12] The move of the treasury function meant that a critical aspect of BCCI's business was not under the clear purview of the Bank of England; the result placed the interests of UK depositors under threat.

In addition to verifying that the accounts showed a 'true and fair' view, the auditor was required to act as a reporting accountant to the Bank of England. This gave rise to a clear conflict of interest, particularly in the area of assessing previous work. The policy of having the same accounting firm acting as external auditor and reporting accountant was positively encouraged by the Bank, based on the argument that this approach led to greater efficiency because of the knowledge the audit had already accumulated about the client. However, the Treasury Select Committee which reported on Barings Bank found that the weaknesses which led to the collapse raised particular issues about the dual capacity of the external auditor. The committee recommended that the Bank of England use a different firm, fully independent from the auditors of the financial statements, to conduct the s. 39 reports under the Banking Act 1987.[13]

The problems associated with over-reliance on the use of external auditors have resulted in some re-examination of their use by the FSA, as will be seen later. But first it is appropriate to outline and analyse the professional standards that govern their work, given that these guidelines are those to which third-party regulators require external auditors to conform when undertaking work for them. It is important to analyse the legal liability of external auditors to third parties like regulators to determine whether they are in common law legally accountable for their acts or omissions.

---

11 Minutes of the meeting with Price Waterhouse, available at www.csustan.edu/aaba/aaba.htm, at p. 175.

12 *Inquiry into the Supervision of the Bank of Credit and Commerce International*, The Right Honourable Lord Justice Bingham, House of Commons, HMSO, July 1992.

13 Treasury Select Committee, Barings Bank and International Regulation, First Report, para. 22, p. xii. The Arthur Andersen Report also noted concerned expressed by staff at the Supervision and Surveillance Division about the lack of independence occasionally shown by reporting accountants: Arthur Andersen & Co SC (1996) *Findings and Recommendations of the Review of Supervision and Surveillance* (Arthur Andersen Report), London, Arthur Andersen Consulting, July, at p. 13.

Professional Guidelines

The financial audit remains an important facet of corporate governance that makes management accountable to shareholders for its stewardship of a company.[14] It is the board of directors' responsibility to prepare the financial accounts and ensure general compliance with the UK Companies Act 1985;[15] this assurance should be provided independently.[16] An audit under the Companies Act 1985 s. 235 requires the auditor to verify whether the financial statements give a 'true and fair view' of the financial health of the company.[17] But notwithstanding the importance placed on the audited accounts, one must also highlight their limited shelf life. According to Hobhouse J, the utility of the audited accounts diminishes with the passage of time as more up-to-date sources of information are published which provide a better idea of the financial viability of firm.[18]

The audit is based on a contractual relationship expressed by a letter of engagement between the auditor and the client.[19] The letter indicates the responsibilities of both the auditor and the board of directors, and details the scope of the audit and the nature of the engagement.

The auditor is required to undertake the work in accordance with professional standards and ethics.[20] These are said to be merely guides to interpretation rather

---

14 *Caparo Industries plc v. Dickman* [1990] 1 All ER, 568: 'It is the auditors' function to ensure, so far as possible, that the financial information as to the company's affairs prepared by the directors accurately reflects the company's position in order, first, to protect the company itself from consequences of undetected errors or, possibly, wrongdoing... and second, to provide shareholders with reliable intelligence for the purpose of enabling them to scrutinise the conduct of the company's affairs and to exercise their collective powers to reward or control or remove those to whom that conduct has been confided', at p. 583; APB, International Standard on Auditing 200, Objective and General Principles Governing an Audit of Financial Statements.

15 Companies Act 1985, ss. 226–227; *Barings plc v. Coopers & Lybrand* [1997] 1 BCLC 427, at p. 435; see also *Bank of Credit and Commerce International (Overseas) Ltd (in liquidation) and Others v. Price Waterhouse and Another (No. 3)*, *The Times*, 2 April 1998.

16 *Report of the Committee on the Financial Aspects of Corporate Governance* (1992) (Cadbury Report), London, Gee Publishing; Committee on Corporate Governance (1998) *Report of the Committee on Corporate Governance* (Hampel Report), London, Gee & Co.

17 The expression 'true and fair' is rather controversial and it is reasonable to assert that simply 'true' is the appropriate word. See generally Bird, P. (1984) 'What is "a true and fair view"?', *Journal of Business Law*, September, 480; Bird, P. (1985) 'Group accounts and the true and fair view', *Journal of Business Law*, June, 364; Lasok. K. P. E. and Grace, E. (1987) 'The true and fair view', *Company Lawyer*, vol. 10, 13; McGee, A. (1991) 'The "true and fair view" debate: A study in the legal regulation of accounting', *Modern Law Review*, vol. 54, 874.

18 *Berg & Sons v. Adams* [1993] BCLC 1045, 1055.

19 Auditing Practices Board, International Standard on Auditing 210, Terms of Audit Engagements.

20 ISA 200, n. 14 above.

than instruments of legal responsibility.[21] The audit guidelines state that the auditor is required to express an opinion articulated in the form of a 'true and fair view' of whether 'the financial statements are prepared, in all material respects, in accordance with an applicable financial reporting framework'.[22] This requires the auditor to 'plan' and 'perform' the audit with an 'attitude of professional scepticism' by critically assessing for instance the validity of the audit evidence and the representations made by management.[23] The auditor needs to examine the audit evidence used to make up the financial statements to provide 'reasonable assurance' that the statements are 'free from material misstatements'.[24]

The idea of 'professional scepticism' underpins the audit, and in the literal sense suggests an evaluation that does not accept the audit evidence at face value but questions the soundness of the information and data given. This requires the auditor to act with a certain degree of vigilance by being circumspect and cautious about the evidence. Scepticism and vigilance are interdependent in terms of ensuring that the audit is seen to be independent and objective. When circumstances suggest the possibility of fraud or error, the degree of inquisitiveness and scepticism should increase concomitantly and should express itself by seeking to obtain evidence from independent sources to verify for instance the representations made by management.[25]

The Question of Independence

The audit of financial accounts to reflect a 'true and fair view' has to comply with the ethical guidelines set by the Auditing Practices Board (APB) to ensure it is undertaken with the appropriate level of integrity, objectivity and independence.[26] The literal definition of 'independence' connotes the idea of not being under the influence of another, being able to withstand the demands of people and willing to seek verification of their opinions.[27] The legal definition highlights the responsibility that may be placed on an individual to provide another opinion to solve a problem.[28] This is also espoused in the guidelines, which elaborate extensively on how the auditor is expected to achieve independence. For example, the guidelines require auditors to demonstrate objectivity by expressing their opinion on the financial statement in an impartial manner based on 'all the available audit evidence and their professional

21 *Lloyds Cheyham & Co. Ltd v. Littlejon & Co.* [1987] BCLC 303; *Esanda Finance Corporation v. Peat Marwick Hungerfords* [1997] 71 ALJR 448. McHugh J, at p. 475, refers to *Columbia Coffee & Tea Pty Ltd v. Churchill* [1992] 29 NSWLR 141.

22 ISA 200, n. 14 above, at para. 2.

23 Ibid., at para. 6.

24 Ibid., at para. 8.

25 See International Standard on Auditing 500, Audit Evidence; International Standard on Auditing 580, Management Representations, respectively.

26 APB, Ethical Standard 1: Integrity, Objectivity and Independence, (reissued December 2004) at www.frc.org.uk/apb/index.cfm.

27 OUP (1996) *Compact English Dictionary*, Oxford, Oxford University Press, at p. 504.

28 *Potato Marketing Board v. Merricks* [1958] 2 All ER 538, 548.

judgement'.[29] They also require the auditor to 'adopt a rigorous and robust approach and… be prepared to disagree, where necessary, with the directors' judgement'.[30] In addition the audit needs to be free of 'financial, employment, business and personal relationships' between auditor and client to demonstrate the audit was completed independently.[31]

The reliance placed on the audit report by the stakeholders in the financial markets has called into question the reliability of the auditors' judgement when their work is not confined to the report but includes a large volume of non-audit work.[32] It is also a mistake to think it is only the sale of non-audit services to an audit client that undermines the impartiality of the auditor: it involves the relationship as whole and the culture of dependence that ensues from it.[33] Therefore, the principle of auditor independence is not simply a question that is asked when a client is secured. It is a continuous obligation, evolving over time. In many respects the longer the relationship continues, the more rigorous the monitoring needs to be.

The ethical standards exist within a paradox: they require the auditors to regulate client interests themselves on an ongoing basis while accepting that non-audit work does challenge auditor independence. The volume of non-audit work sold to an audit client has been one indicator of the perception that auditing is simply a route to sell more profitable business services. In providing non-audit services (such as accounting services, other audit services, consultancy, corporate transactions, internal audit, information technology, mergers and acquisitions, regulatory compliance, restructuring and tax), there is the chance that the auditors will exceed the limits of their statutory responsibilities. This concern continues regardless of the fall in non-audit fees now received by auditing firms. The 2003 survey by *Financial Director* magazine for the first time found a decline in non-audit business in comparison to the year 2001–2002;[34] this trend has continued, as shown in the 2006 survey as well.[35]

The magazine bases the trend on the concern audit committees have about auditors undermining their degree of independence by undertaking non-audit work for a company. While audit fees have increased significantly due to regulatory

---

29 APB, n. 26 above, at para. 5.(reissued December 2004), at para. 5.

30 Ibid.

31 Ibid., at para. 12.

32 Sikka, P. (1998) 'The impossibility of eliminating the expectations gap: Some theory and evidence', *Critical Perspectives on Accounting*, vol. 9, 299; Puxty, A., Sikka, P. and Willmott, A. (1997) 'Mediating interests: The accountancy bodies' responses to the McFarlane Report', *Accounting and Business Research*, vol. 27, 323, at p. 339; Humphrey, C. (1992) 'The audit expectations gap – Plus ça change, plus c'est la même chose?', *Critical Perspectives on Accounting*, vol. 3, 137.

33 The US Cohen Commission in 1978 first brought to the public platform the idea of an 'expectations gap': American Institute of Certified Public Accountants (1978) 'Report conclusions and recommendations of the Commission on Auditor's Responsibilities', reprinted in *Journal of Accountancy*, April, 92.

34 *Financial Director*, 2003 survey.

35 *Financial Director*, 2001 survey; *Financial Director*, 2002 survey; *Financial Director*, 2004 survey; *Financial Director*, 2005 survey. *Financial Director*, 2006 survey, available at www.financialdirector.co.uk/financial-director/features/2165245/tenth-audit-fees-survey.

changes, the issue needs to be placed in context of the level of non-audit fees as a proportion of the total fee to the auditor: non-audit fees account for between 40 and 300 per cent of audit fees, and in one case 800 per cent. Therefore non-audit work still represents the bulk of the work performed for the client, even though the 2006 survey indicates a decline.[36]

The survey indicates the audit contract is effectively a lead to sell non-audit work. Accounting firms on occasion set audit fees at less than the market rate, which is called 'low-balling', to secure audit contracts, and simply compensate for this low rate by providing non-audit services.[37] This means that concern for fees can make the auditor more an advocate for the firm than an appropriately objective professional. A number of studies have been undertaken into this issue, and the general conclusion is that low-balling could cause a decline in the quality of audit work by its tendency to reduce the number of actual auditing hours put into an assignment. The *FD* survey points out the emphasis placed on the speed with which audits are completed and signed off. The implication is that auditors are under pressure to cut the number of days the audit takes to complete – leading to quality assurance concerns.

The Accounting Investigation and Discipline Board

The Accounting Investigation and Discipline Board (AIDB) (formerly the Joint Disciplinary Scheme – JDS) deals with high-profile cases of misconduct by chartered accountants.[38] The JDS, however, is still responsible in the interim for cases referred to it before the AIDB took over. The JDS is required to determine whether the conduct and quality of the work in question has fallen below that which is reasonably expected from its members. This can be illustrated by looking at some of its 'high-profile' decisions. The auditing failures relating to the Mirror Group pension fund, regulated by IMRO, are a good example of a firm that did not show the appropriate degree of scepticism in its work. The auditing firm, then known as Coopers & Lybrand, and individual partners were fined for their failures to report to IMRO various regulatory breaches by the Mirror Group.[39] The report highlights a number of deficiencies that undermine the audit. The tribunal held there was a

---

36 Ibid.

37 Ezzamel, M. (1996) 'Some empirical evidence from publicly quoted UK companies on the relationship between the pricing of audit and non-audit services', *Accounting and Business Research*, vol. 27, 3; Barkess, L. and Simnett, R. (1994) 'The provision of other services by auditors: Independence and pricing issues', *Accounting and Business Research*, vol. 24, 99; DeAngelo, L. (1981) 'Auditor independence, "lowballing", and disclosure regulation', *Journal of Accounting and Economics*, vol. 3, 113; Lee, C. J. and Gu, Z. (1998) 'Low balling, legal liability and auditor independence', *Accounting Review*, vol. 73, 533; Gregor, A. and Collier, P. (1996) 'Audit fees and auditor change: An investigation of the persistence of fee reduction by type of change', *Journal of Business Finance & Accounting*, vol. 23, 13.

38 To date the AIDB has not published a decision so the responsibility still lies with the JDS to preside over cases.

39 JDS Tribunal (1998) 'Report into 35 complaints against Coopers & Lybrand Deloitte ("The Firm") and 20 complaints against John Steven Cowling ("Mr Cowling")'.

severe lack of adherence to IMRO rules and deficient audit practice in establishing primary audit facts, consideration of third parties and reviews and overviews of its operations.[40] Although the Maxwell affair took place between 1988 and 1991, before auditors had a duty to report certain circumstances to regulators, the lapse still raised concerns about the objectiveness of auditors and their failure to report to IMRO inadequacies identified in an interim audit.[41]

Management representations can provide only limited assurance when the extent of a fraud is being determined.[42] This was a criticism raised by the JDS tribunal in the audit failures surrounding the Maxwell affair. The auditors accepted that their approach to some of the work, such as the treatment of loans and related-party transactions, was not undertaken with a 'detached eye'.[43] This highlighted the need to be far more sceptical when considering the degree of reliance placed on management representations.

While the level of auditors' scepticism and vigilance during the auditing process is an essential consideration in determining whether they have performed their duties with appropriate skill and care, further criteria, such as efficiency and competence, are equally necessary. These facets of the standard of care came under scrutiny by the JDS in the action against Spicer and Oppenheim, the auditors of Atlantic Computers plc.[44] The key facts concerned the way Atlantic leased computers to its clients: the flexibility of the leasing agreements had stark financial consequences. The 'walk agreements' meant that Atlantic Computers was exposed to the risk of clients not renewing the lease, which would have a significant adverse effect on profits for the company. The case invoked a number of the provisions of the auditing standards and guidelines, and allegations of non-compliance were made on the basis of provisions contained in Operational Standard 101, Guideline 201 (Planning, Control and Recording), Guideline 203 (Audit Evidence) and Guideline 402 (Events After the Balance Sheet Date).[45] The JDS tribunal held that the 1988 accounts for Atlantic Computers did not show a 'true and fair view' of the actual or potential liabilities. Moreover, no provisions were made for the actual or contingent liabilities in respect of the leasing arrangements. Matters that should have caused concern were not investigated in any significant detail; consequently, according to the tribunal, there were serious audit failings. This attracted penalties of censure and a fine of £100,000 and costs for bringing the proceedings.[46]

The collapse of Barings calls into question the role of management, auditors and regulators. Information about internal failures was available for all three parties to

40 Ibid., at para. 11.

41 Ibid., at para. 24.

42 Ibid., at para. 29.

43 Ibid., at para. 22.

44 JDS Tribunal (1997) 'Case No. 04/97, before Sir John Bailey KCB, Chairman, Mr F E Worsley FCA and Mr J C Platt FCA. In re: *Complaint against Messrs Spicer and Oppenheim*.

45 Ibid. These standards governed the audit for 1988 and have been repealed.

46 Ibid., para. 31.

discover what Leeson was doing.[47] Coopers & Lybrand audited Barings, including its overseas subsidiaries.[48] The complaints before the tribunal identify a number of failures at Barings that could have been discovered if the approach to the audit had been effectively evaluated to ensure the integrity of the work. The case fundamentally calls into question the reliance placed on the internal controls at Barings, and a lack of observance of the audit guidelines to determine whether the accounts gave a 'true and fair view'. For example, the discrepancy in the margin payments to Leeson could have been discovered if C&L had independently verified the data with the Singapore International Monetary Exchange (SIMEX) rather than relying on information generated by Barings. The JDS tribunal into the audit of Barings calls into question the reliance placed on information given by its management. This information should have been independently verified, particularly when a firm was engaged in derivatives business.

The BCCI[49] closure also brought into question the work of the external auditors responsible for the audits of its accounts as well as other parts of the group.[50] The BCCI saga is without doubt one of the major financial scandals both domestically and internationally. It was closed with losses totalling £9 billion, and resulted in the prosecution of a host of senior directors implicated in the massive fraud. In 2006 the external auditor PriceWaterhouseCoopers (PWC) was fined in total £975,000 by the JDS tribunal for failures to show the whole picture of the way BCCI was managed in its annual audit reports, thus not giving a true and fair view of the state of its financial affairs; this was conduct that fell short of what was reasonably expected of a member firm. The complaints related to the audits for 1987 and 1988 respectively, which were supposed to be prepared in accordance with International Accounting Standards (IAS). For example, PWC did not comply with IAS 24 as a result of its failure to disclose the link between BCCI and ICIC Group as a 'related part relationship' in its 1987, 1988 and 1989 audits, in particular the share ownership between the two and the security provided for the lending to ICIC by BCCI.[51] In addition PWC failed to determine whether the loan loss provision for the 1987 accounts reflected the level of lending and bad debt provision for the year, particularly for business with the CCAH and Gulf Group, both major clients of BCCI: PWC was found not to have obtained sufficient audit evidence to 'enable it to draw reasonable conclusions therefrom', which it could only have done if it 'obtained additional appropriate

---

47 *Report of the Board of Banking Supervision Inquiry into the Circumstances of the Collapse of Barings*, London, HMSO, 18 July 1995; Barings Futures (Singapore) Pte Ltd Investigation pursuant to section 231 of the Companies Act (Chapter 50) *The Report of the Inspectors appointed by the Minister for Finance, M. L. C. San and N. T. N. Kuang, Partners of Price Waterhouse*, 6 September 1995; Arthur Andersen Report, n. 13 above; *Re Barings plc (No. 5), Secretary for Trade and Industry v. Baker and others (No. 5)* Ch D [1999] 1 BCLC 433.

48 JDS Tribunal (2002) 'Report: Coopers & Lybrand, Gareth Maldwyn Davies and Andrew Charles Turner', 29 April.

49 For a brief background to the closure see p. 9.

50 JDS Tribunal (2006) 'Complaints against the United Kingdom Firm of Price Waterhouse', before Adrian Brunner QC, Chairman, 25 January.

51 Ibid., at p. 26.

evidence about the value of the security and its enforceability' and 'the adequacy of claim loss provisions against the Gulf Group related lending'.[52] However, the question of whether the auditors should shoulder all the blame is highly questionable, as discussed below.

The Auditor's Liability to the Client

In addition to disciplinary actions brought by the profession, the external auditor is exposed to action by the client in common law for liability under contract law. The external auditor is obliged to exercise reasonable care in its work for the client. To ascertain whether an auditor has exercised such care the circumstances need to be assessed on a case-by-case basis. In *Re Kingston Cotton Mill* Vaughan Williams J said there is '[n]o doubt he is acting antagonistically to the directors in the sense that he is appointed by the shareholders to be a check upon them'.[53] However, the auditor is not required to enter the audit engagement with suspicion, but should undertake it on the basis that if suspicion does exist then an obligation exists to 'probe it to the bottom'.[54]

The standard of knowledge, skill and care required is that expected of a reasonably competent auditor. The court needs to consider whether the act or omission departs from 'general practice'.[55] In such a case, 'general practice' is interpreted to mean the typical behaviour of a skilled person accepted by a 'responsible body' of opinion.[56] An individual is not required to have a high level of skill:[57] the act or omission will be simply judged on whether it departs from 'general practice'.[58] Indeed, there can be a body of professional opinion that contradicts general practice, and negligence is not said to ensue if the person follows the former rather than the latter. The auditing standards outlined above, given their broad discretion, inevitably give rise to differing opinions about auditing practices. In such circumstances, provided the auditor can justify his actions on the basis of a responsible body of opinion, he would be considered not to have been negligent. The court also needs to consider the likelihood of the risk occurring to determine whether an auditor, for instance, would have attempted to avoid creating the risk in the first place,[59] and take into account the precautionary measures that a reasonable and prudent professional would take in the circumstances.[60] This is to determine whether the possible precautionary measures would have been apparent to a person of his or her level of skill.[61]

---

52 Ibid., at pp. 42 and 52 respectively.
53 *Re Kingston Cotton Mill Co.* [1896] 1 Ch 6, 11.
54 *Re Kingston Cotton Mill Co. (No.2)* [1896] 2 Ch 279, 288–289.
55 *Kraji v. McGrath* [1986] 1 All ER 54, 61.
56 *Bolam v. Friern Mgmt Comm.* [1957] 2 All ER 118, 122.
57 *Glasgow v. Muir* [1943] 2 All ER 44, 47.
58 *Bolam*, n. 56 above, at p. 122.
59 *Bolton v. Stone and others* [1951] 1 All ER 1078, 1083.
60 *Latimer v. A.E.C. Ltd.* [1952] 1 All ER 1302, 1305.
61 *Ibid.*, at p. 1306.

Contributory negligence

The external auditors are an obvious target, given the perception that they are awash with money and thus more able than those in management to pay damages if 'bad' audits lead to failures. But company failures are not simply the result of bad audits; the underlying stewardship of the company plays an obvious, if not sole, part, which means the level of damages extracted from auditors must be calculated with that in mind. In such circumstances the auditors need to show that the directors and management failed in their duty of reasonable care towards the company, so partly contributing to their own downfall and the losses ensuing. The auditors use the defence of contributory negligence to get the courts to apportion damages more equitably among the parties that caused the loss. In such circumstances the courts have to look at the acts and omissions of all the parties and assess how each contributed to the ensuing loss to the company by weighing up the various causes of the loss.[62] The Barings collapse provides a good illustration of how the courts trawl through the factual evidence and calculate the level of damages the auditors will ultimately pay as a result of their failures.

Barings Bank

Barings collapsed as a result of Nick Leeson's trading activities in Singapore, which led to massive losses totalling £827 million, causing its parent company Barings Bros & Co to be placed in the hands of the administrators.[63] Barings Futures Singapore (BFS) sought damages from the external auditor, Deloitte & Touche (D&T), for its part in the collapse.[64] The claim for damages was brought by BFS against D&T for the period between 1992 and 1995. In this case, Evans-Lombe J decided that BFS was only entitled to a proportion of the damages because of its failure to manage Leeson's activities. The damages were reduced by 50 per cent in the early period and by 80 per cent in the later period up to April 1994, after which BFS was said to be wholly at fault for its losses.[65]

BFS alleged that D&T was negligent on a number of counts during the audits completed in 1992 and 1993; this contributed to the collapse by D&T failing in its duty to undertake the audits with the appropriate level of care. BFS alleged that D&T, *inter alia*, failed to take into account that Leeson controlled front and back office; failed to confirm and reconcile all balances and positions; did not detect that ¥670 million had been treated as received and confirmed on the wrong date; failed to review the use of the 88888 account; failed to discover the open option positions on the 88888 account; and failed to investigate the excess margins deposited at SIMEX.[66]

62 *Daniels v. Anderson CA (NSW)* 16 ACSR (1995) 607.

63 *Report of the Board of Banking Supervision Inquiry*, n. 47 above; Barings Futures (Singapore) Pte Ltd Investigation, n. 47 above.

64 *Barings plc v. Coopers & Lybrand* [2003] EWHC 1319 (Ch) (unreported).

65 Ibid., at para. 7.

66 Ibid., at paras 469–471.

D&T had proposed that the BFS audit should take a substantive approach rather than a controls-based approach. This decision was based on the fact that the audit involved no real serious concerns because BFS was an execution-based broker. Given the relatively low risk posed in auditing such a company, the method was considered appropriate.[67] Evans-Lombe J decided that BFS posed no more of a threat of unauthorised trading than any other similar-sized brokerage firm. D&T was not required to step up procedures to capture Leeson's activities and had planned the audit with the appropriate level of care necessary for a low-risk brokerage client.[68] On the face of it BFS did not pose a high audit risk and there appeared to be no reason for more procedures to be put in place. The substantive method required D&T to verify the information provided by BFS and its associated companies by independent means to give a complete record of its business transactions. According to Evans-Lombe J, D&T was not negligent in the procedures applied to audit BFS.[69]

BFS's financial situation could only have been undermined by Leeson's fraudulent manipulation of the positions taken by BFS to disguise the ¥670 million hole in the accounts.[70] In this process a discrepancy arose as to when the actual funds were received in the infamous 88888 account at BFS.[71] The BFS records indicated that it was 30 September, when in fact the funds were received on 1 October. Leeson had deleted that entry in the accounts so the funds appeared to fall into the previous accounting period. The discrepancy between the dates was a fact BFS considered D&T should have picked up during the audit, as it appeared to be window-dressing the actual financial position. This issue gave rise to examination of various guidelines concerned with material mis-statements and auditing procedures. While no formal convention existed regarding the receipt of funds, common sense should prevail in the simple rule that inaccurate records of receipts were considered, in the words of Evans-Lombe J, an 'untruth'.[72] It was contended by Evans-Lombe that D&T was negligent, as it should have got independent verification of when the funds were received from Barings Securities London (BSL) and not simply have accepted the explanations given by BFS. This failure was considered by Evans-Lombe to have been the cause of the subsequent losses.[73]

BFS contended that D&T was negligent by failing to investigate the anomalies, which would have revealed the use of the 88888 account and the unauthorised trading.[74] The argument that it relied on the representations of management to explain the discrepancy was inadequate. According to Evans-Lombe J, the timing of margin payments needed to be thoroughly investigated once the auditors were alerted to the imbalance as it raised concerns.[75] On the basis of these facts, Evans-

67 Ibid., at para. 474.
68 Ibid., at paras 543–545.
69 Ibid., at paras 586–588.
70 Ibid., at para. 589.
71 Ibid., at para. 609.
72 Ibid., at para. 622.
73 Ibid., at para. 652.
74 Ibid., at para. 663.
75 Ibid., at para. 679.

Lombe concluded that D&T was negligent in not investigating the issues surrounding margin payments.[76]

In order to gauge how fault should be apportioned, Evans-Lombe first considered the 'fault-line' between D&T and Barings' management in the saga.[77] To undertake this task he asked whether the 'chain of causation' from D&T's negligence to the ultimate loss sued for was broken as a result of the acts or omissions of Barings' management, and if so when did it break?[78] On the evidence, Evans-Lombe concluded that by the end of April 1994[79] Barings' management had a considerable amount of information about Leeson's activities that gave rise to serious suspicions of unauthorised trading. Barings failed to investigate those suspicions, which broke the chain of causation between D&T and the ultimate losses. Therefore Barings, through the failures of its own management, contributed to the ensuing losses. Evans-Lombe J sought to clarify on whose shoulders the responsibility for Leeson's activities was to fall.[80] The board of directors at BFS had delegated responsibility for the management of its business to individuals both inside and outside the company, on the basis of a parent and subsidiary rather than a broker and customer relationship, so it was responsible for the ensuing failures. In these circumstances, individual managers needed to accept that they had management responsibility for BFS business even when their companies, BSL and Barings Securities Japan (BSJ), were also its customer and it undertook business on SIMEX on their behalf. The extent to which the acts and omissions by management contributed to their own losses ultimately reduced the damages levelled at D&T.[81]

The final counterclaim initiated by D&T was the defence provided by s. 727 of the Companies Act 1985.[82] This defends an action of negligence based on evidence that the party acted honestly and reasonably. The court has the discretion to permit the party to be excused either partially or fully from liability. The application of the provision in *D'Jan*[83] was successful, although it is unique given the unusual facts of the case. The directors of the company were the individuals who were most likely to be harmed by their acts and omissions. The case evidenced little gross negligence on the part of the directors, which further justified the application of the provision. The evidence in the BFS and D&T case was considered by the former not to be of a trivial nature, even though it did not give rise to allegations of dishonesty. According to Evans-Lombe J, while the evidence pointed to the existence of negligence it was limited to a technical nature and was not 'pervasive and compelling'. Consequently s. 727 could reasonably be applied in those circumstances. However, Evans-Lombe decided that D&T had already benefited from being excused partially on the basis

76 Ibid., at para. 690.
77 Ibid., at para. 693.
78 Ibid., at para. 826.
79 Ibid., at para. 892.
80 Ibid., at para. 897.
81 Ibid., at para. 1069.
82 Ibid., at para. 1125.
83 *Re D'Jan of London Ltd Copp v. D'Jan* [1994] BCLC 561.

of its counterclaim of contributory negligence, so giving rise to a similar result in the end.

The Barings decision shows the court's attempt to realign the relationship between the auditor and the company to reflect its statutory foundation: to assess the stewardship of the company on behalf of the shareholders based on the accounting information provided by the company. The decision certainly reaffirms that the auditor is not, as noted before, an 'insurer against company losses'. In addition it highlights that auditors are not exposed to the same level of damages for negligence as they were in the past, regardless of the failures of directors and management to perform their responsibilities with reasonable care.[84]

The small fee charged for the audit of BFS also played a part, albeit a small one, in determining the level of blame placed on the shoulders of D&T, as it acted as an indicator of the level of work envisaged for such a low-risk audit. The decision reaffirms the auditor's responsibility to exercise scepticism only when audit evidence gives rise to a suspicion that material mis-statements may exist in the accounts, not at the commencement of the audit. The auditors acted with reasonable care despite the possibility of other methods of auditing the financial statements that may or may not have drawn out the mis-statements. Nevertheless, the auditors failed to investigate the discrepancies when issues required them to probe further, as required in the auditing guidelines discussed above and as 'common sense' would suggest. But despite the failures of the auditors the management failures continued long after the audits were complete. Indeed, it suffices to say that management failings were the only cause of the losses in the latter part of Barings' existence. Finally, the level of fault placed on the shoulders of the external auditors was not systemic by any means; as Evans-Lombe J contended, the negligence was more of a 'technical' and 'minor' nature at the lower end of the spectrum.

The FSA's Use of External Auditors

The work of the external auditor is still important to the FSA's decision-making process despite the criticisms levelled above.[85] For example, the external auditor will assist the FSA with information on financial resources, and report issues of material significance regarding a firm undertaking deposit-taking business. The FSA places the responsibility for appointing a suitably experienced external auditor on the regulated firm.[86] It is the responsibility of the firm and the external auditor to ensure the auditor is independent in accordance with professional and ethical guidelines.[87]

The FSA also needs to satisfy itself that the external auditor is sufficiently independent, considering the fact that the degree of independence may decline over time. The regulated firm is required to cooperate fully with the external auditor, including giving access to the firm's records.[88] The work of the auditor may raise

84 *Re London and General Bank* [1895] 2 Ch 166.

85 FSA, Supervision Manual, Chapter 3, para. 3.2.1G, SUP 3.

86 SUP 3 3.4.1G and 3.4.2R.

87 SUP 3 3.4.7R.

88 SUP 3 3.6.1R.

concerns about the business of the regulated firm. In such circumstances the firm is expected to disclose those concerns to the FSA if they could, *inter alia*, result in the accounts being qualified.[89] The external auditor also has a responsibility to cooperate with the FSA and provide it with information to make an informed decision about the firm's compliance with its rules, standards and guidelines.[90] This relationship is reciprocal: the FSA also has a responsibility to cooperate with the auditors to assist them with their work.[91]

Given that the FSA relies on reports provided by external auditors to make regulatory decisions,[92] it should come as no surprise that it has in place powers to disqualify or prohibit auditors from acting for a regulated firm if they breach their duty towards the regulator. The FSA highlights the sensitivity surrounding disqualification, so the imposition of the sanction needs to be proportionate to the breach of duty. However, the scope of reasons for disqualifying or prohibiting an auditor has been extended to cover not just issues connected with appointment but also issues concerning professional conduct *per se* deemed to call into question the individual's or firm's professionalism.[93] The seriousness of the breach would be assessed in the light of the FSA regulatory objective that was threatened, such as consumer interests, market confidence or increasing the likelihood of financial crime occurring at the regulated firm. Furthermore, the FSA can take into account any previous action taken by the governing professional body against the auditor, thus matters not relating to the financial services industry could be taken into account to gauge whether the auditor is fit and proper to undertake the audit of a regulated firm. The sanction is not simply limited to firms but also applies to individuals.

The Auditors' Right and Duty to Report to Regulators in the Financial Sector

The traditional relationship between external auditor and client is one of confidentiality within which the auditor does not have the authority to communicate his findings to others. However, the financial services industry is an exception to that rule. The Banking Act 1987 first conferred a right on auditors to communicate any matter of which they might became aware regarding the business or affairs of an authorised institution. This right placed on the auditor an obligation to fulfil the objectives of the legislation while acting for the client. This requirement to communicate was not accepted easily by the auditing profession, but it was given a choice between either a duty to communicate with the regulator or the more contentious responsibility of detecting fraud and error. The working group set up by the ICAEW (Institute of Chartered Accountants in England and Wales) with the Bank of England considered the imposition of the latter too onerous. However, pressure after the closure of BCCI and the recommendations by Lord Justice Bingham to extend the scope of the duty was overwhelming. The right and duty to report to the regulator in the financial

89 SUP 3.7.2G.
90 SUP 3.8.
91 SUP 3.8.9G.
92 ENF 17.
93 ENF 17.4.5 G.

sector were soon articulated in the profession's auditing standards, which have recently been revised.

The new SAS 620 is a revised edition of the first statement regarding communication with the regulator in the financial services sector issued in 1994.[94] It provides a statutory duty that the auditors of a regulated entity should bring to the attention of the regulator information they come across during the ordinary course of performing the audit. Such information includes any matter considered relevant to the regulator's remit of responsibility and any matter of material significance to the regulator. SAS 620 provides a 'general' duty to report to the regulator if information obtained during the audit warrants that course of action. A right to report also exists if a matter falls outside this definition but warrants being passed on to the regulator to protect the public interest. The new standard provides guidelines on the expression 'in the capacity of an auditor'. It takes into account the fact that information about the audit client can be obtained either directly or indirectly when parties involved in the audit also act in another capacity for the client. This requires the audit firm to be much more aware of the non-audit services it provides to the client, and places on the audit partner a responsibility to plan the audit so that it captures the various different associations the firm may have with the audit client. The auditor must report to the regulator information about those other services if they are considered to affect 'adversely' the regulated entity's compliance with the necessary regulatory requirements. This in many respects advocates the principle of taking a holistic examination of audit and non-audit work carried out by a firm so that the impact of the relationships and businesses can be taken into account from a regulatory perspective. In general this solves the issue arising from the BCCI saga of tax liability management, which could raise regulatory implications.[95]

Qualification of Bank Accounts

Banks are unique institutions in that they are vulnerable to a run if adverse opinions about them are disclosed to the capital markets and depositors. Disclosures such as these could result in their demise or pose a risk of contagion.[96] Information about the well-being of banks has to be cautiously disclosed, hence the concern about providing an adverse opinion on a set of bank accounts. Notwithstanding this, measures exist to ensure that the regulator is made aware of problems during bilateral and trilateral discussions. Bilateral discussions do create a tension in the trust relationship between external auditor and management, simply because the audit fee is paid by the institution and yet the auditor is discussing its private business with a third party.[97] Management will inevitably see the auditor as a person working in the interests of

94 Auditing Practices Board (2004) *The Auditors' Right and Duty to Report to the Regulators in the Financial Sector*, May.

95 *Inquiry into the Supervision of the Bank of Credit and Commerce International*, note 12 above.

96 See pp. 2–3.

97 Interview, 25 January 2001, with external auditors of institutions authorised under the Banking Act 1987.

regulators, shareholders and depositors. In any regulatory environment the external auditor must have all the interests equally in mind. This is because an adverse report would place the interests of depositors at risk – a risk which shareholders have clearly undertaken as investors. The auditor is providing a service to regulators: he must assist and bridge the gaps principally in the areas of fraud, error and conflicts of interest. Consequently, qualification of the financial accounts of a bank is not a simple decision. In these cases, auditors are required to notify the FSA if they intend to qualify the accounts in accordance with ss. 235(2)(3) and 237 of the Companies Act 1985.[98] The bank would also have to consider whether it should notify the FSA of a possible qualification of the annual financial statements, even if the qualification is no more than a comment on an aspect of its accounts.[99]

The reluctance to qualify financial statements raises serious dilemmas for auditors, especially when a problem arises more than six months after an audit and losses are exposed or, worse, the institution collapses. Despite the concerns expressed by the auditors of BCCI, that bank's accounts were not qualified. According to Plaistowe of the ICA, the possibility of causing a run on a bank 'is always a question which you have to have in your mind when you are auditing a bank'. However, 'if any auditor were in a position that he had doubts about the accounts of a company such that he wanted to qualify those accounts then that is, indeed, what he should do'.[100] But the general consensus in the case of BCCI is that the extent of the fraud and its deliberate concealment were such that it was too much to ask the auditors and supervisors to 'uncover the deliberate and well designed fraud'.[101]

The Skilled Person

The policy of using the external auditors of a regulated firm to act in the capacity of skilled person has not been completely abandoned. This is somewhat surprising given the criticism it generated during the previous regulatory regime governing banks.[102] However, the skilled person is not used to the same extent as its predecessor, the reporting accountant: as the FSA annual statistics show, in 2003 only 28 reports were commissioned, which fell to only 19 reports in 2004.[103] So the FSA has taken a more cautious approach to the use of external auditors acting as skilled persons, and relies on a variety of methods of supervision and investigation.

98 SUP 3, para. 3.2.2G.

99 SUP 3.7.2G.

100 Treasury and Civil Service Committee (1992) Banking Supervision and BCCI: International and National Regulation, Minutes of Evidence, 29 January, *The Institute of Chartered Accountants in England and Wales (ICAEW) Mr W I D Plaistowe, Mr P R Chapman and Mr B R Nelson*, London, HMSO, at p. 31, q. 106.

101 The Treasury Select Committee relied on Price Waterhouse's argument that 'even the best planned and executed audit will not necessarily discover a sophisticated fraud, especially one where there is collusion at the highest level of management and with third parties'. Fourth Report, Evidence, pp. 59–60, cited p. xvii. See Chapter Six, Legal Accountability of Financial Regulators.

102 Arthur Andersen Report, n. 13 above, at p. 13, para. 68.

103 FSA (2005) *Annual Report*, at p. 156.

The FSA has the authority under s. 166 of the FSMA 2000 to notify a 'skilled person' to provide it with 'a report on any matter'. The appointment of the skilled person is contractual and the report is addressed to the directors of the regulated firm. The FSA provides rules governing the appointment of auditors and skilled persons in its Supervision Manual.[104] These measures go some way to reducing any conflict of interest when skilled persons are required to act objectively in assessing matters for which they were responsible in another capacity, such as the client's auditors.[105] SUP 3 stresses the importance of undertaking audit work independently and avoiding conflict of interests with the firm. The FSA decides whether the auditor breaches the independence rule by referring to the ethical guidance provided by the profession. Thus the onus is on the firm to ensure steps are taken so that it has an independent auditor. These proposals go some way to place the issue of independence on the regulatory agenda, but the current internal arrangements may not necessarily ensure auditor independence.[106]

The FSA can appoint a skilled person to report to it as part of its monitoring, diagnostic, preventive or remedial work to assess the risks posed to its regulatory objectives. It thus has the power to initiate a report for the purpose of carrying out an investigation into issues that may relate to a particular sector of the industry or an individual firm.[107] For example, the FSA's decision to impose a fine on Abbey National plc[108] of £800,000 for its failure to handle with due care and skill the complaints resulting from its mis-selling of endowment mortgages was based on the findings of a s. 166 skilled person report into the matter. The scope of the report included reference to the whole complaints-handling process put in place by Abbey to deal with endowment mis-selling. It specifically referred to the consistency with which it dealt with complaints, and this was one of the main reasons for imposing such a large fine. This enforcement action demonstrates the reliance the FSA places on the expertise and findings of skilled persons. For example, the FSA's justifications for imposing the fine were based on the fact that the skilled person found Abbey *inter alia* to have failed to ascertain the customers' attitude to risk.[109]

The Liability of the External Auditor to Third Parties

The potential liability of external auditors for failure to undertake their responsibility with reasonable care to audit the accounts of a client is much more straightforward in comparison to their potential liability to a third party that may not be privy to the contractual relationship but relies on their findings.[110] This section analyses the duty

104 SUP 3.5 and SUP 5.4.8.

105 Ibid., SUP 5.4.8(5)(c).

106 See pp. 88 92.

107 FSMA 2000, ss. 167–168.

108 FSA (2005) 'Final Notice: Abbey National plc', 25 May.

109 Ibid., para. 4.24.

110 *Candler v. Crane Christmas & Co.* [1951] KB 164; although the dissenting opinion in the case by Lord Denning was subsequently approved in *Hedley Byrne and Heller & Partners Ltd* [1963] which held it was wrongly decided; and *Caparo*, n. 14 above, at p. 582.

of care that can be placed on a third party like the FSA which relies on the work of the external auditors to make a broad range of decisions, from authorisation to enforcement, on the basis of the auditors' findings. The guidance provided by the FSA gives rise to a clear duty for the external auditors to take reasonable care, even though they are mainly instructed by the client (the regulated firm) and the contract exists between the external auditors and the firm in terms of what the engagement requires. The FSA has formalised the relationship between itself and external auditors to avoid the potential uncertainty regarding whether a duty of care exists or not (as would be the case by relying on the common law position) by putting in place a formal obligation to take reasonable care.

The common law position depends on whether the courts determine that the external auditor owes a duty of care to a third party which may rely on its findings. The courts have applied the criteria articulated in *Caparo* of 'foreseeability, proximity and whether it is just, fair and reasonable' to decide whether a duty of care exists. The application of the test meant it was only 'just, fair and reasonable' for a duty to be owed to shareholders as a whole for the specific purpose of determining the stewardship of the company rather than reasons to do with investment decisions. The *Caparo* case refers to the principle of 'proximity' to ascertain whether a duty of care exists. The idea of proximity in relation to third parties requires consideration of whether the auditor's advice is given on the basis that it will be relied upon for a particular purpose which has been outlined to him; the adviser knows that the information will be communicated to the advisee for the purpose stated; and the adviser knows that the particular third party will rely on it to make the specified decision.[111] The application of this criterion inevitably narrows down the range of individuals who may claim an auditor owed them a duty of care. For example, auditors do not generally owe a duty of care to creditors,[112] investors[113] or a prospective purchaser.[114]

Law Society v. KPMG[115] is an interesting case as it relates to the potential liability of a reporting accountant to the Law Society (as the regulator of solicitors) for damages in the tort of negligence for the accountant's failure to qualify its report about a firm which was commissioned by the Law Society. The Court of Appeal decision in the case affirmed Vice Chancellor Sir Richard Scott's decision, thus cementing in principle the expansion of the incremental approach of the tort for claims for economic loss by not restricting the duty of care to cases where it is only 'fair, just and reasonable to do so'.[116] In this case the failure to qualify the report culminated in continued malpractice at the firm of solicitors, and prevented the Law Society from intervening and avoiding losses as a result of compensation claims. According to Scott, the relationship between the reporting accountant and the Law

111 *Caparo*, n. 14 above, at p. 589.

112 *Al Saudi Banque v. Clark Pixley* [1989] 3 All ER 361; *Berg & Sons v. Adams* [1993] BCLC 1045.

113 *Anthony v. Wright* [1995] BCC 768.

114 *James McNaughton Papers Group Ltd v. Hicks Andersen & Co.* [1991] 1 All ER 134.

115 *Law Society v. KPMG Peat Marwick and Others*, *The Times*, 6 July 2000.

116 *Professional Negligence* (2000) '*Law Society v. KPMG Peat Marwick* Court of Appeal, 29th June, 2000', case report, *Professional Negligence* vol. 16, 186.

Society was 'sufficiently proximate' to warrant due care. In this case, provisions of the Solicitors Act 1974 required the accountant to alert the Law Society to the possibility of improprieties in the conduct of the solicitors' practice, and that those improprieties could lead to claims for compensation.[117] The most problematic issue in determining whether a duty of care existed was whether the expectation of due care was 'just and reasonable'. This required consideration of policy to determine whether it is necessary to expand the incremental approach of the tort of negligence to encapsulate the relationship between the Law Society and the reporting accountant. The vice chancellor made the points that damages arose only from the undetected misappropriation of funds, which consequently led to the loss to the compensation fund; and the fact that such reports were annual meant the unqualified report would stand until the next reporting opportunity detected the misappropriation, so limiting the opportunity to uncover the wrongdoing.

The Role of External Auditors in the USA

The Securities and Exchange Commission (SEC) has a broad range of powers governing investor protection in the US securities market.[118] In its remit is oversight of auditor independence.[119] It plays a very influential role in the auditing profession and the guidelines and standards that govern its work. Generally, external auditors in the USA are members of the American Institute of Certified Public Accountants (AICPA), which is responsible for overseeing the professional conduct of members and ensuring they comply with auditing standards. The standards devised by the Accounting Principles Board (APB) provide guidance on the competency and independence which audit work is required to achieve, so that reasonable care is taken. The standards also govern the way the audit should be completed so that the auditor can provide an opinion on the financial statements and indicate whether they comply with the appropriate accounting standards. In addition to the AICPA, the Sarbanes Oxley Act 2002 requires all public companies to be audited by accounting firms that are registered with the newly formed Public Company Accounting Oversight Board set up specifically to oversee the auditing of public companies. This body intends to devise specific auditing standards for public companies, incorporating the standards produced by the AICPA.[120] The professional guidelines, as amended by the Sarbanes Oxley Act, reassert the importance of the external auditor acting with the appropriate

117 Ibid., at p. 187.

118 Kammel, A. J. (2005) *The Law of International Banking Institutions: A Comparative Analysis*, Vienna, Mille Tre, at p. 402.

119 Securities Exchange Act 1934, s. 2. For a historical overview of external auditing see GAO (1996) *The Accounting Profession, Major Issues: Progress and Concerns*, report to the Ranking Minority Member, Committee on Commerce, House of Representatives, Washington, DC, General Accounting Office, GAO/AIMD-96-98, at pp. 26–28.

120 PCAOB Annual Report 2003, available at www.pcaobus.org/documents/PCAOB_2003_AR.pdf.

level of independence. In particular they regulate the provision of non-audit work to the client.[121]

The US approach to banking regulation and supervision is generally characterised as an on-site system of monitoring the safety and soundness of authorised banks.[122] However, the degree of on-site and off-site regulation does vary between the US regulators.[123] Notwithstanding the reliance placed on regulatory oversight, external auditors do have a significant role to play in assisting the regulator with its decisions about the safety and soundness of a bank.[124] The audit of US banks is governed by s. 112 (codified as s. 36) of the Federal Deposit Insurance Corporation Improvement Act 1991 (FDICIA).[125] The annual accounts are required to be audited by an independent public accountant in accordance with generally accepted auditing principles and s. 37 of the FDICIA.[126] The auditor is required to determine whether the financial statements are presented fairly in accordance with general auditing principles and the requirements set out by the respective regulator. The auditor is also required to implement procedures to gauge the extent to which the insured institution is compliant with the necessary standards, rules and regulations. The management of the bank is responsible for preparing the annual statements, which need to comply with generally accepted accounting principles set by the profession and the bank regulator. The annual accounts also need to include a statement by the chief executive officer (CEO) and chief financial officer (CFO) indicating management responsibility as to the adequacy of the internal controls and compliance with the safety and soundness requirements of the respective regulator.[127] The insured institution is required to cooperate with the public accountant by providing the necessary information to complete the financial audit. The onus is placed firmly on management to have in place an effective system of risk management to produce reliable and accurate financial statements. The external auditor is required to assess and report on the management's assertions of the effectiveness of the institution's internal controls.

121 Zinski, C. J. and Pacioni, M. R. (2003) 'Sarbanes-Oxley Act of 2002: Financial institution compliance', *Banking Law Journal*, March, 191.

122 Group of Thirty (1994) *Defining the Role of Accountants, Bankers and Regulators in the United States*, Study Group Report, Washington, DC, at pp. 25–29.

123 See US Federal Reserve Division of Banking Supervision and Regulation (2001) *Commercial Bank Examination Manual*, Section 1000.1, Examination Strategy and Risk-Focused Examinations, at p. 2.

124 Ferguson, R. W. (2001) 'Certified public accountants: Partners in financial stability', paper presented at American Institute of Certified Public Accountants National Conference on Banks and Savings Institutions, Washington, DC, 8 November, available at www.federalreserve.gov/boarddocs/speeches/2001/20011108/default.htm, at p. 4. For an analysis of safety and soundness see pp. 69–72.

125 Section 112 codified as FDICIA 1991, s. 36, available at http://thomas.loc.gov/cgi-bin/query/F?c102:3:./temp/~c102yz39A4:e14351.

126 This section of the FDICIA provides policy guidelines surrounding the level of capital a bank may hold and the significance attached to them when problems arise that threaten the deposit insurance fund.

127 Badawi, I. M., Elifoglu, I. H., Latshaw, C. A. and Zollo, R. A. (2003) 'New interagency guidance on the internal audit function', *Bank Accounting & Finance*, October, 32.

Interestingly, the onus is on management rather than the regulator to define the remit of the audit programme so that it covers those areas deemed to be of a significant risk. The Federal Reserve indicates the reliance it places on external auditors' work in their examination of a bank. This is based on the perceived advantages of having an external audit, namely to enhance the accuracy and reliability of regulatory reports, improve internal controls and benefit from the efficiency of a risk-based approach to regulation. The Federal Reserve also points out other benefits of external auditors regarding non-audit work: they can act in other capacities such as advising on the adequacy of internal controls, taxation and management information systems. In the latter case, separate external auditors would need to undertake the non-audit work in accordance with the AICPA's professional standards.

In the US system external auditors are not utilised by all banks in the same way, so the approach is very much a two-tier system: one governing public banks and the other small non-public insured banks. The USA requires an independent audit on an annual basis of banks with assets totalling $500 million or more.[128] In the case of small banks which are not subject to other audit requirements set by the SEC, the Federal Reserve encourages the adoption of an annual audit as part of their overall risk management plans. The rationale behind the policy is to allow more flexibility by reducing the regulatory burden on small institutions. In the policy guidelines small institutions are recommended to adopt an annual audit of financial statements. However, the guidance also recommends alternatives, such as an annual examination of the effectiveness of internal controls governing financial reporting, an audit of the balance sheet or an annual state-required examination.[129] The alternatives obviously do not equate to a full annual financial audit in terms of its extensive planning and procedures to test and verify the assertions made by management and the reliability of the financial statements; they cover only one aspect of what may feature in a full audit of financial accounts. The objectives and scope of the various types of audit are the responsibility of the management and audit committee of the institution. Input by the regulator would be useful here, considering it is going to rely on the information provided by the external auditor to determine the scope of its own examinations. In these circumstances, management may be rather conservative about their business and the risks it poses to the insured fund. This risk is particularly significant with the annual state-required examination, which can be carried out by an institution's own management.

The Federal Reserve, as indicated above, advocates the use of external auditors. However, the rule governing independent annual audit is not applicable across the board and nor is it a continuous obligation; it is compulsory for only the first three years of a bank's charter. The external audit may not be an absolute guardian against corporate abuse but it does remain a useful component in assessing the stewardship of the company. This was indicated in strong terms after the review of the savings and

128 12 USC, § 1831m and § 1831n.

129 *Federal Register* (1999) 'Interagency policy statement on external auditing programs of banks and savings associations', *Federal Register*, vol. 64, No. 187, 28 September, Rules and Regulations, available at www.wais.access.gpo.gov.

loans disaster in the 1980s.[130] The GAO report pointed to concerns about the overall approach to corporate governance in banks, not just the problems associated with annual audits. In the savings and loans collapse, of the 39 banks that failed during this period four were never audited and 23 had not been audited in the previous year. Moreover, six of these 23 banks had not been audited for the last two years prior to the collapse. Notwithstanding the limits of the independent audit, it does provide some degree of deterrence against corporate abuse. The lack of or inconsistent approach to auditing simply enabled management to manipulate their financial position to disguise the problems present within the banks. In particular, serious internal control failures were more likely to be picked up by an independent audit and brought to the attention of senior management so they could act on the information. While the GAO report provided a number of recommendations to improve financial regulation and supervision, such as annual audit of insured banks, it did not indicate the scope of the rule, i.e. all insured banks, large and small, annually. As indicated above, the audit of bank financial accounts remains applicable only to certain banks for limited time periods.

The demise of Superior Bank in 2002 highlighted the point that issues still remain surrounding the role of external auditors in the US supervisory process.[131] The bank's main business was concentrated on originating and securitising mortgages for customers of low credit quality. The business was not appropriately managed, leading to a high concentration of risky assets which were not accurately valued, giving rise to the impression that the bank was highly capitalised.[132] Once the regulator did its own valuation of the bank's assets it became clear that the bank was significantly undercapitalised. The inappropriate valuation of the bank's assets continued for a considerable length of time, which led to the question as to why the external auditors failed to spot the matter and raise it with management and regulators. This incident brought to the fore the issue of auditor competence, independence and the reliance placed on the auditor's opinions by the regulator. For instance, the external auditors provided advice on evaluation techniques which turned out to be flawed.[133] Notwithstanding the GAO report's general support for the use of external auditors to assist the regulators, it also expressed an important warning about them being over-reliant on the audited accounts.[134] According to Bies, auditors are not concerned about the substance of the accounts, but rather the form.[135] It is submitted that auditors are not drawing to the regulator's attention internal control deficiencies. Moreover, they

130 GAO (1991) 'Failed banks: Accounting and auditing reforms urgently needed', GAO/AFMD-91-43, April, at pp. 41–46.

131 GAO (2002) 'Bank regulation: Analysis of the failure of Superior Bank FSB, Hinsdale, Illinois', GAO-02-419T; Johnson, C. A. (2004) 'The failure of Superior Bank FSB: Regulatory lessons learned', *Banking Law Journal*, January, 47, at p. 59.

132 GAO, ibid., at p. 9.

133 Ibid., at p. 10.

134 Ibid., at pp. 15–16.

135 Bies, S. S. (2003) 'Restoring our confidence in bank controls and financial statements', paper presented at Conference of State Bank Supervisors, Ashville, NC, 30 May, available at www.federalreserve.gov/boarddocs/speeches/2003/20030530/default.htm, at p. 4.

are applying auditing standards, i.e. a materiality standard linked to annual accounts, which causes a number of anomalies. According to the governor, external auditors should not apply such a standard to an attestation report because (from a regulator's perspective) the deficiencies they come across provide information about the quality of the internal controls.

This is further exacerbated because the external auditors rely on the internal audit function within the bank to produce the attestation report by basing their conclusions on its work. This does not lead to the appropriate level of quality assurance, given the fact that the internal audit may not be independent from management.

To reduce the likelihood of regulatory concerns going undetected, the federal regulatory agencies have the authority to request working papers from an external auditor engaged under s. 36(g) (3) (A) (i) by an FDIA-authorised institution.[136] The rationale for the policy is twofold: firstly to gather a better understanding of the bank's systems and controls, and secondly to evaluate the auditor's opinion based on the evidence submitted by management governing the financial statements. The FDIC is granted this right before an external auditor takes up an appointment with an insured institution. The engagement letter grants the examiners access to all the accountant's or auditor's working papers and other material to do with the institution. However, this policy is not mandatory when it comes to institutions below the s. 36 threshold; it is simply left to the discretion of the external auditor to agree to the request. The policy is further assisted by the annual examination, where the examiner has the authority to request all correspondence between the auditor and management to be disclosed as part of the review. Notwithstanding the discretionary form regarding the request for working papers from institutions below the s. 36 threshold, the FDIC request is couched in rather coercive tones of persuasion, indicating that failure to comply would be deemed a contravention of the policy statement.

The Federal Reserve is initiating new guidelines to enable it to enforce the appropriate level of professionalism within the external auditing profession with a range of sanctions. According to Hughes and Gfeller, 'accountants auditing non-public financial institutions will now be motivated to audit for fraud as vigorously as their counterparts do when auditing public companies'.[137] The broad scope of the rules means that auditors will need to be familiar with the other links they have with the client and any connected group of entities so that these do not jeopardise or threaten the audit engagement. The basis of the move is to ensure auditors undertake their responsibilities with the appropriate rigour expected by the examiners relying on their opinions about the well-being of the bank. The power to suspend or debar an auditor is based on such grounds as a lack of the requisite qualifications to undertake the audit; knowingly or recklessly engaging in conduct that results in a violation of the applicable professional standards; acts or omissions of negligence; and aiding

---

136 Elifoglu, I. and Thompson, J. W. (2000/2001) 'When may examiners review auditors' workpapers?', *Bank Accounting & Finance*, November/December, 51.

137 *Federal Register* (2003) 'Removal, suspension, and debarment of accountants from performing audit services', *Federal Register*, vol. 68, Rules and Regulations; Hughes, J. D. and Gfeller, C. F. (2003) 'Federal bank regulators seek greater power over "broken accounting profession"', *Bank Accounting & Finance*, June, 21.

or abetting 'a material and knowing or reckless violation of any provision of the Federal Bank and securities law'.[138] These acts or omissions would give rise to either the firm or the individual being removed, suspended or debarred.

Conclusion

The audit of financial statements is an important aspect of corporate accountability. Despite the pressure for more accountability of the external auditor's work, its necessity is without doubt. In many industries, notably financial services, regulators have in one form or another attempted to harness auditors' skills to assist them with their responsibilities. In many respects the use of external auditors further legitimises the function of regulation by harnessing a market tool for public ends. The work of the regulator and external auditor does share some similarities – for instance, verifying the accuracy of the financial representations made by management, with whom the responsibility for preparing the financial statements rests. However, caution is focused on whether the public objectives of financial regulation can be achieved by private entities that ultimately act in their own interests of commercial profit. These concerns were warranted when the role of the external auditor and reporting accountant were undertaken by the same firm, and the purchase of non-audit work was not regulated in the same manner as it is now. While the new changes do not prohibit the provision of non-audit work to the audit client, they certainly place the issue in a climate of caution to avoid overfamiliarity. The change in direction by audit committees on the topic of non-audit work, post-Enron, demonstrates the real concern companies have about the risk to their reputation if allegations of overfamiliarity are made. However, the relationship between the auditor and client can become over time too familiar, and so call into question whether the auditor can maintain the appropriate degree of vigilance and scepticism required by the profession. Industry pressure to complete audits in record times and at least cost exacerbates this fragile relationship. The collapse of Barings demonstrates that external auditors can risk liability when relying on management representations. However, whether they should be burdened with a significant amount of legal responsibility should be challenged when the case goes to the Court of Appeal. It is advocated, as demonstrated at first instance but to a higher degree, that management should bear the highest proportion of legal responsibility for failures within their companies.

In order to reduce the likelihood of public interests being undermined, external auditors need to be regulated by the regulator using them so that their independence can be assured and conflicts of interests are reduced. The broad authority the FSA now possesses to disqualify external auditors or skilled persons from working in the financial services industry allows it to exercise more influence over them. The FSA has also adopted a more holistic approach to the work accountants and auditors within a firm provide to the same client. The BCCI collapse demonstrated how non-audit work does have detrimental implications for regulators. The move by the FSA to make auditors consider these types of risks when planning the audit is a positive

138 *Federal Register*, ibid., at p. 48257.

step forward to ensure the audit is better informed about the implications of this work and the duty auditors have to inform the regulator when concerns arise. However, the FSA approach is similar to the traditional approach in that it can use skilled persons to undertake a report on any matter it considers necessary, but this does not preclude the FSA from undertaking its own on-site investigations. The possible move towards requiring skilled persons to report on the effectiveness of internal controls, as they do for building societies, will further the FSA rationale for using them.

The US position is premised on an on-site system of supervision, so the use of external auditors will be limited. However, this does not preclude their use to assist the regulatory examination process to gauge whether banks are operating in a safe and sound manner. The emphasis on the on-site approach may explain why the use of external auditors is not as regulated as it is in the UK. The US approach is focused on the rationale of using the external audit to examine the financial statements of the insured institution, but it does not extend beyond that as it does in the UK, where extra auditor functions are acquired. While an external auditor is advocated strongly, it is not applied consistently across all authorised institutions regardless of size. The adoption of other forms of audit will not provide the same depth of scope as an audit of annual financial statements. Management representations will not always be reliable, so caution needs to be incorporated into the weight examiners place on such statements. This is to some extent mitigated by the examiners' right to seek disclosure of working papers relating to a client. Moreover, the adoption of enforcement sanctions proposed by the Federal Reserve will also strengthen the regulator's position to punish work considered by the external auditor as being below professional standards. This approach very much mirrors the one adopted by the FSA only recently. Finally, while considerable change has taken place to strengthen the independence and standards surrounding the work of an external auditor, the reliance placed on management representations by external auditors is one factor that needs to be monitored closely to ensure independence.

Chapter 6

Legal Accountability of Financial Regulators

Introduction

The rationale for bank regulation and supervision is based on the desirability of maintaining financial stability, and protection of the interests of depositors is intrinsically linked to this. The mechanisms to protect these interests arise through public regulation and supervision rather than through private means. The obligation a bank has to depositors are inextricably limited by the fact that the bank-depositor relationship is simply one of debtor and creditor, so the mechanisms to hold banks accountable is limited in general corporate law. Thus banks have no need to consider the interests of depositors unless public regulation is put into the equation and provides a framework in which they can operate. The mechanisms to protect depositor interests involve compliance with statutory provisions and rules that have been put in place by the regulator; indeed, the regulator has a general responsibility to satisfy itself that banks are in continuous compliance. This ultimately requires those conferred with the responsibility of exercising regulatory powers to act in good faith and in accordance with the general fiduciary duties associated with their employment. Thus it is important to analyse how depositors are protected if a bank fails – can they seek compensation for the losses they sustain, and damages if the compensation is not considered adequate?

In this chapter the legal accountability of regulators for their decisions is explored, broadly focusing on the legal responsibilities of those exercising public functions and the protection afforded to them in common law and statute. It will outline the alternative mechanisms for holding the regulated and regulators accountable to both the regulated and depositors rather than have these matters dealt with in the courts. The first section explores the fiduciary duty of public employees generally, in particular the obligation they have to act in the interests of their employer rather than for personal gain. This is important, as it reflects the general obligations of employees working for public bodies such as the FSA; the FSA code of conduct elaborates on these obligations to protect the integrity of the regulator from the unique conflicts of interests that arise from its work. FSA employees are required to abide by the code of conduct during their employment, as failure to comply could have wider repercussions of a public nature, such as undermining the credibility of the regulator. The second section examines the exposure of financial regulators to liability in tort of negligence. It will outline the rationale for an implied immunity given that a financial regulator acts in the interests of depositors as a whole rather than individually, and highlight that Parliament has put in place an official system of compensation which in some respects deals with the losses that would ensue from a bank closure. The third section will outline express immunity as set out in the FSMA 2000. It will look at the recent Privy Council decision where express immunity did not protect the regulator from acts or omissions deemed to be outside the scope of the legislation. The implications for the financial regulators are discussed, given that decisions to safeguard market confidence may have to be made in a short time with a limited amount of information. The fourth section explores the alternative mechanisms in place to deal with matters that could give rise to liability in common law were it not for the fact that an implied immunity and indeed a statutory immunity are in place. The alternative mechanisms essentially deal with the failures of both the regulated and regulator via the Depositor Compensation Scheme, Ombudsman Scheme and Independent Complaints Commissioner. These mechanisms will be described with the use of examples to illustrate some of the work they undertake. The fifth section analyses the tort of misfeasance in public office, the exception to implied and express immunity for claims in the tort of negligence. This section will explore the ingredients of the tort and its focus on actions in bad faith by referring to the *Three Rivers* litigation that has recently been discontinued in a cloud of heavy judicial criticism. The sixth section focuses on aspects of legal accountability of financial regulators in the USA. It will first outline and describe the statutory rules and regulations public employees are required to comply with, in particular the fact that such employees expressly act in the interests of the USA rather than the public body which employs them. Additional rules and regulations exist on top of those general ones, and pay particular attention to the types of conflicts of interests that can arise in the financial sector. The issue of immunity is also considered, and the liability of federal regulators after the savings and loans crisis in the 1980s and 1990s that gave rise to compensation payments by the US government. Finally, the seventh section will provide some concluding points and comparative observations about the UK and US approach.

Public Responsibilities

A regulator having responsibilities which are conferred by statute is accountable for the way it exercises it duties both politically and legally. Ultimately these duties are performed by its employees, and those holding senior positions such as directors will be individually accountable for their acts or omissions – not just to the employer, but also to the government department or select committee responsible for the sector. These employees are required to undertake their duties in good faith and in compliance with a host of equitable obligations: fidelity, loyalty, confidentiality, not profiting from one's position and avoiding conflicts of interest. These are incorporated expressly or implicitly in the contract of employment, which governs the way the regulator expects them to exercise their responsibilities on a day-to-day basis.[1] The

1 Rideout, R. W. and Dyson, J. C. (1983) *Rideout's Principles of Labour Law*, London, Sweet & Maxwell, at p. 74; Clarke, L. (1999) 'Commentary: Mutual trust and confidence, fiduciary relationships and the duty of disclosure', *Industrial Law Journal*, vol. 28, 348.

responsibility to ensure employees are complying with these disparate obligations lies with the employer, which has the power to dismiss employees for not exercising their duties in accordance with those obligations. Indeed, it is the employer, the public body, that will have its reputation damaged if those it employs do not exercise their responsibilities in good faith in the interests of those they are collectively serving, whether it is the regulated, depositors, investors or other stakeholders such as the government.

The relationship between employer and employee can be construed to be fiduciary, where a person undertakes to act for another person by placing their own self-interests to one side. According to Lord Herschell in *Bray v. Ford*,[2] a person is not allowed to put himself in a position where his interest conflicts with his duty, thus prejudicing the interests he is meant to protect. The principle provided by Lord Loughborough is also pertinent: 'he, who undertakes to act for another in any matter, shall not in the same matter act for himself'.[3] This has been interpreted to mean that fiduciaries cannot put themselves in a position where their obligations to the fiduciary are compromised,[4] and that a person in such a position should not profit from his position.[5] For example, Lord Nicholls highlighted the point in *AG v. Blake*[6] where a former member of the Secret Intelligence Service (SIS) wrote about his experience in the SIS in his autobiography. The Attorney General wished to prevent him from profiting from the obligation to the SIS he had undertaken when he entered into service. It was held that he had a duty of confidentiality which was similar to a fiduciary obligation, for which an account of the profits was necessary in the public interest. According to Lord Nicholls, 'equity reinforces the duty of fidelity owed by a trustee or fiduciary by requiring him to account for any profits he derives from his office or position. This ensures that trustees and fiduciaries are financially disinterested in carrying out their duties.'[7]

Equally important is the equitable principle of confidentiality, which is central to the relationship of trust between a public regulator and the industry it is supervising. According to Gurry, confidence is formed whenever one party (the confider) imparts to another (the confidant) private or secret matters on the express or implied understanding that the communication is for restricted purposes.[8] This duty of confidentiality does not come to an end once the individual has left his employment, as the confidentiality attaches to the information itself and thus continues.[9] For instance, in the decision of *Jonathan Cape* [1975] a cabinet minister whose work diaries were due for publication was prohibited until such time as the

2 *Bray v. Ford* [1896] A C 44, 51.
3 *Wichcote v. Lawrence* (1798) 3 Ves 740, 750.
4 *Chan v. Zacharia* [1983] 53 A L R 417, 435.
5 Public Bodies Corrupt Practices Act 1889, s. 2(b).
6 *Attorney General v. Blake* [2000] 3 WLR 625.
7 Ibid., at p. 280.
8 Gurry, F. (1985) 'Breach of confidence', in Finn, P. D. (ed.) *Essays in Equity*, London, Sweet and Maxwell, at p. 111.
9 Rideout and Dyson, n. 1 above, at p. 82.

collective ministerial responsibility he had been assigned had lapsed.[10] The latter point, highlighted by Megarry J, is considered in *AG v. Guardian Newspapers*,[11] where the Attorney General sought an injunction to prevent the newspaper from serialising extracts from the book *Spycatcher*. It was held that a person who has a duty of confidentiality should be prevented from disclosing information known to be secret; this emanates from both contract and equity. However, in order to establish that it is against the public interest it must be proven that disclosure was likely to damage or had damaged such interest. In this instance, the utility of the injunction against the newspaper was undermined by the worldwide publication of the book, which disclosed its content.

FSA Code of Conduct

The expectations of those responsible for exercising public functions are a prominent issue in the UK, and part and parcel of a move towards better standards of behaviour in public life.[12] The introduction of a code of conduct by the FSA to outline the standards of behaviour it expects of its employees in its role as regulator of the financial system is no surprise.[13] The importance attached to the code is quite obvious given the powers of the FSA and the broad range of responsibilities within its remit. While the right of third parties to claim damages in the tort of negligence against the FSA and its employees is expressly restricted in the FSMA 2000, it does not absolve the FSA from ensuring its employees exercise reasonable care in their day-to-day responsibilities.[14]

The code of conduct draws on some of the rules explained above in its guidance to employees and executive members when dealing with matters they may encounter while fulfilling the fiduciary duties associated with the execution of their responsibilities. The formalisation of standards of behaviour in a code of conduct avoids uncertainty as to what is expected of employees. Indeed, the weight attached to the code is elevated by the fact the FSA requires mandatory compliance by employees, with the possibility of dismissal if it is not adhered to.[15] It emphasises the importance of avoiding a third party being able reasonably to conclude a breach of the code as a result of acts or omissions of an employee, and consequently the FSA as employer, if an interest is not disclosed.

This means the code of conduct is part and parcel of a broader accountability and governance framework. It also includes a catch-all provision which requires the

10 *Attorney General v. Jonathan Cape* [1975] 3 WLR 606. This principle does need examining in light of the principle of disclosure in the public interest – see *Lion Laboratories v. Evans* [1984] 3 WLR 539.

11 *Attorney General v. Guardian Newspapers* (No. 2) 1 [1990] A C 109.

12 Woodhouse, D. (2003) 'Delivering public confidence: Codes of conduct, a step in the right direction', *Public Law*, Autumn, 511; Belcher, A. (1998) 'Codes of conduct and accountability for NHS boards', *Public Law*, Summer, 288.

13 FSA (2004) *The Financial Services Authority Code of Conduct*, available at www.fsa.gov.uk/pubs/staff/code_conduct.pdf.

14 For an explanation of this duty see Rideout and Dyson, n. 1 above, at p. 96.

15 FSA, n. 13 above, at p. 4.

employee to disclose 'any other significant relationship of any description, including professional, personal, financial or family relationship' held in connection with or capable of affecting a relevant organisation. Employees must disclose formally both present and past interests to the line manager and ethics officer, whose role is to ensure FSA staff comply with the code.

The FSA code of conduct sets out the scope of its remit to be effectively the financial system it regulates, designated as 'relevant organisations'. It places responsibility for compliance with the code on the employee, but it also encompasses the actions of the employee's family if the employee takes the ultimate financial decisions. So its scope is much broader than simply the execution of individuals' day-to-day responsibilities and how they should act, and includes those who may act on their behalf to achieve some personal goal.

The code of conduct is explicit in its expectations that 'work must be carried out in an environment which is free from any suggestion of improper influence' according to accepted rules of behaviour.[16] This is an attempt to set out clearly the culture expected to prevail in the working environment. It embarks on this by firstly addressing conflicts of interest that may arise in the course of an employee exercising FSA responsibilities. Such conflicts are covered by providing that the whole organisation needs to ensure that all interests which could arise in daily work and may conflict are disclosed. The code does not expand on the possible conflicts in an explicit way: it is left to the discretion of the individual to disclose any possible interests that 'could conflict'. It follows the point made above that an individual must not 'exploit or appear to exploit to our personal advantage, any personal or professional relationships'. For example, a 'financial' or 'personal' relationship could be either connected to or affected by the decision the employee is going to make.[17] The benefit that could accrue from such an act could be financial or a promise of future employment.

The code also governs more practical relationships an employee may have with a 'relevant organisation'. It refers *inter alia* to investments and other financial products such as mortgages, collective investment schemes and bank accounts. The relationship that may ensue and the interests therein do differ, so the code of conduct treats them differently as well. In the first case employees are made aware of the criminal offence of insider dealing: an employee who deals or arranges a deal in securities as a result of access to unpublished price-sensitive information is committing a criminal offence which could result in a prison sentence or a fine.[18] To avoid allegations of insider dealing the employee has to get clearance before dealing in such securities. In the case of other products and services the code is more flexible, since such products give rise to a lower probability of a 'gain', unlike dealing in securities.[19] If a conflict of interest does arise the individual employee is obliged to disclose it.

---

16 Ibid., at p. 6.

17 Ibid.

18 Ibid., at p. 9.

19 Ibid., at p. 11.

The code also covers the receipt of gifts and hospitality given during the course of employees dealing with, for instance, regulated firms or persons. While the FSA is not discouraging its staff from building good relations with the industry, it does need to ensure this does not give rise to 'criticism' and indeed 'undue influence'. To avoid being compromised the individual needs to exercise 'common sense' and ensure any likely conflict of interest is factored into the weight attached to any decision. The code specifically addresses the issue of gifts valued over £25, which need to be declared to the head of department and surrendered to the ethics officer to make suitable arrangements to give them to charity or dispose of them. It also addresses whether or not hospitality can be received in the form of meals or tickets for an event. While the FSA encourages its employees to get to know the relevant organisations, it requires them to avoid 'frequent', 'lavish' or 'expensive' and 'exclusive' forms of hospitality which could imply 'a sense of obligation' or 'bias' in their decision-making.[20]

The implications for the FSA of such breaches would be damage to its reputation and credibility as a public regulator, resulting in a loss of confidence if it were considered widespread. Evidence of this poses serious implications for the employee as well, given that the individual could be dismissed. However, it is not completely clear on how many occasions the code has been breached as the information is not available in the FSA annual reports. This leads to a general conclusion that either such information is not disclosed or no breach has occurred. Both conclusions give rise to criticism: shedding light on such matters would enhance the credibility of the FSA by explicitly showing that it is dealing with such issues seriously, as it does with enforcement matters generally. The idea that no breach has occurred is somewhat surprising, and calls in to doubt whether the whole area is effectively monitored or independently reviewed. While this is not suggesting that every minor digression should be publicly investigated, the simple act of addressing breaches even in a general way is a move to improve the standards of those given responsibility for regulating and supervising the financial system.

Liability of Financial Regulators

Implied Immunity

Financial regulators have statutory responsibility for authorisation, supervision and enforcement. However, a breach of a statutory function does not automatically give rise to a legal right to damages by a third party. Depositors cannot rely on the fact that the bank is authorised by the regulator and continuously supervised to establish an obligation to protect their individual rights in law, although in practical terms a case can be made. This task may seem simple when a failure to exercise statutory responsibilities to regulate and supervise institutions causes loss to depositors. For example, in *Yuen* the depositors claimed the Hong Kong regulator would have known the bank in question was being managed fraudulently.[21] This was clear in

20 Ibid., at p. 13.

21 *Yuen Kun Yeu v. Attorney General of Hong Kong* [1987] 2 All ER 705.

Davis v. Radcliffe,[22] in which the Treasurer and Finance Board of the Isle of Man were sued for breach of statutory duty for their failure to supervise. The court held the regulator did not owe a statutory or common law duty of care to individual depositors but acted in the interest of the public as a whole. In such actions the courts have been unwilling to establish a duty of care, let alone to hold that a breach arose and the resultant loss is recoverable. While the loss to depositors is foreseeable, 'proximity' is required: the courts need to ask whether it is 'fair and reasonable for the duty of care to be owed to the person concerned'.[23] In such circumstances the courts have sympathy for depositors who place their money with a bank only to find that it is insolvent, but they have not been prepared to make a regulator (third party) responsible for the failures of authorised institutions arising from their lack of prudence and carelessness.[24]

The courts have justified curtailing a public body owing a duty of care on a number of other grounds. The initial concern centres on regulatory bodies acting in a defensive manner. In *Hill* it was alleged that the police failed to apprehend the Yorkshire Ripper,[25] which could have prevented the murder of his last victim. The decision was that a duty of care did not obtain for reasons of public policy and in the light of a previous decision that such a duty is not owed to individual members of the public. It was considered that the duty of care has 'an inhibiting effect on the exercise of… judgement', leading to the argument that speedy decisions would not be taken because a defensive approach would be adopted. In addition, the question of limited resources plays an obvious part in whether or not investigations or inspections take place in any given regulatory regime.[26] It is suggested that imposing a duty could mean regulators divert resources from other areas simply to avoid having actions taken against them. According to Lord Keith in *X v. Bedfordshire*, who decided that no duty of care was owed with regard to children's welfare and education, it would mean resources would have to be used by the authorities to prepare a case for defence.[27] Alternatively, as Lord Steyn decided in *Elguzouli*, they could simply act in a way to protect themselves from an action in negligence.[28] This can lead to a situation where further regulatory intervention is not actually necessary, so the costs would not justify the benefits of greater vigilance or onerous safety measures. The final policy reason is that the plaintiffs in cases such as *Stovin* and *Hill* had other means of gaining compensation for loss or damage, through private or public insurance schemes. In such instances, as Hoffmann LJ notes in *Stovin*,[29] the 'denial of liability does not leave the road user unprotected' when there is compulsory insurance. Distinct remedies for liability for damages mean that Parliament has to some extent addressed the question of compensation.

---

22 *Davis v. Radcliffe* [1990] 2 All ER 536.

23 *Dorset Yacht Co. v. Home Office* [1970] AC 1004.

24 *Johnson Matthey Plc v. Arthur Young and the Governor of the Bank of England* [1989] 2 All ER 105, 110.

25 *Hill v. Chief Constable of West Yorkshire* [1988] 1 WLR 1049, 1055.

26 Ibid., at p. 1056.

27 *X (Minors) v. Bedfordshire County Council* [1995] 3 WLR 152.

28 *Elguzouli-Daf v. Commissioner of Police of the Metropolis* [1995] 2 WLR 173.

29 *Stovin v. Wise* [1996] 3 WLR 388.

The financial services sector does have formal arrangements to deal with and compensate individuals for the failures of private firms and even the regulator. In addition a compensation system is in place to protect banking, securities and insurance customers who may lose money as a result of their service provider being put into administration or its permission to undertake regulated activities terminated. The deposit insurance scheme attempts to protect the relatively small depositor who may experience such a loss. However, the rationale for the introduction of such systems has not necessarily been based on consumer interests but rather to protect the banking system from its own misdeeds in pursuit of new business that would benefit the economy.[30] Nevertheless, the intrinsic feature of a deposit insurance system is to protect depositors and mitigate the risk of a bank run, which can ensue when depositors seek withdrawal all at once.[31] But in the case of deposit protection systems not all depositors are protected and nor is there 100 per cent compensation, so some claiming of damages by way of compensation is still an issue which needs to be considered.

Express immunity

A formal express immunity against claims for damages has been a provision of UK banking regulation since the enactment of the Banking Act 1987. It has also been a key provision internationally, and is indeed endorsed by international standards bodies like the Basel Committee in its Core Principles.[32] The rationale for this immunity mirrors the implied reasons for not imposing a duty of care on a public regulator, as highlighted above. However, political opposition to this formal immunity against such claims has been significant in the UK in light of the power the FSA wields as a single regulator. The right to pursue a claim in damages is seen as one way of balancing the power disparity between the FSA and the financial services industry;[33] for example, the Centre for Policy Studies draws attention to the problems of an investigation undertaken by the FSA that is ill-founded but results in a firm losing business or collapsing as a result of a loss of business without it being able to sue the FSA for damages for its failures to take reasonable care.[34]

Nevertheless, the express immunity in the FSMA 2000, Sch. 1, s. 19(1), exempts the FSA from liability:

30 *The Licensing and Supervision of Deposit-Taking Institutions*, Cmnd 6584, London, HMSO, August 1976, at p. 6.

31 Campbell, A. and Singh, D. (2007) 'Legal aspects of the interests of depositor creditors: The case for deposit protection systems', in Campbell, A., Labrosse, R., Mayes, D. and Singh, D. (eds) *Deposit Insurance*, Basingstoke, Palgrave.

32 Delston, R. (1999) 'Statutory protections for banking supervisors', World Bank, available at http://www1.worldbank.org/finance/html/statutory_protection.html, Appendix 1: Survey of relevant laws.

33 *Joint Committee on Financial Services and Markets, First Report* (1998/99), part v. Accountability, paras. 135–141.

34 McElwee, M. and Tyrie, A. (2000) *Leviathan at Large: The New Regulator for the Financial Markets*, London, Centre for Policy Studies, at p. 49.

'Neither the Authority nor any person who is, or is acting as, a member, officer or member of staff of the Authority is to be liable in damages for anything done or omitted in the discharge, of the Authority's functions.'

An exception is Sch. 1, s. 19(3):

'(a) if the act or omission is shown to have been in bad faith; or
(b) so as to prevent an award of damages made in respect of an act or omission on the grounds that the act or omission was unlawful as a result of section 6(1) of the Human Rights Act 1998.'[35]

This express immunity protects both the FSA and its employees from a claim for damages against them. However, in a recent case the protection afforded by such statutory immunity has been called in doubt if the act or omission is purportedly outside the statutory requirements. *Gulf Insurance Ltd v. The Central Bank of Trinidad and Tobago*[36] referred to the way the Central Bank intervened to deal with serious problems at the Trinidad Co-operative Bank Ltd. To help with the rescue the Central Bank of Trinidad and Tobago (the Central Bank) was conferred additional powers to assist with problems in a crisis situation. The Central Bank intervened to save the bank by restructuring its management and providing new capital; this was converted into shares, culminating in the Central Bank being the majority shareholder. The bank did, it seems, make a successful recovery. In light of this, Gulf Insurance Ltd sought to take advantage of the bank's new fortunes and bought a 0.54 per cent share in it. However, during this time two other banks also experienced problems and so the Central Bank again duly intervened to rescue them on similar terms as with Trinidad Co-operative; in addition a plan was devised where all three banks would be amalgamated into one bank. A feasibility study was carried out, but the asset structure of the three banks was found to be weak, and this fact was subsequently leaked to the press. In light of this information being publicly disclosed the risk of a bank run was clear, so the Central Bank quickly intervened by immediately putting in place a new management structure at the three banks to see through the amalgamation and the creation of a new bank called First Citizen Bank Ltd. The consequence of this quite simply was that Trinidad Co-operative Bank now held no assets but was exposed to certain liabilities. Gulf Insurance as a part-shareholder of Trinidad Co-operative sought to have the vesting of its assets to the new bank void as it was *ultra vires* and unlawful; it also sought judicial review to have the amalgamation deemed null and void, and damages.

---

35 In the case of this exception, s. 6(1) refers to a right to a fair hearing, so it is not of any real use to a depositor who has incurred losses resulting from the acts or omissions of the FSA. It does not set aside the legal protection afforded to the FSA because it prevents the depositor from seeking damages in the tort of negligence, but essentially ensures individuals are not denied a right to a fair hearing. Given that immunity to claims for damages falls into the realms of a jurisdiction's law, this exception is of limited benefit to a depositor.

36 *Gulf Insurance Ltd v. The Central Bank of Trinidad and Tobago*, Privy Council Appeal No. 78 of 2002, 9 March 2005. I would like to thank Charles Proctor at Bird & Bird for bringing this to my attention.

The Court of Appeal dismissed the case for judicial review and the claim in damages on the basis that there was insufficient evidence. In addition, the court made reference to the protection afforded to the Central Bank by the statutory immunity from such claims.[37] The penultimate appeal against the decision claimed that the amalgamation of the banks' assets was undertaken without a proper valuation of the assets by an independent valuer as required under 44D(1)(vi) of the Central Bank and Financial Institutions (Non-Banking) (Amendment) Act 1986.[38] The fact that the Governor of the Central Bank had made the decision was not sufficiently independent. Thus the transfer of assets from Trinidad Co-operative Bank was not lawful and on that basis Gulf Insurance sought judicial review and damages.

The Privy Council decided in favour of Gulf Insurance and agreed damages in conversion should be paid given that the failure of the Central Bank to get an independent valuation was unlawful. The Privy Council conferred a more restrictive interpretation of the immunity articulated in 44H than the wide construction given by the Court of Appeal in the previous decision; it took exception to the fact that the Court of Appeal was effectively including acts by the Central Bank that were '*purportedly*' within its powers when in fact what it sought to do was not in its power. The decision delivered by Lord Hoffmann provides that 'provisions of this nature should be restrictively construed. They should not be treated as a license for unlawful expropriation without compensation, provided only that the acts are done in good faith and without negligence.'[39]

The Privy Council decision is very significant for regulators and central banks seeking to act in the public interest to prevent and manage fallout from a bank failure that may pose systemic risks to the financial system. Such scenarios give rise occasionally to circumstances that may not have been considered when the legislation was first introduced. Where the regulator for all intents and purposes acted in good faith and without negligence then a wide construction to the immunity should be given on the underlying justifications for implied immunity examined above. The interpretation of the immunity strongly suggests that a regulator or central bank still needs to be careful to act lawfully, even in difficult and unusual circumstances which may necessitate a decision in a matter of minutes or hours rather than days and weeks; such a decision can later be construed as unlawful because the bank regulator does not have the statutory mandate to take such actions, even though it has acted in good faith to avoid contagion and systemic risk. This case must be distinguished from a regulator exercising its discretion at the parameters of its legal powers. However, it still provides a stark reminder that regulators need to act in a lawful manner to avoid future claims in damages which may not be countered by the protection afforded in the legislation.

---

37 Ibid. The actual reason for the decision is not clear in the appeal to the Privy Council. On the cross-appeal the court was satisfied that the Central Bank had acted for a proper purpose, which was to avoid damage to the financial system and the domino effect of one bank failure leading to others also failing.

38 A new part was included titled 'Special Emergency Powers of Bank' numbered s 44C – 44AA Gulf Insurance (2002) at para. 2, ibid.

39 Ibid., para. 53.

Alternative Mechanisms of Accountability

The FSA is required under the FSMA 2000 to introduce alternative mechanisms of accountability for consumers and regulated firms. The single Ombudsman Scheme, Compensation Scheme and a new Independent Complaints Commissioner are the central pillars of this system of accountability. Individuals with an issue about the way financial firms undertake their business or a complaint about the FSA failing in some way to carry out its work properly have a port of call for an independent party to deal with their claims and act accordingly rather than having to make a claim for some form of compensation through the courts. These alternative mechanisms provide a system of redress for consumers to seek some compensation for failures, whether at a firm or regulatory level, to act with the appropriate level of care and which have caused them financial loss. In many respects it is a less costly route than seeking remedy through the courts, where the individual would be required to finance the action. Indeed, the FSMA 2000 attempts to guide individuals to these forms of redress rather than pursuing a claim through the courts; it also provides routes for the claims to be dealt with given the limitations placed on a court action succeeding against the regulator, for instance in the tort of negligence. (The exception to this is an action in bad faith, which is addressed below.) The issue that arises is how do these alternative routes provide redress for the consequential losses that have ensued from the act or omission?

Depositor Compensation System

The move towards a single regulator brought with it a single compensation scheme to replace the individual schemes that existed pre-FSMA 2000 for the UK financial services industry. The FSMA 2000 simply provides the framework for the compensation scheme;[40] its parameters in terms of how it operates and is administered are set out separately.[41] The objectives of a formal scheme, as highlighted by the FSA, are to secure 'the appropriate degree of protection for consumers and maintaining confidence in the financial system'.

The overall management of the compensation scheme is rather complicated. The FSA is not responsible for its administration, albeit it is obligated to set up the scheme. Responsibility for operating and administering compensation is placed on the shoulders of a separate corporate body, the Financial Services Compensation Scheme Ltd (FSCS), which has deemed itself a 'fund of last resort'. It handles compensation claims relating to accepting deposits, designated investment and insurance business, insurance mediation and mortgage advice/arranging, all regulated by the FSA. However, the FSCS, although it has separate legal personality, is not an independent body as such from the FSA with its own rule-making powers, nor is it placed on an equal footing to the FSA in terms of dealing with issues that may arise. It is to all intents and purposes reliant on the FSA to confer responsibilities that it can effectively exercise and not to place an undue constraint on the FSCS to

40 FSMA 2000, Part XV.

41 FSMA 2000, s. 213.

raise sufficient funds to meet the costs incurred in discharging its duties. The FSA and FSCS are required to cooperate with one another in such matters as sharing information and dealing with issues that will give rise to public scrutiny.

The UK scheme has a narrower remit than some of its international counterparts. Since 1982 the UK has had in place an explicit 'paybox' scheme that confers responsibility to raise funds and compensate those eligible when a bank is liquidated. The responsibility of deposit insurers can range from a 'paybox' system where the agency has a narrow role to ones where the agency has significant additional functions, such as being a regulator and insolvency practitioner; there are a myriad permutations as to what the scheme can look like. Regardless of which approach is considered better from a policy position, one significant factor in deciding on the role of the agency has to be the level of resources, both financial and human, which are available to it.

The FSCS on the face of it simply administers a 'paybox' scheme. This requires it to pay compensation when a firm regulated to undertake deposit-taking business is put into administration or liquidation and is 'unlikely or likely to be unable to meet claims against it'. However, in the UK the responsibility for dealing with administration, liquidation and winding-up proceedings falls on accounting firms. In the previous regulatory regime the Bank of England tried to ensure as far as possible the claims made by depositors after bank insolvency were met through the liquidation process to reduce the burden on the public compensation scheme.[42]

The FSCS will only make compensation payments to those who are eligible and provided the individual firm is a participating firm. Those eligible are normally individuals for whom it would be virtually impossible to determine the financial status of a bank. The rules and guidance basically indicate an 'individual' is eligible provided it is not *inter alia* an 'unregulated firm', 'overseas financial services institution', supranational institution, 'local authorities', 'collective investment schemes', 'pension funds', 'directors and managers of the relevant person in default', 'body corporate of the same group' or 'persons holding 5% or more of the capital of the relevant person in default'. The FSCS can also determine an individual is ineligible 'if they are of the opinion that they are responsible for, or have contributed to, the relevant person's default' – this could potentially include employees who have perpetrated a fraud, for example. In this matter it is reliant on the official receiver's opinion in accordance with the UK Insolvency Act 1986.

The UK scheme only compensates those with a protected claim, which basically means an individual with an account at a credit institution (deposit-taking institution). A firm is determined to be in *default* when the FSA, FSCS or judicial authority determines it is 'unable to satisfy protected claims against it; or likely to be unable to satisfy protected claims against it'. This requires the FSCS to work with the administrator and liquidator to identify who is in default and ultimately to whom compensation is owed; it also has to work closely with the FSA as the regulator of financial services. In this respect the FSCS is allowed to assist the FSA when it identifies a firm 'is unable, or likely to be unable, to repay its depositors'.

42 *Re Goodwin Squires Securities Ltd* (1983) *The Times* Law Reports, 22 March, pp. 204–205.

The scheme does not, somewhat controversially, provide 100 per cent compensation to those eligible. The idea that the person insured should share some of the risk is very common in general insurance contracts, and some jurisdictions, including the UK, have introduced co-insurance into the deposit protection scheme for bank depositors. In fact, when the deposit protection scheme was first introduced in the UK no degree of total protection was provided and all depositors were subject to an element of co-insurance. It was not until 1995 that the level of co-insurance was reduced, when cover was raised to 90 per cent of the first £20,000 on deposit. All deposits were still subject to an element of co-insurance, however. The current scheme provides 100 per cent cover limited to a relatively modest £2,000; above this up to £33,000 90 per cent of the deposit is protected. The UK scheme thus only pays out a maximum of £31,700 to any one individual with a protected claim.

Co-insurance presents an added problem, which is that many depositors will not have their claims paid in full and will therefore continue to be creditors of the failed bank. Where co-insurance applies to the entire amount of deposits then all depositors will be unsecured creditors in the liquidation proceedings. This complicates the process and will normally lead to both additional expenses for the liquidator and a delay in completing the winding-up process. The presence of thousands of small claims, as was the case in the UK in the BCCI liquidation, is undesirable – it is preferable if they can be removed from the process, as is typically the case where a reasonably generous level of full cover is provided.

The time scale in which claims are to be processed and compensation paid to depositors has also raised concerns. The UK position is rather vague on the speed with which payments should be made. Under the relevant EU legislation compensation to depositors should be paid within 90 days of a valid claim being lodged with the FSCS; an extension to six months is permitted in exceptional circumstances. According to the FSCS, 'after a firm has been declared in default, we generally aim to pay compensation within six months of receiving a completed application form'. Why it should take so long in the UK is unclear, and this approach would appear to be in contravention of the EU directive.

The Independent Complaints Commissioner

The FSA is required by the FSMA 2000 to have in place a complaints procedure to deal with issues that have been raised about the way it has undertaken its responsibilities.[43] The responsibility for dealing with such issues lies with the new and independent Complaints Commissioner,[44] which was introduced to allow consumers and firms to seek redress for losses caused by the acts or omissions of the FSA.[45] The mandate of the Complaints Commissioner is to deal with 'allegations of misconduct by the FSA';[46] it will address 'acts or omissions' such as 'mistakes and lack of care', 'unreasonable delay', 'unprofessional behaviour', 'bias and lack of integrity'

43 COAF 1.1.1(1)G.
44 COAF 1.1.1(2)(G).
45 COAF 1.3.
46 COAF 1.4.1G.

in cases where complainants think the FSA's investigation is unsatisfactory.[47] The Complaints Commissioner functions alongside the Financial Services and Markets Tribunal rather than with it: this is because the function of the former is to investigate procedural failures rather than the FSA's legislative functions. The FSA's exercise of discretion as to its general policy on a matter does not necessarily fall within the scheme – a criticism raised by the Complaints Commissioner in its inquiry into the accountability of regulators.[48] Nevertheless, this does not mean issues related to the FSA's exercising of its discretion cannot be investigated, as it is the allegation that triggers the investigation, so the Complaints Commissioner's work does to some extent protect against unfettered FSA discretion. The guidance sets out the procedure to be followed for a complaint to be properly dealt with by either the FSA or the Complaints Commissioner.[49] The complaint is first handled by the FSA, which bears the initial responsibility to investigate the issue and remedy it if it considers itself at fault in an incident from which a loss ensued. The FSA and the Complaints Commissioner will ultimately need to determine whether the FSA acted reasonably when it undertook the task in question. The Complaints Commissioner will deal with the complaint if the person is not satisfied with the FSA's decision, by reviewing the case and ultimately carrying out its own investigation;[50] it has at its disposal appropriate resources to carry on the investigation, including any external assistance it deems is required.[51]

The FSA and the Complaints Commissioner can recommend a range of remedies to deal with the fallout from FSA acts or omissions.[52] If the complaint is deemed 'well founded' the complainant could be offered an apology, rectification of the administrative systems that resulted in the complaint or compensation on an *ex gratia* basis.[53] The offer of compensation is some recognition at least of the fact that failures by the FSA can cause loss or damage, even though the courts have curtailed this kind of action by putting in place implied immunity from such suits, and as indeed the government has done with a statutory immunity unless the claim is one of bad faith. The move towards a formal remedy is in some respects the result of the difficulty of having to deal with complaints by individuals who on a pragmatic level desire some form of remedy, even if it is a mere apology, rather than having their complaints simply dismissed. Examination of some of the complaints illustrates the constraints placed on the FSA – by its own admission, 'misunderstanding' and 'mistakes' can result from the pressures placed on its employees in the exercise of their normal

---

47 Ibid.

48 Complaints Commissioner (2003) 'The Constitution Committee: Inquiry into the accountability of regulators to citizens and Parliament', submission by the Complaints Commissioner for the Financial Services Authority, April, at para. 30.

49 COAF 1.5.

50 COAF 1.5.4G–1.5.9G.

51 COAF 1.5.10G.

52 COAF 1.5.4G.

53 This is not available for cases that fall within the transitional period before the FSA took on full responsibility for the financial services industry, even if a complaint is upheld. For an illustration of this point see Final Report on Complaint GE-L0544, 27 September 2005.

daily work[54] – and also the extent to which it tries to deal with issues, occasionally going beyond the call of duty. The number of complaints in comparison to the tens of thousands of issues the FSA must handle on a day-to-day basis is an indication of the relatively small number of cases that it formally addresses each year.[55] For example, the annual report of the Complaints Commissioner for 2003/04 indicates that 178 enquiries and complaints were received, mostly concerned with the FSA's supervisory function and administrative responsibilities. The other reasons for complaint arose from particular financial services, such as pensions and endowment mortgages.[56] The report does note that the Complaints Commissioner has not upheld a complaint on the basis of 'gross misconduct', so one can infer that the complaints which have been upheld probably evidence some element of mistake or negligence rather than anything more culpable.

The work of the Complaints Commissioner and the FSA in this area can be illustrated by looking at some of the complaints made and the action taken.[57] The reports identify the nature of the complaint and the way it was dealt with during the initial investigation by the FSA. For example, complaint GE-1008[58] was an investigation into the FSA's failure to process a resignation from a previous self-regulatory body so that the individual could register membership with the FSA; the complainant thought there was 'excessive and unreasonable delay' in dealing with the request. The Commissioner, while articulating the process that needed to be carried out by the FSA, indicated the communication between the parties was not 'clear' or 'timely'. It therefore recommended the FSA should give an apology for its failure to communicate the implications of late payment of membership fees, and that better procedures be put in place to deal with complaints that may not go through the designated channels. Finally, the Complaints Commissioner recommended a payment of £354.12 as a 'gesture of goodwill'. In response the FSA considered the findings and agreed to address the recommendations by apologising, changing procedures and making the *ex gratia* payment to the complainant.[59] The recommendation by the Complaints Commissioner to the FSA to pay compensation is very rare.[60] In another instance the FSA was called into question about whether an existing authorised entity that wanted to change its legal status from a partnership to a limited company was required to submit a new application for authorisation. The investigation by the Complaints Commissioner exposed uncertainty about this point, exacerbated by the uncertainty in the legislation and the FSA Handbook on the matter. The first part of the complaint referred to the lack of response on the matter and the cost incurred by the firm when it changed its legal status: the recommendation, in favour of the firm, was for better training at the FSA so that

54 Final Report on Complaint GE-L0097, 22 December 2003.

55 See www.fsa.gov.uk/Pages/About/complaints/index.shtml.

56 Complaints Commissioner (2004) *Annual Report of the Complaints Commissioner 2003/04*, at p. 17.

57 The complaints are anonymised.

58 Final Report on Complaint GE-1008, May 2002.

59 FSA 'Response to the Complaints Commissioner's Report GE-1008', May 2002.

60 The author only found one other instance where compensation was recommended to be paid to the complainant.

such issues could be addressed as expeditiously as possible. The second part referred to the FSA's legislative function so it fell outside of the complaints scheme. The Commissioner recommended payment of £100 compensation for 'distress and inconvenience caused'.[61] In response the FSA reported that it had put in place steps to improve training in this area and initiated steps to improve the application form for authorisation. Finally it increased the *ex gratia* payment to the firm from £100 to £250.[62]

The FSA Ombudsman Scheme

The Financial Ombudsman Scheme has been a key mechanism for consumers to seek redress against financial firms once all procedures at a firm level to deal with the complaint have been exhausted.[63] The utility of the Ombudsman Scheme has received considerable attention in light of the reliance consumers have come to place on it to deal with their complaints rather than seeking redress through the courts – the scheme thus ultimately reduces court congestion.[64] The fact that the Ombudsman operates solely for the financial services industry effectively means it is a more efficient way of dealing with disputes between financial providers and consumers. The move to a single Ombudsman Scheme has brought with it benefits: for instance, a consumer who may previously have been unaware which scheme would be the appropriate one to contact because of the number of ombudsman schemes in operation now has a single port of call. Indeed, the statutory footing it now has means that the perception of the Ombudsman acting in the interests of the industry that funds it is diminished. It has also resulted in a formal system of complaints handling at both firm and Ombudsmans level to deal with issues in an efficient and timely manner, which was not the case under the previous regime.[65]

The Financial Ombudsman Scheme is established by Part XVI of the FSMA 2000 with the responsibility to deal independently with disputes in an efficient manner with 'minimum formality'.[66] The FSA is responsible for setting up a body corporate, referred to as the 'Scheme Operator',[67] which is the Financial Ombudsman Service Ltd (FOS).[68] The FOS is a separate body with a management structure to administer

61 Final Report on Complaint GE-L0287, 3 March 2005.

62 FSA, 'Response to the Complaints Commissioner's Report GE-L087', 3 March 2005.

63 Cartwright, P. (2004) *Banks, Consumers and Regulation*, Oxford, Hart, at p. 175; James, R. and Morris, P. E. (2002) 'The Financial Ombudsman Service: A brave new world in ombudsmanry', *Public Law*, Winter, 640; Morris, P. E. (1987) 'The Banking Ombudsman: Part 1', *Journal of Business Law*, March, 131; Morris, P. E. (1987) 'The Banking Ombudsman: Part 2', *Journal of Business Law*, May, 199; Ferran, E. (2002) 'Dispute resolution mechanisms in the UK financial sector', *Civil Justice Quarterly*, vol. 21, 135.

64 Cartwright, ibid., at p. 175.

65 FSA (2002) *Understanding Why Consumers Complain to Financial Suppliers and Their Experiences of Complaining*, July.

66 FSMA 2000, s. 225(1).

67 FSMA 2000, Sch. 17, Part II.

68 DISP 1.

the scheme,[69] and is conferred the responsibility of maintaining a panel of persons to act for the purposes of the scheme as ombudsmen.[70] It is required to appoint one of those panel members as chief ombudsman. The FOS is accountable to the FSA for the administration of the scheme but is not liable in damages for 'anything done or omitted in the discharge, or purported discharge of any functions'.[71]

The responsibility of dealing with consumer complaints rests with the firm to which a complaint is directed: ultimately it is the catalyst for the complaint and should thus take responsibility for resolving it. The FSA requires firms to have in place effective mechanisms to handle consumer complaints in an efficient manner.[72] This is to ensure that the number of complaints that are not resolved between the firm and the consumer and are passed on to the FOS is kept to a minimum. The firm is required to 'have in place and operate appropriate and effective internal complaints handling procedures' which can deal with 'expressions of dissatisfaction' about its 'failure to provide, a financial service', whether justified or not.[73] The internal procedures must be able to deal with the whole process: receiving, responding to, referring and investigating complaints.[74] The resources a firm needs to devote to comply with this must reflect the business it undertakes, its size, complexity and the number of complaints it is likely to handle.[75] If it decides redress is necessary the firm is required to pay 'fair compensation for any acts or omissions for which it was responsible and comply with any offer of redress which the complainant accepts', which could simply be a formal apology.[76] The complainant needs to allow the firm a sufficient amount of time to deal with the matter before seeking redress through the FOS. The 'final response' by the firm must direct complainants to the FOS if they are still dissatisfied.

The FOS will deal with an 'eligible' complaint by a 'dissatisfied complainant' if it falls into its jurisdiction.[77] Once a complaint is received by the FOS it must deal with it quickly and with minimum formality.[78] The FOS will seek initial representations from both parties and has the power once these have been heard to dismiss the complaint if it is considered to have no merit,[79] resolve it through mediation and propose a settlement or investigate the complaint. In 2004 42 per

69 FSMA 2000, Sch. 17, cl. 3.

70 FSMA 2000, Sch. 17, cl. 4.

71 FSMA 2000, Sch. 17, cl. 10.

72 DISP 1.

73 DISP 1.2.1R.

74 DISP 1.2.4G; see also DISP 1.4 1.5.

75 DISP 1.2.5G.

76 DISP 1.2.17R; see also 1.2.18G–1.2.20G.

77 DISP 2.2.1G; FSMA 2000, s. 226. The Financial Ombudsman will deal with a complaint under its 'compulsory jurisdiction' if *inter alia* the complainant is eligible and the respondent is authorised at the time of the act or omission; it will deal with a complaint under its 'voluntary jurisdiction' if it is not included in its compulsory jurisdiction, such as activities not formally regulated by the FSA but where the firm has entered into a contractual agreement. DISP 2.6.1R.

78 DISP 3.

79 DISP 3.3.

cent of cases were dealt with through mediation, and in only 8 per cent of cases did the Ombudsman exercise the right to have the final decision.[80] The parties could be invited to a formal hearing if the Ombudsman considers it necessary, and their full cooperation will be required in terms of the correspondence and other evidence necessary to determine the complaint.[81] The Ombudsman must, as a result of this, determine 'what is, in his opinion, fair and reasonable in all the circumstances of the case',[82] taking into account the 'relevant law', 'regulations', 'regulators' rules' and 'guidance and standards', 'relevant codes of practice' and 'good industry practice'.[83] The FOS could require the firm to pay 'fair compensation for the financial loss or for loss or damage'.[84] The compensation element could be for 'pain and suffering', 'damage to reputation' or 'distress or inconvenience'.[85] The Ombudsman has the authority to award a maximum of £100,000, which can in some circumstances be exceeded if it considers it 'fair compensation'.

The FOS exercises a specific responsibility distinct from that undertaken by the FSA. However, the issues it considers can overlap if the FSA considers some form of regulatory, supervisory or enforcement action could be warranted. The FOS and FSA have set up 'wider implications units' within their respective organisations to act as 'gateways' to determine whether matters they encounter have implications such that the FSA will either take regulatory action or assist the FOS in its investigation with evidence it has gathered itself.[86] This work is formally addressed jointly by the FSA and FOS, and case studies are published to illustrate some of the issues that have wider implications. For example, in case study WI-01[87] the FOS received a large number of complaints regarding allegations of mis-selling of a specific investment product across the country, giving rise to suspicion about the sales techniques. The FOS notified the FSA, following which an investigation was carried out into the matter: the FSA imposed a significant penalty and ordered compensation payments commensurate with those awarded by the FOS. In case study WI-AO5[88] the matter in question was raised by the firms to which a number of complaints had been directed, as it gave rise to wider implications. This case related to cheques written to banks and building societies eventually being put into the accounts of third parties, a common industry practice. The firms sought to discuss this with the FOS and FSA; but while both recognised the wide implications of the case given the potential fraud

80 FSA and FOS (2004) *FSMA 2 Year Review: Financial Ombudsman Service*, at pp. 11–12.

81 DISP 3.5.

82 DISP 3.8.1R.

83 Ibid.

84 DISP 3.9.1G.

85 DISP 3.9.2R.

86 FSA (2005) *Feedback on CP05/4 FSMA 2 Year Review: Financial Ombudsman Service Procedural Rules*.

87 Ombudsman and FSA case studies, 'Alleged widespread mis-selling of an investment product by a large firm', WI-01, available at www.ombudsmanandfsa.org.uk/case_studies/wi-01.htm.

88 Ombudsman and FSA case studies, 'Banking practice Fraudulent diversion of cheques', WI-AO5, available at www.ombudsmanandfsa.org.uk/case_studies/wi-05.htm.

that could be perpetrated, it was considered that the matter could more appropriately be addressed by civil law and the industry itself rather than through regulatory intervention. The industry associations, namely the British Bankers Association and the FSA, came to an agreement in 2005 to phase out this practice by October 2006.

Exception to Statutory Immunity: The Tort of Misfeasance in Public Office[89]

The tort of misfeasance in public office has a long history, with roots dating back to 1364.[90] It is a unique tort, as it is only applicable to those exercising public functions[91] for what may be described as an 'ulterior or improper purpose' which is contrary to the 'public good'.[92] It can only be initiated against public officers exercising public functions – an issue which was not in dispute in the *Three Rivers* case.[93] The tort of misfeasance in public office is a remedy for acts or omissions of a very serious nature where there is evidence of some form of bad faith. This places misfeasance at the latter end of the *ex-post-facto* civil liability spectrum in the category of a punitive

89 This chapter does not discuss EU liability. For an analysis of it see Tison, M. (2005) 'Do not attack the watchdog! Banking Supervisor's Liability after Peter Paul', *Working Paper Series, WP 2005–02*, Financial Law Institute, Universiteit Gent.

90 Evans, R. C. (1982) 'Damages for unlawful administrative action: The remedy for misfeasance in public office', *International Comparative Law Quarterly*, vol. 13, 640.

91 The tort of misfeasance in public office is only applicable to those exercising public functions, but who actually exercises public functions is not entirely clear – does it only apply to those in public office or does it also include employees as well? The concept of a public office has traditionally been construed as distinct from being a mere employee of a public body, thus giving rise to specific forms of personal liability. See Fredman, S. and Morris, G. (1989) *The State as Employer: Labour Law in Public Services*, London, Mansell, at p. 74. However, public functions are not solely exercised by those in public office but are undertaken by a vast number of employees conferred with responsibility to perform statutory functions in the public interest on a daily basis. In the traditional sense a public officer is entrusted by statute with functions to be performed in the public interest or for public purposes. See *Whitelegg v. Richards* (1823) 2 B & C 45; *Sutherland Shire Council v. Heyman* (1985) 157 CLR 424. This is illustrated in the leading definition of public office, see *R v. Whitaker* [1914] 3 K B 1283. This definition gives rise to a narrow interpretation of those responsible for exercising public functions as it emphasises the person as a holder of an office, whereas most public functions are carried out by employees without such privileges. This is evident in the earlier decision by Best C J in *Henly v. Mayor & Burgesses of Lyme* (1828) 5 Bing 91,107, which expanded the scope of public officer to include employees. In the more recent decision in *R v. Bowden* [1996] 1 WLR 98, 101 the reasoning of Best C J is further cited as support for an extension of public office -- to include employees exercising public duties for the purpose of the offence of misconduct in public office.

92 *Jones v. Swansea* [1989] 3 All ER 162, 186.

93 *Three Rivers DC v. Bank of England* [2000] 3 All ER 1; *Three Rivers DC v. Governor and Company of the Bank of England (No. 3)* [1996] 3 All ER 558; *Three Rivers DC v. Governor of the Bank of England* (CA) [1999] 11 Admin LR 281.

civil sanction.[94] In light of the seriousness of the claim it is more difficult to establish, as the courts must consider the subjective mind rather than the objective standard of care prevalent in negligence. The tort of misfeasance is thus not merely a form of negligence in another guise applied to those in public office. The courts have been very clear not to allow parties simply to graft such claims on to a tort of negligence action.[95] The nature of misfeasance is distinct, in that it is a claim of bad faith.[96] Its scope in public office is not confined to unlawful administrative acts: it includes elements of misuse of power, not just the invalidity of an act or omission.[97] This distinguishes actions constituting a tort of misfeasance from actions that constitute a tort of negligence and breach of statutory duty against public authorities. According to Clarke J, at first instance the tort should not be equated with gross negligence because in an action on misfeasance in public office the subjective state of mind must be established.[98]

The Three Rivers *Saga*

The question of whether the Bank of England can be sued was finally settled by the House of Lords in the interests of the depositors who lost millions when the Bank of Credit and Commerce International was closed in July 1991.[99] A motion that it can be sued was carried by the House on a two-thirds majority, thus bringing to an end eight years of scrutinising the tort of misfeasance in public office. In that judgment the House of Lords sought to consider whether a reasonable cause for action could be made against the Bank on the evidence, which would ultimately need to fulfil the criteria to establish misfeasance in public office, to determine whether the plaintiffs' allegations warranted a full hearing or should be struck out on the grounds that there was no case to answer. The plaintiffs alleged that the loss to depositors resulted from the Bank's failure to carry out its responsibilities under the Banking Act 1987, and that the failure enabled BCCI to accrue losses of billions of pounds through its fraudulent activities around the globe. In the *Three Rivers* action the plaintiffs sued the Bank for damages in misfeasance in public office and for inadequate implementation of the European First Banking Directive.

The plaintiffs' action was brought as a charge of misfeasance in public office rather than as a charge of negligence given the express immunity examined above against such actions. To enable them to bring a case for liability in misfeasance against the Bank, the plaintiffs needed to establish the existence of either malice evidenced by an intention to injure or knowledge that a public officer did not have authority to act

94 Ibid. The House of Lords indicated it had similarities to the criminal offence of misconduct in public office: *Bowden*, n. 91 above, at p. 8; *R v. Newham LBC, ex p Watkins* (1994) 26 HLR 434.

95 *Lam v. Brennan* [1997] 3 PLR 22.

96 *Three Rivers* [2000], n. 93 above.

97 *Jones*, [1989] n. 92 above; *Takaro Properties Ltd v. Rowling* [1978] 2 NZLR 314; *Bourgoin SA v. Ministry of Agriculture Fisheries and Food* [1985] All ER 585; *Northern Territories v. Mengel* [1995] 69 ALJR 527.

98 *Three Rivers (No 3)* n. 93 above at p. 578.

99 *Three Rivers DC v. Bank of England* [2001] 2 All ER 513.

as he had. The allegations made by the plaintiffs point to the failures of specific bank officials rather than the Bank *per se*, citing two former Bank Governors who acted in bad faith by licensing BCCI in 1979 when they knew that it was unlawful to do so; shutting their eyes to what was happening at BCCI after the licence was granted; and failing to effect the closure of BCCI despite information (available by the mid-1980s) that warranted its closure. The cause of action also included other general issues: the Bank granted a licence to BCCI despite the fact that it did not satisfy paras 7, 8 and 10 of Schedule 2 of the Banking Act 1979 (and Schedule 3 of the Banking Act 1987). The plaintiffs alleged that the Bank had placed too much reliance on the powers of s. 3(5) of the Banking Act 1979, and later s. 9(3) of the Banking Act 1987, and upon assurance from the Luxembourg Banking Commission (LBC) and the Institut Monetaire Luxembourgeois (IML) that the management and financial status of BCCI SA were both sound. The plaintiffs further alleged that the Bank was not entitled to rely on the LBC and IML assurance because, in its own opinion, those institutions were not competent to give assurance about BCCI's management or financial soundness: the Bank itself was dissatisfied with the supervision of BCCI SA's activities by LBC/IML. Nevertheless, the Bank permitted BCCI (Overseas) to carry on an unlicensed deposit-taking business when it knew BCCI (Overseas) Central Treasury conducted its business from 100 Leadenhall Street, London. Moreover, it permitted both BCCI SA and BCCI (Overseas) to use a banking name to which they had no entitlement in law.

The Requisite State of Mind in Misfeasance

Abuse of office is at the heart of misfeasance in public office, which arises as some form of deliberate dishonesty or bad faith.[100] Best CJ[101] said that the tort consisted of a public officer who 'abuses his office either by an act or omission the consequences of that is an injury to an individual'. The tort has, for example, been shown to be analogous with 'gross abuse of legal power', which is the antithesis of the proper use of power by a public officer.[102] The underlying basis of the tort in this context is the abuse of public power; this is present as two alternatives rather than in one cumulative way, where the public officer's act or omission is underpinned by malice through 'spite or ill will',[103] or where the public officer has knowledge that the act or omission is unlawful, which is a modern articulation of the tort. However, notwithstanding its long history in the *Three Rivers* saga, reliance was placed on the more modern articulations of the tort rather than the older decisions. The more recent decisions recognise the two separate limbs of the tort rather than applying a broad

100 *Elguzouli-Daf v Comr of Police of the Metropolis* [1995] QB 335.

101 *Henley v. Motor of Lyme* [1828] 5 Bing. 91, 107. Other cases are cited as providing a wider ambit for liability: *Brasyer v. Maclean* [1875] LR 6 PC, which is supported by the later decision of *Farrington v. Thompson* [1959] V R 286, at p. 293, although the latter case is rejected in *Pemberton v. Attorney-General* [1978] Tas SR, Chambers J, at p. 29.

102 *Roncarelli v. Duplessis* [1959] 16 D L R 2, Rand J, at p. 706.

103 *Ashby v. White* [1704] 2 Ld Raym 938, 695.

notion of malice to the facts of a case.[104] The old cases did not outline the nature of the tort either exhaustively or consistently, particularly not the all-important degree of knowledge and foresight required in the second limb of establishing the existence of a tort, which has received a lot of attention given its relevance to most factual scenarios.[105]

The Two Limbs of the Tort

The early decisions in the tort of misfeasance in public office recognised the different ways in which the tort could be established. Usually, malice was the essential component in the evidence of its existence. The old cases tend to focus on malice without clearly defining the term. In *Bromage*[106] malice in fact and in law were distinguished, in that malice in fact focused on ill will whereas malice in law focused on a wrongful act undertaken with an unjustifiable intention. The other decisions tended to focus on both facets of malice. According to *Harman*,[107] malice could be inferred from the conduct of the public officer or, as in *Cullen*,[108] in some improper motive for an act. Clarke J at first instance concluded that the early decisions interpreted malice in a number of ways specific to the facts of the case, which gave rise to a wide interpretation of malice and, without defining it, recognised that it subsists in the act or omission of the individual.[109] This led Clarke J to conclude that malice as a concept was wide enough to be interpreted not only as targeted malice or spite but also as wrongful acts done intentionally without just cause or excuse. Interestingly, in *Rawlinson*[110] Barker J noted that malice descends into the realms of reckless indifference, thereby suggesting that it is not simply confined to the first limb of misfeasance. The wide interpretation of malice in case law legitimately encompasses the elements of the second limb of the tort because of the central idea of abuse of power. For example, in *Roncarelli*[111] the plaintiff's licence to sell alcohol, which was normally renewed annually, was cancelled because of his association with petty criminals whom he would bail if they were Jehovah's Witnesses. It was noted by Rand J that the public officer's statutory duties do not include a duty to cancel licences on the grounds applied to the licence in question. The act was deemed a gross abuse of statutory power, intended to punish by destroying the plaintiff's livelihood.[112]

The second category of the tort is clearly recognised but is somewhat uncertain in terms of its constituent elements; the authorities have not clarified the mental

104 *Bourgoin*, n. 97 above.

105 *Three Rivers DC* [2000] n. 93 above, at p. 7.

106 *Bromage v. Prosser* [1825] 4 B & C 247.

107 *Harman v. Tappenden* [1801] 1 East 555.

108 *Cullen v. Morris* [1819] 2 Stark 577.

109 *Bromage*, n. 106 above. Bayley J interpreted malice to mean 'ill will against a person, but in its legal sense it means a wrongful act, done intentionally without just cause or excuse', at p. 254–255.

110 *Rawlinson v. Rice* [1997] 2 NZLR 651.

111 *Roncarelli*, n. 102 above.

112 *Roncarelli*, Ibid., at p. 706.

elements of this second category. Like the first, the second limb consists of an act or omission which is an abuse and is deemed unlawful or invalid. For Clarke J, the second limb of the tort was the central issue of the preliminary ruling in *Three Rivers (No. 3)*. The existence of the second limb is made out in both the earlier[113] and more recent decisions.[114] It is important to establish when knowledge is sufficient to constitute a tort of misfeasance, and whether liability can arise when persons simply know an act or omission to be beyond the powers of their office.[115] According to Lord Diplock, an act that is known to exceed the powers of an office can satisfy the second limb.[116] This was endorsed by the House of Lords decision in *Calveley*, which accepted 'failure to establish reasonable cause' as satisfactory.[117] However, the decision in *Mengel* objected to the inclusion of 'constructive knowledge' in the duty of care concept,[118] thus placing the tort in a context of validity broader than abuse of office.[119] The question of validity focuses on the conduct of the public officer rather than simply on the invalidity of the act or omission: it must be established that the officer knew the act in question was beyond his powers.[120] Occasionally defendants in misfeasance actions do admit they knew their act was invalid, or the evidence clearly suggests that knowledge existed.[121]

The House of Lords followed the opinion of Clarke J that nothing less than actual knowledge or recklessness is sufficient. According to the opinions in *Mengel*, recklessness was regarded as sufficient for the first limb of the second category of the tort, where a public officer recklessly disregards the means of ascertaining the extent of his or her power.[122] Clarke J placed particular reliance on Brennan J and Deane J, who had agreed that reckless indifference to the possibility of injury is sufficient. Clarke J further refined the difference between knowledge and recklessness by referring to the *Eurysthenes*.[123] According to Lord Denning, 'knowledge' consists not only of being in the possession of positive knowledge but also instances in which 'turning a blind eye' is apparent. If a suspicious man 'turns a blind eye' to the truth and refrains from enquiry so that he will not know it for certain, then he is to be regarded as knowing the truth. It appears, therefore, that 'turning a blind eye' is far more blameworthy than mere negligence. Negligence in not knowing the truth is not equivalent to avoiding knowledge of it. Lord Denning's 'turning a blind eye'

---

113 *Farrington*, n. 101 above, at p. 293.

114 *Bourgoin*, n. 97 above; *Mengel*, n. 97 above.

115 *Three Rivers (No. 3)*, n. 93 above, at p. 569.

116 *Dunlop v. Woollahra Municipal Council* [1981] 1 All ER 1202.

117 *Calveley v. Chief Constable of Merseyside* [1989] 1 All ER 1025.

118 *Mengel*, n. 97 above, at p. 541.

119 *Beaurain v. Scott* [1813] 3 Camp. 388; *Pickering v. James* [1873] L R 8 C P 489.

120 *Three Rivers (No. 3)*, n. 93 above. Clarke J placed particular reliance on *Mengel*, Brennan J, at p. 546.

121 *Bourgoin*, n. 97 above; and earlier *Farrington*, n. 101 above.

122 *Mengel*, n. 97 above, Brennan J, at p. 554, and Deane J, at p. 546, recognised the importance of reckless behaviour in public officers.

123 *Three Rivers (No. 3)*, n. 93 above, at p. 579; particular reference is made to *Cia Maritima San Basilio SA v. Oceana Mutual Underwriting Association (Bermuda) Ltd* [1976] 3 All ER 243, at p. 251.

essentially amounts to Peter Gibson J's 'wilfully shutting one's eye to the obvious' or 'wilfully and recklessly failing to make such inquiries as an honest and reasonable man would make'.[124] Clarke J used these concepts to underpin his own views about state of mind and suggested that recklessness in the subjective sense is necessary. The House of Lords emphasised '[r]ecklessness about the consequences, in the sense of not caring whether the consequences happen or not, will satisfy the test'.[125]

The Court of Appeal accepted Clarke J's interpretation of the second limb of the tort but placed emphasis on the notion of dishonesty, thereby introducing additional criteria into the equation for determining the form and sufficiency of 'knowledge'.[126] The idea of dishonesty, according to Hirst LJ and Walker LJ, informs and permeates the ingredients of the tort,[127] equating it to the idea of abuse in the tort. This point was reiterated by Lord Nicholls, who proposed that acts of dishonesty should be distinguished from acts of negligence, and that 'knowingly' was required as a description of acts or omissions in that 'darker spectrum' of public office where misfeasance must surely reside. In the light of the concern expressed by Millet J and Lord Nicholls, the Court of Appeal added 'dishonesty' to the equation of knowledge.[128] According to Auld LJ (dissenting opinion), dishonesty is 'something more which distinguishes it from other forms of civil wrong and prevents the tort from overflowing its banks';[129] the tort should be simply established by proving that the public officer disregards his duties or does not honestly perform his duties without recognising the perils.[130] According to Lord Hope, the issue of dishonesty or bad faith is a question of 'fact and degree' which can only be for the trial judge to consider in light of the evidence.[131] For Lord Hobhouse (No. 3) (dissenting) the plaintiffs needed to be more specific when making such allegations: in his opinion the plaintiffs should be required to set out the case for dishonesty in their statement of claims rather than simply leave it and 'hope that something may turn up during the cross-examination of a witness at the trial'.[132]

Duty to the Depositors

The House of Lords addressed the question as to whether the BCCI claimants had an interest which required protecting to determine whether they can sue the Bank. The Court of Appeal, departing from the opinion of Clarke J, at first instance introduced a requirement of sufficient proximity between the defendant and plaintiff

124 *Societe Generale pour Favouriser le Developpment du Commerce et de l'Industrien France SA* [1992] 4 All ER 161, at p. 235.

125 *Three Rivers* [2001], n. 99 above, at p. 532.

126 *Mengel*, n. 97 above, at p. 185; see also *Garrett v. AG* [1997] 2 NZLR 332; *Rawlinson*, n. 110 above.

127 *Three Rivers* [1999], n. 93 above, at p. 334.

128 Ibid.

129 Ibid., at p. 440.

130 Ibid.

131 *Three Rivers* [2001], n. 99 above, at p. 534.

132 Ibid., at p. 569.

as a precondition for establishing misfeasance.[133] The proximity requirement is used to curtail the existence of a duty to take reasonable care in order to prevent claims on policy grounds from an unascertainable class of individuals.[134] This effectively limits the existence of such a duty and prevents a flood of claims against regulators. According to Clarke J, these policy considerations were necessary to curtail the scope of the duty of care in an action in the tort of negligence,[135] but not in a case involving an allegation of misfeasance.[136] The House of Lords concurred with Clarke J that such mechanisms were not needed to curtail a claim in misfeasance because the plaintiffs would have to overcome the difficulty of establishing the necessary state of mind of the defendant before they could succeed. The hurdle of establishing deliberate abuse of power through either of the two limbs has the effect of protecting a regulator against over-zealous plaintiffs.[137] Their Lordships stated that the requirement to be satisfied was establishing the requisite state of mind, and determining loss would probably ensue. This was sufficiently difficult effectively to rein in the unique tort.[138]

Causation and Misfeasance in Public Office

The questions of causation and the remoteness of damage are crucial to establish that the act or omission caused the loss and this was the kind of damage that would ensue. These require consideration of the degree to which the relevant facts fulfil the allegations, which is a concern more appropriate for a trial judge to determine, and whether the loss was caused by the defendant's act or omission or whether it was too remote. On common-sense principles,[139] an act or omission must provide more than just the occasion or opportunity to sustain loss,[140] particularly when regulatory bodies have a wide discretionary authority that makes the ascertaining of causation problematic.[141] The issue here is whether the Bank's alleged misfeasance was an effective and direct cause of the ensuing loss, or whether it merely provided the occasion for the loss because the Bank did not have day-to-day control of BCCI and its activities.[142]

Misfeasance also requires consideration of whether damage needs to be foreseeable or foreseen. This is crucial in determining that the necessary 'state of

133 *Three Rivers* [1999], n. 93 above, at p. 342.

134 *Yuen Kun Yeu*, n. 21 above, at p. 192.

135 *Governors of Peabody Donation Fund v. Sir Lindsay Parkinson & Co. Ltd* [1985] A C 210, at pp. 240 241.

136 *Yuen Kun Yeu*, n. 21 above, at p. 196; Davis, n. 22 above, at p. 827.

137 *Three Rivers (No. 3)*, n. 93 above, at p. 584.

138 *Three Rivers* [2000], n. 93 above, at p. 10.

139 *Cork v. Kirby Maclean Ltd* [1952] 2 All ER 402, at pp. 406–407. This is notwithstanding the fact that the 'but for' test has limitations where there are multiple causations.

140 *Galoo Ltd (in liq.) v. Bright Grahame Murray (a firm)* [1995] 1 All ER 16, Glidewell LJ, at pp. 16 19.

141 McBride, J. (1979) 'Remedy for unlawful administrative action', *Cambridge Law Journal*, vol. 38, 323, at p. 334.

142 *Three Rivers (No. 3)*, n. 93 above, at pp. 628 629.

mind' was present, which in turn is crucial in evaluating the facts, in the light of that standard, to determine whether the tort of misfeasance is an extension of the tort of negligence. The ultimate question is whether foreseeability of harm is appropriate in this context. An important point to bear in mind is that foreseeability of harm in its own right does not necessarily mean that an action in negligence will succeed; a number of safety nets to curtail a duty of care need to be overcome.[143] According to Watkin J,[144] foreseeability is simply the first condition to establish – the courts have to take into account other factors in the loss or damage claim, including the nature of the event or act, and more importantly matters of public policy.

The House of Lords articulated the test to determine whether the losses suffered by the plaintiffs were the sort of losses recoverable in law. The test delineated by Clarke J was considered appropriate. He dismissed the test that the claimants would have to prove the Bank actually foresaw the losses as a result of its acts or omissions. The House of Lords placed emphasis on Clarke J's reasoning as it made 'new law': the test is simply whether the damage was foreseeable.[145]

The issue of damage being foreseen or foreseeable in a quest to establish misfeasance was in an uncertain state before Clarke J's emphasis on actual foresight placed it on a much clearer footing, though for Auld LJ that was still an insecure one.[146] Clarke J was of the view that the basis of the tort should be more stringent than merely the knowledge that an act was unlawful. He proposed that liability should be more 'closely confined' to include 'acts which are calculated in the ordinary course to cause harm... or with reckless indifference to the harm that is likely to ensue'.[147] Clarke J rejected the interpretation in *Bourgoin* by Mann J, and was of the view that knowledge that an act is invalid, coupled with foresight that its commission would probably cause damage to the plaintiff, is enough.[148] This conclusion follows Brennan J in *Mengel*, who stated that 'causation of damage is relevant; foreseeability of damage is not'.[149] This is notwithstanding the fact that the majority decision in *Mengel* thought foresight of harm was sufficient but not in terms of establishing knowledge. Clarke J recognised that there was no support in his conclusion for the opinion that reasonable foresight is sufficient at the second stage. The inclusion of 'foresight of harm' is a logical extension of how knowledge is established: it is now actual knowledge plus a positive state of mind, or recklessness with advertence to consequences as distinct from inadvertence to consequence, which constitutes negligence.[150] Lord Steyn explains that the tort of misfeasance provides a remedy against executive and administrative abuse of power without exposing public officers who act in good faith to 'unmeritorious actions'.[151]

143 *Dorset Yacht Co.*, n. 23 above, at p. 1030.

144 *Lamb v. Camden London Borough Council* [1981] 1 QB 625, 642.

145 *Three Rivers* [2000], n. 93 above at p. 12.

146 *Three Rivers* [1999], n. 93 above, at p. 442.

147 *Three Rivers* (No. 3), n. 93 above, at p. 540.

148 *Bourgoin*, n. 97 above, at p. 602.

149 *Mengel*, n. 97 above, at p. 547.

150 Kneebone, S. (1996) 'Misfeasance in a public office after Mengel's case: A "special" tort no more?', *Tort Law Review*, July, 111, at p. 135.

151 *Three Rivers* [2000], n. 93 above, p. 12.

House of Lords (No. 3)

The articulation of the ingredients of the tort of misfeasance required the House of Lords to address the all-important issue of whether the claimants could progress to the next stage for a full trial of the evidence.[152] The House sought to address this by examining the preliminary evidence presented at this stage of the case to ascertain whether the plaintiffs had pleaded a reasonable cause of action. Lord Hope set out the long history of BCCI into four broad periods, from its licensing to undertake banking business to its closure after the Price Waterhouse Report in 1991. The plaintiffs made several claims, including the fact that the Bank gave BCCI a licence by relying on the Luxembourg authorities when it should not have done so, and subsequently its failure to take responsibility for supervising BCCI although its main business was undertaken in the UK. The House of Lords decision at this stage in hindsight gave the plaintiffs a right to go on a fishing expedition for further evidence, and indeed submit claims against individuals at the Bank at various stages of the proceedings. This may not be surprising given the relatively long history of this bank closure, and thus the encyclopaedia of facts and issues that needed to be ploughed through to ascertain whether a case existed.

The Bingham Report

The crucial piece of evidence in the *Three Rivers* saga is the Bingham Report.[153] The inquiry highlights the long history of BCCI, in particular the relationship between the Bank and BCCI. The terms of reference of the inquiry were:

- what did the UK authorities know at all relevant times?
- should they have known more?
- what action did the UK authorities take in relation to BCCI at all relevant times?
- should they have acted differently?
- what should be done to prevent, or minimise the risk of, such an event recurring in the future?

The House of Lords decision questioned the reliance placed on the Bingham Report by Clarke J and the Court of Appeal, thereby calling into question the usefulness of the report: on the one hand they held it to be of limited value, and on the other they were relying on its findings to determine whether the case should be struck out.[154] Their decision supported the dissenting opinion of Auld LJ, who questioned the right to treat the Bingham Report as effectively conclusive. According to Lord Hobhouse, the critical issue was whether to rely on the Bingham Report or dismiss its decision,

152 *Three Rivers* [2001], n. 99 above.

153 Ibid., at p. 523.

154 Ibid., at p. 524. See also Lord Hobhouse, for whom Clarke J and the Court of Appeal made appropriate use of the Bingham Report, reaffirming Clarke J's conclusion that the plaintiffs' case should be struck out for want of sufficient evidence to establish dishonesty, at p. 570.

not on whether one agrees with it.[155] The BCCI inquiry could not be equated with the type of investigation that would ensue from a civil trial of the issues arising from the affair. The report by Bingham LJ was not a full public inquiry under the Tribunals and Inquiry Act 1921 but an inquiry arranged voluntarily by the Bank, and His Lordship had no power to compel the attendance of witnesses. It is submitted that Clarke J and the Court of Appeal placed too much emphasis on the report in determining whether the case should be struck out. On the other hand, there was no other report or evidence before the court. While both Bingham LJ and Clarke J were critical of the Bank's conduct, both were reticent about considering the Bank liable for the failures in its supervision of BCCI. Clarke J's initial conclusion, like Bingham LJ's, blames the collapse and losses incurred by depositors and creditors on BCCI alone, because of the 'systemic fraud' that it perpetrated. The Lords' majority decision calls into question the opinion of Clarke J that the report's terms of reference require an investigation into the Bank's knowledge of the BCCI affair. The Lords suggested that the plaintiffs must obtain the evidence that underpins Bingham LJ's findings to flesh out the case against the Bank, which could only happen if a trial was allowed.

The Preliminary Conclusions

The complexity of the case is shown by the chronological evidence provided by the Bingham Report about the Bank's responsibilities as a third party for the losses. According to Lord Hope, not all of the allegations could simply be struck out, and it would be unreasonable to strike out the whole claim. Lord Hobhouse estimated the trial would last for a year at least and, being a case without real prospect of success, would use a disproportionate amount of resources and court time. Their Lordships suggested that the appropriate test to determine whether the case should be struck out is not whether it is bound to fail but whether it has any 'real prospect of success'. The Lords were at pains to make clear that the question of whether the case should be struck out did not necessarily mean that the allegations are not proven. Their Lordships' decision called into question Clarke J's conclusion that the case was bound to fail because there was little likelihood of further evidence becoming available to the plaintiffs in support of their claims. It was thus accepted that the claim should proceed on a purely objective basis and without any preconditions regarding its outcome. The unreported Three Rivers was considered to have left more unanswered questions, which led to the conclusion that a full trial is the only route for getting to the bottom of the BCCI affair.

Clarke J considered chronologically a number of allegations, including the original granting of a licence to the divestment by Bank of America, the continuing supervision of BCCI and the issues surrounding the relocation of Central Treasury operations, which happened in the period preceding its closure.[156] On the basis of these allegations, Clarke J had to determine whether the Bank knew, believed or suspected that BCCI would collapse, that a rescue package would not be secured and

155 Ibid., at p. 524.

156 Singh, D. (1999) 'Misfeasance in public office: The case of banking supervision and BCCI', *European Financial Services Law*, vol. 6, 128.

that losses to potential and future depositors would occur. Clarke J held the Bank had no case to answer. It had not dishonestly granted a licence to BCCI, nor should it have revoked its licence or authorisation once it knew, believed or suspected that BCCI would collapse. It is to be noted, however, that at first instance and in the Court of Appeal it was recognised that in some circumstances the supervision had been ineffective. However, the Court of Appeal agreed with Clarke J that the claimants could not establish that the Bank actually knew BCCI would probably collapse or that it would not be rescued. Serious issues in respect of the probity of BCCI reveal a picture far worse than even the most sceptical critic could have suspected.

However, the House of Lords was not so dismissive. Lord Hope emphasised the importance of ascertaining whether evidence could be available to support the allegations made by the plaintiffs, which ultimately claim the Bank acted in bad faith. What the plaintiffs were seeking to establish is 'that the Bank knew that the likely consequences were that depositors and potential depositors would suffer losses, wilfully disregarded the risk of the consequences or was recklessly indifferent to the consequences' – in other words, either knowledge or reckless indifference, as examined above.[157] For Lord Hope the precise nature of the state of mind to establish the tort is a question of degree and risk which can only be dealt with at a trial. The plaintiffs alleged the Bank acted in bad faith by over-relying on the assurances it was given by LBC/IML regarding BCCI's financial soundness. In addition LBC/IML had clearly notified the Bank that they were unable to carry on adequate supervision of BCCI. In light of this it was alleged the Bank knew the consequence of its unlawful reliance on LBC/IML was that BCCI was effectively not licensed or authorised during this period, giving rise to risks to both existing and future depositors. In relation to the Bank's failure to revoke BCCI's licence and authorisation, evidence of major losses in its Central Treasury and a money-laundering indictment in Tampa, Florida, establish prima facie a failure on the part of the Bank to exercise its powers. Given the limited evidence available it was in the opinion of Lord Hope difficult simply to dismiss the claim during the latter period of BCCI's history, when the Bank knew if a rescue package was not put together then BCCI would collapse and this would result in loss to depositors.

The Tomlinson Decision (2006)

The success of the plaintiffs in finally having their day in court was a tremendous victory, albeit short-lived, as the lawsuit against the Bank was later brought to an abrupt end when the creditors called on Deloittes, the liquidators for BCCI who brought the case against the Bank in misfeasance in public office, to discontinue it.[158] Tomlinson J's judgment is very critical to say the least, calling parts of the whole legal campaign 'cynical and grotesque' and 'inhumane'. It in many respects brought new insights to the actual evidence available, and indeed the lengths to which lawyers on behalf of the depositors went to establish their case of dishonesty against the Bank and its officials; it also featured the longest opening speech in English

157 *Three Rivers* [2001], n. 98 above, at p. 531.

158 *Three Rivers DC v. Bank of England* [2006] EWHC 816.

legal history by the claimants. The Bank succeeded in its claim for costs against the liquidator, totalling £73 million. The Tomlinson decision reviewed the claims made by the depositors against the Bank and sheds new light on the whole saga.

The judgment addresses some of the claims: suffice it to say that they were based on weak or contradictory grounds, which resulted in the plaintiffs continuously changing their claims against the Bank when their previous claims could not be substantiated in light of the evidence that arose from the disclosures made for the trial. First, the claim regarding the over-reliance on LBC/IML to supervise BCCI was considered flawed, given the fact that such practice was general for overseas banks with a branch presence in the UK. The claimants also accused the Bank of not revoking BCCI's authorisation when a rescue was not forthcoming. But new evidence clearly indicates the Bank did evaluate the risk posed by not revoking its licence or authorisation, but considered the likelihood of a rescue a real possibility. Secondly, the claim alleged failure by the Bank to carry on consolidated supervision. Tomlinson J highlighted the changing nature of bank supervision, comparing the practices then with those now: the plaintiffs were simply acting from a vantage point of hindsight to claim that the Bank acted dishonestly by not undertaking consolidated supervision. The evidence clearly showed that the Bank had considered the matter and its implications with all concerned, which does not support the claim that the Bank acted dishonestly by not exercising its power to carry out consolidated supervision. The third claim was that the grant of a licence to BCCI was an act of misfeasance, in that the Bank acted dishonestly by unlawfully licensing it while knowing it placed depositors at a serious risk of loss. This included implying that Bank officials manipulated proceedings for the drafting of the First Basel Concordat so that the supervision of international banks by home and host states was not sufficiently addressed to capture the problems associated with supervising BCCI at the time.[159]

The US Approach to Accountability of Federal Bank Regulators

Federal bank regulators are required, like all those undertaking public functions, to exercise their responsibilities in the national interest rather than simply that of the agency or department for which they work.[160] This is part of a wider legislative move to improve the accountability of those exercising public functions after the Watergate crisis. The Office of Government Ethics established by the Ethics in Government Act 1978 is responsible in conjunction with the executive agencies and branches of government, which *inter alia* include the Department of the Treasury (including the OCC and OTS), the FRS and the FDIC, for ensuring high ethical standards of behaviour by its employees; the ultimate aim is to maintain public confidence in the government's ability to conduct its business with 'impartiality' and 'integrity'.[161] This requires public officers and employees to exercise their responsibilities with

159 Ibid., paras 109–115.

160 5 CFR, Ch. XVI, § 2635.101.

161 5 CFR, Part 2600, 'Organization and Functions of the Office of Government Ethics', § 2600.101.

'loyalty to the Constitution, laws and ethical principles above private gain'.[162] According to Thompson, government ethics are a 'way of reminding officials that they are accountable to the public, that they primarily serve not their administrative superiors or even their own consciences but all citizens'.[163]

The law relating to the fiduciary duty of public officers and employees is set out in 5 CFR and supplemented by further regulation, legislation and guidance.[164] These regulations are enforced by both the agency and the Director of the Office of Government Ethics. They provide for the appointment of an ethics officer at individual agencies to oversee compliance with ethical issues at the agency level.[165] The role of ethics officers has been described in many ways in light of the role they play: from 'mullahs of the US Government' to a 'priesthood of ethics counsellors'.[166] One of the more useful descriptions is that of 'educator', as suggested by Thompson, to ensure public employees comply with the spirit of ethical rules and standards and understand what they aim to achieve.[167]

The general provisions are very prescriptive and focus on a whole array of matters that may undermine an employee's impartiality, whether directly or indirectly, ultimately damaging the confidence the public places in them. Despite these prescriptive standards the federal bank regulators have supplemental rules to which their employees are required to adhere. These expand on the general regulations to address some of the more specific conflicts of interests employees may be exposed to while undertaking their responsibilities as, for instance, examiners or supervisors. The circumstances that call into question an individual's impartiality can occasionally be dealt with at an agency level; nevertheless, the high expectations placed on public officials and employees are such that most matters which give rise to material conflicts are regulated.

Public employees are prohibited from receiving or soliciting gifts, including 'any gratuity, favor, discount, entertainment, hospitality, loan, forbearance, or other item having a monetary value', which literally excludes any kind of gifts or services.[168] This is to avoid public employees benefiting from their position or exploiting their status for personal gain, because if it were not for their position they would not have been offered the gift or service in the first place.[169] The exceptions to the general rule are limited: for instance, gifts valued at $20 or less could be accepted provided the accumulative total of individual gifts from any one person does not exceed $50 in a calendar year.[170] Individuals who have received gifts are required *inter alia* to return the gift, pay the donor its market value or give it to charity. Employees are also prohibited from receiving gifts from their subordinates unless they are for one-off

162 5 CFR, § 2635.101(b)(1); Thompson, D. F. (1992) 'Paradoxes of government ethics', *Public Administration Review*, vol. 52, 254.

163 Ibid., at p. 255.

164 5 CFR, § 2635.105.

165 5 CFR, § 2638.201.

166 Thompson (1992) n. 162 above.

167 Ibid., at p. 258.

168 5 CFR, § 2635.202(5)(b)(1)–(7).

169 For exceptions see 5 CFR, § 2635.204.

170 5 CFR, § 2635.204(a).

events such as marriage or retirement; it would not be acceptable to give presents for birthdays or even Christmas.

The standards also provide measures to deal with conflicts of interest that can arise from personal financial matters.[171] Public employees are either disqualified or prohibited from having particular financial interests, either directly or imputed through a family connection, 'if the particular matter will have a direct and predictable effect on that interest', whether it is to achieve a gain or avoid a loss accruing.[172] In certain instances employees may be prevented from holding a particular financial interest if it would disqualify them from undertaking critical aspects of their duties because they would be deemed 'materially impaired' or it would 'adversely affect the efficient accomplishment of the agency's mission'.[173] For example, federal bank regulators like the OCC are prohibited either personally or through their spouse or children from holding or even recommending securities of commercial banks, state chartered banks or bank holding companies.[174] This prohibition does not extend to more generic investments such as mutual funds or collective investment funds offered to the public – it does not extend to deposit accounts, for example.[175] A number of other restrictions also exist: for instance, borrowing from national banks is prohibited unless it is a spouse relying on their own credit. However, compliance with this is dependent on an individual's responsibilities: at the OCC, for example, an examiner of banks would be required to comply but not a non-examiner.[176] Even in the case of obtaining a credit card the supplemental rules prohibit bank examiners getting them from banks they are responsible for examining.[177] Despite these broad-brush prohibitions, the ethics officer could in certain circumstances exercise discretion in such matters if it is clear that a conflict of interest will not arise.

In addition to financial interests, an individual's personal and business relationships are regulated as they can also impair a public employee's ability to exercise their responsibilities.[178] In such matters the employee must 'avoid the appearance of a loss of impartiality'; to do that the individual needs to be mindful of whether 'a reasonable person with knowledge of the relevant facts would question his impartiality in the matter'.[179] For example, OCC examiners cannot examine a bank where they have a financial interest.[180] Finally, the ethical standards prohibit public employees 'misusing' their position for private gain; for instance, employees may not use non-public information to further their own personal interests by disclosing

171 5 CFR, § 2635.401; see 5 CFR, § 2635.403(c)(1) for a definition of financial interests.

172 5 CFR, § 2635.401.

173 5 CFR, § 2635.403(a),(b)(1)(2).

174 Chapter XXI, Part 3101, 'Supplemental Standards of Ethical Conduct for Employees of the Department of the Treasury'; § 3101.108(a).

175 OCC (2006) *OCC Ethics Rules, A Plain English Guide*, 21 July, available at www.occ.treas.gov/ethics.htm, at p. 4.

176 § 3101.108 (b)(3).

177 § 3101.108 (b)(4).

178 § 2635.501.

179 § 2635.501(a).

180 OCC, n. 172 above, at p. 7.

it to others.[181] The OCC guidance extends this general prohibition to OCC staff using their position to solicit funds for a charitable cause, other than putting up a notice in a common room.

A number of regulations restrict certain senior public officers from obtaining employment within the industry for a year after leaving a post, unless compliance has been waived by the agency.[182] These restrictions govern those senior officers who have had close contacts with those with whom they are seeking future employment, whether for remuneration or not. For instance, the FDIC regulations explicitly provide 'an officer or employee of the FDIC who serves as a senior examiner of an insured depository institution for at least 2 months during the last 12 months of that individual's employment with the FDIC may not, within 1 year after... accept compensation as an employee, officer, director, or consultant from... the insured depository institution'.[183]

Legal Accountability of Bank Regulators

US public bodies and regulators such as federal government agencies are not necessarily immune against claims by individuals in the tort of negligence for their acts or omissions if these are the type of claims private individuals would be liable for in 'like circumstances'.[184] In such cases the USA is the respondent to the claim, albeit it is the act or omission of the federal regulator or agency that has given rise to it.[185] This includes the acts or omissions of an officer or employee of a federal agency 'acting within the scope of this office or employment'.[186] A claim must generally first be put to the federal agency to deal with through its own administrative process; only after exhausting that process can a claim against the USA be initiated.[187] Nor can a claimant pursue a tort of negligence claim in common law: it has to be pursued using the legislative procedure set out in 28 USC.

A number of exceptions do exist, however, to ensure federal agencies are not inundated with claims in tort, resulting in the administrative machinery effectively coming to a halt in a climate of continuous litigation which would distort the way it functions and clog up the courts. Federal regulators have the authority to deal with relatively small claims in the tort of negligence by individuals by alternative means, which then must be reported separately to Congress on a periodic basis.[188] In claims not settled through this process the USA is said to be able 'to assert any defense

181 5 CFR § 2635.703(a).

182 5 CFR § 2635.6019(a)(2).

183 FDIC Rules and Regulations, Part 336, 'FDIC Employees', § 336.12(a)(1).

184 28 USC, § 2674. See also Axelrad, J. (2000) 'Federal Tort Claims Act administrative claims: Better than third-party ADR for resolving federal tort claims', *Administrative Law Review*, vol. 52, 1331.

185 28 USC, § 2679.

186 28 USC, § 2671.

187 28 USC, § 2675.

188 28 USC, § 2672 and § 2673.

based upon judicial or legislative immunity which would have been available to the employee of the United States whose act or omission gave rise to the claim'.[189]

Federal agencies are also exempted from liability if the act or omission emanates from a 'failure to exercise or perform a discretionary function or duty on the part of the federal agency or an employee'.[190] The decisions ultimately taken by bank regulators emanate from broad rules that require a large degree of judgement to be exercised in their application. Indeed, numerous policy issues may need to be considered before a decision is made by a bank regulator, and these may compete with one another. This suggests that a significant proportion of the issues that may be challenged by an individual in a claim could not be pursued against the USA *per se* because federal agencies and their employees would invariably be exercising discretionary functions where choices have to be made. This is aptly discussed in the protracted litigation arising from the liquidation of Franklin Savings Corporation as a result of it being considered to be 'in an unsafe and unsound condition to transact' by the Office of Thrift Supervision.[191] The decision to terminate the bank's operations resulted in a claim in negligence on the part of the regulators for their alleged failure to manage its operations properly during the period when it was in receivership. This resulted in consideration of whether the claim fulfilled the criteria necessary to pursue the USA successfully for compensation – in particular whether it fell within the exception of being classed as a discretionary function for which the regulator would be exempted from liability. In this respect the court applied a 'two-pronged test': first it had to determine whether the issue 'involved an element of judgement or choice'; secondly whether the issue on which a judgement had to be made 'is of the kind that the discretionary function was designed to shield'. In response to the first question the court highlighted that the regulations did not 'require bank regulators to pursue any specific course of action', which would be necessary in any successful claim. In the latter the court determined that the exception to liability was intended to 'shield' federal agencies from these very claims based on individual employees executing decisions with a broad policy mandate.

This immunity protecting the USA from claims in tort of negligence does not extend to the contractual relationships federal agencies enter into with other parties. For example, the USA was not able to avoid liability as a result of the contractual commitments the federal bank regulators entered into with a number of thrifts in the fallout from the savings and loans débâcle during the 1980s and 1990s. The crisis was a result of a poor economic climate at the time with high interest rates, but this was exacerbated by poor regulatory oversight and management of thrifts, and in a number of cases fraudulent activities. According to Citron this period saw a considerable level of 'regulatory forbearance' to avoid a huge spate of closures of insolvent thrifts.[192] To mitigate the extent of the financial impact of the crisis on the

189 28 USC, § 2674.

190 28 USC, § 2680(a).

191 *Franklin Savings Corporation and Franklin Savings Associations v. US and the Federal Deposit Insurance Corporation* 970 F. Supp. 855 (D.C. KS. 1997).

192 Citron, R. D. (2002) 'Lessons from the damages decisions following *United States v. Winstar Corp*', *Public Contract Law Journal*, vol. 32, 1, at p. 10.

public purse, through the Federal Savings and Loan Insurance Corporation (FSLIC) deposit protection fund, the federal regulator put together a scheme to encourage healthy thrifts to merge with their weaker counterparts to forestall the continued crisis and instil an element of confidence in the sector. The implications for the healthy thrifts were obviously serious given that the weaker thrifts were insolvent, thus the impact on the quality of their capital base was something they had to consider before a merger could even be contemplated. The federal regulators gave the prospective thrifts reassurances by devising new accounting rules to avoid the mergers adversely affecting the quality of the capital base and extending the benefits of the new regime for several decades to avoid non-compliance with regulatory capital requirements. The political reaction was considerable, with the enactment of a number of pieces of legislation to stem the crisis: the most significant and far-reaching was the Financial Institutions Reform, Recovery, and Enforcement Act 1989 (FIRREA).[193] Its wide scope reversed the benefits of the mergers initiated by the regulator by dramatically reducing the period for which the liabilities incurred through the mergers could be offset for the purposes of compliance with the regulatory measures for capital. The impact on the merged thrifts was literally to render them not compliant with regulatory capital requirements, resulting in them being technically insolvent; the federal regulators consequently closed those thrifts that were not compliant with the new regime.

The closure of these thrifts resulted in a considerable level of litigation, at the pinnacle of which was the seminal decision of *US v. Winstar Corp.*[194] This litigation focused on the contractual basis on which the thrifts entered into mergers with insolvent counterparts and the resulting breach of contract that arose from the reversal of US government policy through the FIRREA 1989 to rein in the extended supervisory goodwill that was promised when the mergers took place. The *Winstar* case deals with three thrift mergers that resulted in damages for breach of contract. The USA put forward two lines of defence. First, the 'unmistakability doctrine' which requires the US government to establish the terms of the contract was effectively ambiguous, as it did not prevent the government from changing its policy in the future. The grounds on which this defence was denied were *inter alia* that the agreements in question did not adversely impinge on the government's sovereign authority to exercise its future regulatory authority. The agreements required the US government simply to 'do something that did not implicate its sovereign powers at all, that is, to

193 Financial Institutions Reform, Recovery, and Enforcement Act 1989, Public Law No. 101-73, 103 Stat. 183.

194 *US, Petitioner v. Winstar Corporation, et al.* 518 US. 839 (1996). For an examination of this case see Macey, J. R. (1998) '*Winstar*, bureaucracy and public choice', *Supreme Court Economic Review*, vol. 6, 173; Citron, R. D. (2003) 'Culture clash? The Miller & Modigliani propositions meet the United States Court of Federal Claims', *Review of Litigation*, vol. 22, 319; Tishuk, B. R. (2003) 'High time for closure: Yes, the Federal Tort Claims Act applies to the FDIC as receiver', *Annual Review of Banking and Financial Law*, vol. 22, 367; Wei, R. (1997) '*United States v. Winstar*: Renewed government liability arising from the savings and loans crisis', *North Carolina Banking Institute*, vol. 1, 366.

indemnify its contracting partners against financial losses from regulatory change':[195] the contracting parties would not have entered into such contracts unless the healthy thrifts got a clear promise the regulatory requirements would not change. The second defence was the 'sovereign acts doctrine', which also failed. This defence is based on the potential dichotomy between a government fulfilling its public responsibilities through a policy change and its contractual obligations to a private party: a change to public policy could directly impinge on the contractual terms entered into by the government. The 'sovereign acts doctrine' prevents liability for a breach 'resulting from its public and general acts as a sovereign'.[196] The court determined this defence was not applicable to these circumstances as the government had not expressed its intentions to rely on the doctrine and had 'assumed the risk of a change in its laws'.[197]

Conclusion

This chapter has attempted to analyse the legal responsibility and accountability of regulators and their employees – most discussions of legal accountability tend to neglect the fiduciary duties these persons are required to abide by in their day-to-day work. The common law position is quite clear that those in a fiduciary relationship are expected to set aside personal interests that may conflict with professional responsibilities. The FSA code of conduct has sought to build on this principle to ensure its employees are clear about the expectations attached to their duties to avoid undermining its integrity as an organisation. This code of conduct is part and parcel of a broader system of accountability and governance.

The FSA is, like the majority of financial regulators, immune to a claim in the tort of negligence, both implicitly in common law and expressly in the FSMA 2000. The rationale for immunity is based on a number of grounds, but is ultimately designed to allow individual employees the opportunity to work without fear of potential claims for negligence for decisions that may in hindsight be wrong but are based on broad policy couched in discretionary terms which requires them to exercise a significant level of judgement. However, the recent Privy Council decision in *Gulf Insurance Ltd v. The Central Bank of Trinidad and Tobago* provides a new dimension to such statutory immunities, which were perceived to be watertight forms of protection. The case clearly exposes regulators and central banks to a significant risk of liability in what are very difficult circumstances, such as having to manage and prevent a crisis occurring in the financial markets and make decisions based on incomplete information in a very short period of time.

Despite the implied and express immunity against claims in the tort of negligence, policy-makers have put in place alternative mechanisms for firms and individuals to seek redress through the Ombudsman Scheme and the Independent Complaints Commissioner. Whether these can bridge the gap that the courts could technically provide is a point that needs considering further. It certainly provides evidence that

195 *Winstar*, ibid., at p. 887.

196 Ibid., at p. 924.

197 Ibid., at p. 925.

the lack of a duty of care owed for instance by a regulator towards individuals is purely a policy point to protect regulators from a host of claims. The office of the Independent Complaints Commissioner is based on the premise the FSA can get things wrong, and that its acts or omissions can give rise to financial loss to an individual or firm as a result of its mistake, negligence or misconduct. This alternative form of redress has been neglected in the academic literature, which demonstrates that little is known about it in comparison to the Financial Ombudsman Scheme. The compensation system in the UK does not provide a sufficient level of cover for individual depositors, and indeed imposes a responsibility on them which they cannot simply discharge through co-insurance if a bank were to close or collapse. This invariably means depositors will seek redress in the courts, because the cover provided is limited and some claimants are ineligible. The only consolation is the fact that not many depositors have needed to claim: in 2005 a total of £90,000 was paid out, in comparison to a total compensation payout of £201.22 million for all financial services.[198]

The exception to express immunity is a claim in bad faith – misfeasance in public office. Such claims against the Bank have been very controversial in light of the level of judicial scrutiny given to the tort of misfeasance in public office over a number of years, and not forgetting the allegations made against individuals at the Bank in depositor claims which were in the end considered 'grotesque'. The difficulty of pursuing a claim in the tort of negligence has made individuals consider misfeasance in public office as an alternative route to get damages. This is as far from the truth as it can possibly get. The courts in *Three Rivers* explicitly noted their reluctance to entertain such claims if they are simply grafted on to a claim in tort of negligence. Nor do the policy initiatives adopted to provide for a duty of care need extending, in light of the fact that the claimants must establish abuse of office by the said individuals.

The expectations of public employees in the USA are set out in a far more prescriptive manner: reliance is placed on the individual to make disclosures about potential conflicts of interest, but these are regulated far more heavily than in the UK. The sanctions associated with a breach are broad, ranging from a fine to dismissal. Indeed, individual employees are required to abide by a host of rules that simply do not exist in the FSA code of conduct. The rules governing employees holding financial interests in regulated firms prohibit dealing in their individual securities, whereas the UK position allows employees to trade in securities with a warning associated with insider dealing quite explicitly attached. The prohibition on working in the industry extends only to those firms with which an individual has been directly involved through examinations; but such a rule does not exist in the UK at all. In the UK regulators are positively encouraged to build links with regulated firms, and are not prohibited from working in the industry in the future. The position in the USA in many respects places public employees beyond reproach in comparison to their UK counterparts; indeed, in the UK a significant concern has been the relatively high turnover of staff, which could mean that FSA employees are lured into the City by high salaries after a short period in public service.

198 FSCS (2005/06) *Annual Report: Financial Services Compensation Scheme.*

Depositors in the USA are generally eligible to claim compensation for the failures of federal bank regulators unless the act or omission ensued from a discretionary function. This effectively curtails the likely success of any claim made against a federal regulator; what is more, the high level of depositor protection means there are few such claims. However, banks themselves are more likely to claim for losses resulting from the acts or omissions of their respective regulators. The probability of such a claim succeeding is limited by the said exception to the general rule. The immunity provided in the USA is more complicated than its UK comparator, as highlighted by Delston.[199] Despite this the USA has in place alternative mechanisms to provide redress for those who have suffered a loss as result of the acts or omissions of federal regulators. A comparison of the UK and US alternative mechanisms needs further investigation.

199 Delston, n. 32 above.

Index

Abbey Life 21
Abbey National Asset Managers 87, 89
Abbey National plc 88, 171
Accounting Investigation and Discipline Board 160–163
Accounting Principles Board 173
AG v. Blake 183
AG v. Guardian Newspapers 184
Allfirst Bank 149–150
Allied Irish Bank 149–150
American Institute of Certified Public Accountants 173, 175
Arthur Andersen Report 122, 135
Atherton v. FDIC 109
Atlantic Computers 161
audit committees 92–97
Auditing Practices Board 158
Auld LJ 204, 206, 207
AXA Sun Life 134–135

Bank Account Directive 155
Bank of Credit and Commerce International (BCCI)
- Bingham Report 207–208
- international cooperation 66
- lender of last resort 5
- major banking fraud 9
- market rumours 128
- role of external auditors 155–156, 162–163, 169–170
- *Three Rivers* litigation 200–210
- Tomlinson decision 209–210

Bank of England
- Arthur Andersen Report 122
- Bank of England Act
  - 1946 122
  - 1998 15–16
- BCCI closure 5, 156
- Bingham Report 207–208
- discretion 123–125
- enforcement strategy 121–125
- 'lead operators' 16
- lender of last resort 3–6, 15–16
- memorandum of understanding 15–16
- prudential supervision 9–10
- regulation of financial services 10–14
- role of external auditors 168
- role of internal auditor 92
- shaping financial regulation 42
  - *Three Rivers* litigation 200–210
- Tomlinson decision 209–210
- transparency in banking supervision 123–125

Bank of England Act
- 1946 122
- 1998 15–16

Bank of Ireland 89–90
Bank of New England 36
Bankhaus Herstatt 66
Banking Act
- 1933 70
- 1979 8, 9, 54, 66, 85–86. 201
- 1987 8, 13, 60, 66, 86, 93, 122, 155, 156, 168, 188, 200, 201

Banking Code 48
banks
- bank run 8
- Banking Code 48
- capital adequacy 60–65
- consolidated supervision 59–60
- constructive ambiguity 6–7
- contagion 3, 80, 146, 169, 190
- corporate governance 80–82
- depositor creditors 83–86
- deposit-taking business 54–68
- discretion in banking supervision 123–125
- duty to depositors 204–205
- financial stability 2–8, 181

formal regulation 8–14
function of regulation 46–49
internal models 63–65
large exposures 65–66
legal position of directors and senior management 97–105
lender of last resort 3 6
moral hazard 6–7
new era of regulation 14–17
Privy Council 190, 216
qualification of bank accounts 169–170
regulation 7–8, 46-48
role of external auditors 155–173
Shareholders 85–86
supervision 7–8, 46-48
systemic risk 3, 5, 15, 40, 123, 190
transparency 123, 125
US approach to regulatory accountability 210–216
US bank failures 176
US position of bank directors 105–110
US risk-based supervision 72–76
US safe and sound requirements 69–76
value at risk 64
Baring, Francis 4
Barings Bank
Arthur Andersen Report 122
collapse of 9–10
lack of international cooperation 66–67
lender of last resort 5
management failures 99
market rumours 128
role of external auditors 67, 161–162, 164–167, 178
role of internal auditor 92
Barker J 202
Basel Committee
capital adequacy 61–63
Core Principles 58–59, 188
First Basel Concordat 210
role of internal auditor 91–92
Berrill, Sir Kenneth 11
Best CJ 201
'big bang' 1
Bingham LJ 168, 208
Bingham Report 156, 207–208
Blue Arrow affair 123–124
Blunden, Anthony 136
Bourgoin 206
Bray v. Ford 183
Brennan J 203, 206
Briggs v. Spaulding 108
Bromage 202

Calveley 203
Cantley J 102
Caparo 172
Capital Adequacy Directive 61–63
Central Bank of Trinidad and Tobago 189–190, 216
Citigroup Global Markets 88
City Federal Savings Bank 109
City Index 88
Clarke J 200, 202–209
Clarke JA 102
Code for Crown Prosecutors 132
Coleman J 121
Companies Act 1985 79, 97, 155, 157, 166, 170
Complaints Commissioner 193 196
Consolidated Banking Directive 61
constructive ambiguity 6–7
Coopers & Lybrand 160, 162
Cottenham LC 83
County Natwest Ltd 123–124
Cox v. the FSA 103
Credit Agricole 149
Credit Suisse First Boston International 88, 136
Cullen 202

D'Jan 98, 166
Davies, Howard 15
Davis v. Radcliffe 187
Deane J 203
Deloitte & Touche 164 167
Deloittes 209
Denning LJ 121, 203–204
Diplock LJ 203
Dorchester Finance 98–99

Elguzouli 187
endowment mortgage mis-selling 141 142, 171
Engel 139
Equitable Life 12, 29–30
Ernst & Young 135
Ethics in Government Act 1978 210

European Convention on Human Rights 137–138
Eurysthenes 203
Evans-Lombe J 164–167
Evitts, Alan 54
ex parte Austin 121
external auditors
Accounting Investigation and Discipline Board 160–163
Barings Bank 164–167
contributory negligence 164
independence 158–160
liability to clients 163–167
liability to third parties 171–173
non-audit work 159–160
professional guidelines 157–163
qualification of bank accounts 169–170
reporting to regulators 168–169
role in financial regulation 155–173
skilled person 170–171
US approach 173–178
use by FSA 167–173

Federal Deposit Insurance Corporation (FDIC)
conduct of public employees 213
enforcement approach 144–145
membership 33
responsibilities 35
role of external auditors 177
Federal Deposit Insurance Corporation Improvement Act 1991 147, 174
Federal Financial Institutions Examinations Council 35, 40–41
Federal Reserve
financial holding companies 39
responsibilities 34–35, 43
risk-based supervision 74
role of external auditors 175, 177–179
Federal Savings and Loan Insurance Corporation 215
financial conglomeration 13–14
Financial Institutions Reform, Recovery and Enforcement Act 1989 (FIRREA) 109, 144, 146–148, 215
Financial Institutions Supervisory Act 1966 71
Financial Ombudsman Scheme 196–199
financial regulation
see also Financial Services Authority
accountability mechanisms 191–199
adoption of single regulator 1, 25–31
approved persons regime 99–105
authorisation and permission 55–56
capital adequacy 60–65
categorisation of regulated 116–117
choice of enforcement strategy 116–117
civil sanctions 119–121
compensation scheme 188, 191–193
Complaints Commissioner 193–196
compliance-based approach 114–117
consolidated supervision 58–60
consumer perspective 28–31
corporate governance 80–82
courts' position on punitive civil sanctions 120–121
decriminalisation of regulatory offences 118–120
deposit-taking business 54–68
deterrence-based approach 114–115, 117–121
discretion in banking supervision 123–125
distinction between regulation and supervision 46–47
duty to depositors 204–205
education 115–116
enforcement powers 128–135
enforcement strategy 114
express immunity 188–190
Financial Ombudsman Scheme 196–199, 216
fines for misconduct 134–135
function of 46–49
implied immunity 186-188
incentives 115–116
internal models 63–65
international cooperation 66–68
large exposures 65–66
'lead operators' 16
lead regulator 60
legal position of directors and senior management 97–105
liability of regulators 186–190
new era 14–17
position of depositor creditors 83–86
practitioner perspective 27–28
Principles for Businesses 86–97

Privy Council 190, 216
prudential supervision 9 10, 46 49
public responsibilities of regulator 182–186
publicising misconduct 132–134
rationale for 7–8
reporting requirements 57–58
risk and supervision 48–49
risk-based approach 49–53
role of audit committee 92–97
role of external auditors 155–173
role of internal auditor 90–92
sanctions 117–121
self-regulatory organisations 11–13
Senior Management Arrangements, Systems and Controls 88–90
Shareholders' 85–86
threshold conditions 56–57
tort of misfeasance in public office 199–210
transparency in banking supervision 123–125
US approach to regulatory accountability 210–216
US enforcement approach 144–150
Financial Services Act 1986 (FSA 1986)
enactment of 10–11
Personal Investment Authority 12
regulatory approach 13
Financial Services and Markets Act 2000 (FSMA 2000)
accountability mechanisms 191 199
amalgamation of regulatory regimes 17, 26
approved persons regime 99–105
complaints procedure 193
controlled functions 100–101
cooperation with overseas authorities 135–136
damages 184
deposit-taking business 54
enforcement powers 128–135
enforcement system 125–127
express immunity 188–189
Financial Ombudsman Scheme 196
fines for misconduct 134
human rights considerations 137
international cooperation 67–68, 135–136
objectives 84–85
permission 55–56
powers of investigation 127
publicising misconduct 132
regulatory principles 23–24
shareholders' obligations to depositor creditors 86
skilled persons 171
threshold conditions 56 57
Financial Services Authority (FSA)
see also financial regulation
accountability mechanisms 191 199
approach to supervision 56
approved persons regime 99–105
ARROW framework 50
assessment criteria for approved persons 104–105
authorisation and permission 55 56
burden of compliance 131–132
capital adequacy 60–65
cautioning approved firms/persons 131
changing culture of regulation 43
code of conduct 184–186
Complaints Commissioner 193–196, 216–217
consolidated supervision 58–60
consumer awareness objective 20–21
Consumer Panel 24–25, 28–31, 139, 143
consumer protection objective 21–22
control of authorised body 86
controlled functions 100–101
cooperation with overseas authorities 135–136
depositor compensation system 191–193, 217
deposit-taking business 54–68
enforcement powers 128–135
enforcement process review 143 144
enforcement strategy 122, 125–127, 139–144
Equitable Life scandal 29 30
express immunity 188–190
Financial Ombudsman Scheme 196 199, 216
fines for misconduct 134–135
firm risk assessment 51–53
fit and proper test 101–102
formal composition 16–17
handbooks 85
human rights 137–139

internal models 63–65
international cooperation 67–68, 135–136
large exposures 65–66
lead regulation 60
Legal & General tribunal 141–143
market confidence objective 19–20
objectives 18 23, 84–85
powers of investigation 127–128
Practitioner Panel 24–25, 27–28, 140, 143
principles 23–24
Principles for Business 86–97
prudential supervision 45–49publicising misconduct 132–134
'reasonable care' test 87
reducing financial crime objective 22–23
refusing applications for permission 129
Regulatory Decisions Committee 126–127
relationship between regulator and regulated 142–144, 151
reporting requirements 57–58
risk-based approach 49–53
role of audit committee 92–97
role of external auditors 167–173
role of internal auditor 90–92
scope of responsibilities 17–25
Senior Management Arrangements, Systems and Controls 88–90
shareholders' obligations to depositor creditors 85–86
skilled persons 170–171
threshold conditions 56–57
top-down approach 53
varying applications for permission 129–130
withdrawal of approval 102–104, 130–131
Financial Services Compensation Scheme 191–193
financial stability 2–8, 181
First Banking Directive 200
First Basel Concordat 210
First Citizen Bank 189
First National Bank of Buffalo 108
First National Bank of Northern Kentucky 147
Fleurose, Bertrand 138–139
Foley v. Hill 83
Franklin Savings Corporation 214

Ghosh 103
Gibson J 204
Glass-Steagall Act 1933 37–38
Gowan J 102
Gramm-Leach-Bliley Act 1999 (GLB) 38–39, 41–42, 69
Gulf Group 162–163
Gulf Insurance Ltd v. The Central Bank of Trinidad and Tobago 189–190, 216

Hague Convention on the Taking of Evidence Abroad in Civil and Commercial Matters 67
Hall v. Bank of England 123
Hampel Report 81
Han and Yau 139
Harding, Michael 105
Harman 202
Herschell, LJ 183
Hill 187
Hirst LJ 204
Hobhouse LJ 55, 204, 207, 208
Hoffman LJ 187, 190
Hoodless and Blackwell v. the FSA 103–104
Hope LJ 204, 207–209
Hornal v. Neuberger Products Ltd 121
Horne, John 71
House of Lords (No. 3) 207
Human Rights Act 1998 137, 139

immunity 190, 216
India Buildings Friendly Society 101
Insolvency Act 1986 192
Institut Monetaire Luxembourgeois 201, 209–210
Insurance Companies Act 1982 (ICA 1982) 12
internal auditors 90–92
Investment Management Regulatory Organisation (IMRO) 11–12

Jenkins Committee 155
Johnson Matthey Bank 155
collapse of 8
lender of last resort 6
Jonathan Cape 183–184
JP Morgan Securities 138–139

Keith, LJ 187

KPMG 141,172–173

Lai Kew Chai J 67
Law Society v. KPMG 172–173
Leeson, Nick 9, 99, 164–166
Legal & General 141–143
lender of last resort 3–7, 15–16
Long-Term Capital Management 41, 75
Loughborough, LJ 183
Luxembourg Banking Commission 201, 209–210

Mann J 206
Mayhew, David 54
Mayo J 102
McCarthy, Callum 30
McKesson and Robbins 93
Megarry J 184
Mengel 203, 206
Millet J 204
Mirror Group pension scheme 160–161
misfeasance in public office 199–210
moral hazard 6–7
Morgan Grenfell 55
Morrison J 139

National Bank Act 1864 32
Nicholls LJ 183, 204
Nicholls V-C 101
Northern Ireland Insurance Brokers 23

Oaktree Financial Services 129
Office Comptroller of Currency (OCC)
  categorisation of banking business 69–70
  conduct of public employees 212–213
  remedy-based enforcement 145
  responsibilities 34
  risk-based supervision 74–75
  role of 32
Office of Government Ethics 210–211
Overend, Gurney & Co. 4–5
Own Funds Directive 61

pensions mis-selling scandal 28
Personal Investment Authority (PIA) 11–12
Post-BCCI Directive 57
Price Waterhouse 155–156
PriceWaterhouseCoopers 141–142, 162–163
Price Waterhouse Report 207
Public Company Accounting Oversight Board 173

Rand J 202
Rawlinson 202
RDC 141–144
Re A Solicitor 121
Re Kingston Cotton Mill 163
Re Swift 736 Ltd 101
Robinson v. Hall 108
Roncarelli 202
Roque de la Fuente II 72
Rourke, John Edward 101
Royal Liver Assurance 22
Rusnak, John 149–150

Sarbanes Oxley Act 2002 173
SCF Finance v. Masri 54
Scott, Sir Richard 172–173
Scottish Amicable 21
Second Banking Directive 59
Second Consolidated Supervision Directive 59
Securities and Investments Board (SIB) 11
Securities Futures Authority (SFA) 11
Seidman 71
Sergeant, Carol 88
Sheller JA 102
single regulator 1, 25–31
Slade LJ 54–55
Smith Report 94–95
Solvency Ratio Directive 61
Spicer and Oppenheim 161
Steyn LJ 187, 206
Stovin v. Wise 187
Superior Bank 176

Target Asset Management 129
Theodore Goddard 98
Three Rivers litigation 182, 199–210, 217
Tomlinson J 209–210
Tribunals and Inquiry Act 1921 208
Trinidad Co-operative Bank 189–190

USA
  accountability of bank regulators 210
  approach to bank supervision 31–42
  bank failures 176
  'bottom-up' enforcement system 125
  business judgement rule 110

common law standard for bank directors 108, 111
conduct of public employees 211–213, 217
directors' duties 107–108
dual banking system 32–33
enforcement strategy 144–150
Federal Deposit Insurance Corporation Improvement Act 1991 (FDICIA) 147, 174
Financial Institutions Reform, Recovery and Enforcement Act 1989 (FIRREA) 109, 144, 146–148, 215
financial modernisation 40–42
fragility of banking system 37, 43
Glass-Steagall Act 1933 37–38
Gramm-Leach-Bliley Act 1999 38–39, 41–42
Great Depression 37
legal accountability of bank regulators 213–216
legal position of bank director 105–110
move towards regulatory consolidation 36–38
primary regulators 33–36, 43
risk to deposit insurance fund 76
risk-based supervision 72–76
role of audit committee 93
role of external auditors 173–178
safe and sound requirements 69–76
savings and loans 71, 72, 109, 176, 182, 214–215
statutory position of bank directors 109
value at risk 64
US v. Winstar Corporation 215

Vaughan Williams J 163

Walker LJ 204
Walker, Sir David 11
Washington Bancorporation 108, 110
Watkin J 206
Wickramsinghe 138
Winn J 102

X v. Bedfordshire 187

Yamaichi Securities 6
Yuen Kun Yeu 186